GW00537713

Kieron Barry

Five Plays

Numbers
Embassyland
Cumquats
Black Soap
Mahler & Rachmaninov

Roland Egan Press

First published in Great Britain in 2005
by Roland Egan Press

A Roland Egan Book

ISBN 0-9551619-0-8
Printed and bound by Antony Rowe Ltd
Chippenham, Wiltshire
Roland Egan Press

www.rolandeganproductions.com

Ad Majorem Dei Gloriam

Contents

Preface

Reading a script when in the mood for seeing a play is perhaps as satisfying as reading a recipe book when hungry or leafing through a musical score when fed up of silence. In addition there is a particular skill to reading a script; what is simple, obvious and everyday in speech often looks illogical or mannered on the page. ('Yeah', for example, still appears slightly rude and distracting in print but is a cornerstone of inoffensive discourse in the modern age.) A play exists solely on the stage and a script is nothing more glamorous than the instruction manual with which director and actors may assemble it. The script, therefore, is only one element of a play and whilst it allows those not present at a performance to become acquainted with what was said in their absence it is no substitution for the witnessing of events.

Little extraneous information has been included in the text other than the sparsest of stage directions. Where absolutely essential a flashback scene, for example, has been labelled as such but on the whole it seems preferable for a reader to undergo a journey as similar as possible to that of an audience member, gradually piecing together an understanding rather than being told what to think. Furthermore, one is always rewarded by giving the director and actors the greatest amount of freedom of interpretation.

Looking through this collection now I note with surprise that although locations and situations zigzag somewhat chaotically from one play to the next there is an apparent thematic consonance to the whole. Failure looms large for most characters in its various forms; imploding marriages, frustrated careers, unnoticed injustices, missed opportunities, regrets and disappointments. Perhaps this is inevitable in drama; how much more fascinating to us are the reactions of those who learn they are not to receive the prize than the uniform response of the winner.

These five plays were first produced at the Landor Theatre in London between 2002 and 2005 and some of the very happiest moments of my life have been spent in that wonderful theatre.

Kieron Barry
London
November 2005

A note on the text

In these plays the '/' symbol is used to indicate the point at which the next line begins to be spoken over the current line.

NUMBERS

to Justine and Gina

Characters
in order of appearance

Katherine
Isabel
Jennifer
Hetty

Numbers opened at the Landor Theatre, London on Tuesday 1 November 2005 with the following cast:

Katherine	Ellen Collier
Isabel	Nicola Fisher
Jennifer	Anushka Dahssi
Hetty	Catherine Steadman

Directed by	Britten Barry
Designed by	Rebecca Vincent
Stage management	Hannah Ireland
	Marnie Chesterton
	Stuart Griffith

Katherine and Isabel.

Occasionally a distant chapel bell can be heard, together with other sounds of school life in summer – the pock of a tennis ball being hit, distant laughter, birdsong, a piano being practised somewhere etc.

Katherine 'And such was this wide ocean, and this shore More barren than its billows; and yet more than all with a remembered friend I love to ride as then I rode; – for the winds drove the living spray along the sunny air into our faces; the blue heavens were bare, Stripped to their depths by the awakening north; And from the waves sounds like delight broke forth / Harmonising with solitude and – '

Isabel / '*Sound* like delight'.

Katherine What?

Isabel 'Sound like delight', not 'sounds like delight'.

Katherine Disagree.

Isabel Eppur si muove.

Katherine 'And sent into our hearts aerial merriment. So as we rode we talked – ' *(without any gap or change of intonation)* The waves are plural so they're going to make more than one sound, aren't they.

Isabel No, not at all.

Katherine Of course they are.

Isabel No; it's like you'd never say I can't sleep because the cars are making too much noises.

Katherine Too *many* noises.

Isabel No, because that implies a series of noises, not one continual noise, as from the ocean.

Katherine *Continuous*, not continual.

Isabel Can you not just look it up?

Katherine I don't have the text.

Isabel Why not?

Katherine Because I don't need it.

Isabel Yeah, but you do.

Katherine I know it.

Isabel What are *they* going to know anyway?

Katherine I know, but it's expected of me.

Enter Jennifer. She is dressed in a tracksuit or similar. During this scene she changes back into her school uniform.

Jennifer Katherine! Today's the day!

Isabel No; / tonight's the night.

Katherine / 'Sounds' or 'sound', Jennifer?

Jennifer I've absolutely no idea.

Isabel Singular or plural?

Jennifer What is it?

Isabel Surely '*which* is it'?

Katherine Are you not familiar with the text, Jennifer?

Isabel '...And from the waves sounds or sound broke forth harmonising with solitude'.

Jennifer I don't know it.

Katherine Oh, come come, Jennifer; what heresy is this?

Isabel *(noting her appearance)* Is it raining?

Jennifer Is what raining?

Katherine It's for the speech tonight.

Isabel Where's Hetty? I thought she was with you.

Jennifer I thought she was with you. Is it Keats?

Katherine That girl has the punctuality of a hot air balloon.

Isabel *(to Jennifer)* Similar but not quite as good.

Jennifer Byron?

Isabel The other way.

Jennifer Shelley.

Katherine Hurray! Now which is it? From the waves sound or sounds like delight came forth.

Isabel Broke forth.

Katherine Oh bloody hell. Pitch in, Jennifer. Where have you been?

Jennifer Simon's soccer match. I really don't know it.

Isabel Can you not just make a stylistic guesstimate?

Katherine Who won?

Jennifer Well it could be either but 'sounds like' sounds like 'sounds like', which is confusing to the ear so 'sound like' singular might meet a more straightforward response from the reader.

Isabel Or listener in this case.

Jennifer Are you doing it without the text?

Katherine That is the tradition.

Jennifer But doesn't it have to be Catholic.

Katherine Yeah, but everything's Catholic, isn't it. That's what Catholic means.

Isabel Who won?

Jennifer I don't know, I'm afraid; Augustine's were winning but I had to leave ten minutes before it ended.

Isabel What was the score when you left?

Jennifer Err… six nil, I think.

Katherine And was your presence noted from the field?

Jennifer Well it seems unlikely, doesn't it.

Isabel How about your absence?

Jennifer More likely.

Isabel Oh Jens. What are we going to do about your hopeless crush?

Katherine Is it hopeless?

Isabel Hopefully.

Katherine He's only Hetty's brother; I'm amazed he engenders such feelings of despair.

Jennifer I'd always imagined he was adopted or something.

Katherine Jennifer! You must just trust.

Jennifer The truth is I long to sweep him up in my arms –

Isabel / Shouldn't that be the other way round?

Jennifer / – and to say Please, for the Lord's sake look beneath my chatty exterior. I think you'll like the real Jennifer.

Katherine The real Jennifer or the new Jennifer?

Jennifer The new Jennifer.

Isabel What happened to the old one?

Jennifer I trashed it.

Katherine Any news on the invite for the summer?

Isabel I thought she'd already invited you.

Jennifer She said I could stay depending on her other plans.

Katherine I didn't know Hetty had plans.

Isabel I think she's working for some charity or something.

Jennifer But I've worked it all out. In my mind.

Katherine Go on.

Jennifer Picture this. The Fletcher household, tennis, walking, simple country pursuits, my skin glows, accidentally touching his hand as he passes me still lemonade on the patio, he lets it linger but looks away, his face flushed and scarlet, dizzy from the heat, or *is* it the heat? My top two buttons undone – oh, he thinks, if only it were the top three: all in good time, darling Simon, all in good time. Then an uncomplicated family supper of poached salmon and fruit salad, talk of literature and politics I bathe and return downstairs in animal print pyjamas feeling clean and delicious oh so casually lolling by a roaring fire / as we pair up for Trivial Pursuit –

Isabel / Roaring fire? It's the middle of summer, Jens.

Jennifer Forget the fire, then – Hetty wants an early night, Mr and Mrs Fletcher bow out soon afterwards, they love me, stay up as late as you like, won't you, help yourself to a nightcap and then at last we're alone, he and I, and he looks at me with solid, almost angry lust and misty-eyed he blurts towards me and… *(she clicks her fingers climactically)*

Isabel Then what?

Jennifer I don't know. That's the bit I'm unsure of.

Katherine Don't worry, Jens; Hetty will invite you.

Jennifer But even then what do you think he thinks of me?

Isabel Well has he said anything?

Jennifer Apparently he said I have a nice face.

Isabel Oh how rude.

Jennifer Yeah; it's like hello? I've got a body too, you know. Anything you want to say about that?

Isabel Exactly.

Jennifer Or should I just read between the lines?

Isabel What an insult.

Jennifer Absolutely.

Isabel Think yourself lucky. Someone once said I had a nice smile. Can you believe the nerve of that?

Jennifer That is dreadful, isn't it.

Isabel Not even the-whole-of-my-face. Just literally one small part of it. That's like saying… well, I can't think of anything to compare it to.

Jennifer You don't need to – it speaks for itself.

Isabel Well, on the plus side if all else fails there's always Bilbo.

Jennifer Bilbo! Oh God!

Isabel Has he tried to meet your eye yet?

Jennifer Err… I'm not sure.

Isabel If he did you'd know it, believe me. He did it to me and my blood turned to snow.

Jennifer Poor old Bilbo. I feel rather sorry for him in a way.

Isabel Now that *would* be a waste.

Jennifer Come on; show a bit of respect.

Isabel Mr Baggins, then.

The girls briefly sing 'Bilbo! Bilbo!'

Jennifer But Simon and I are meant to be. He loves me 89% according to the alpha-numeric name conversion formula.

Katherine Come on, Jens; he's only human.

Jennifer Is he?

Isabel Barely human.

Jennifer I might remind you that the question still remains re. Byron.

Katherine / Shelley!

Isabel / Shelley!

Katherine As I seem to recall I was arguing for 'sound' singular and Isabel against. What was your conclusion, Jennifer?

Jennifer Oh, it wasn't worth drawing, really.

Katherine Oh to blazes with all this. I can't be bothered with the speech now. Let's just leave it.

Jennifer I wouldn't worry, Katherine – you've still got over ninety minutes to get the hang of it.

Katherine Is that the time?

Isabel People aren't going to remember your speech, Katherine –

Katherine / Glad I'm making the effort.

Isabel / – they'll just remember the announcement that you're the new Head Girl.

Katherine No no; don't jinx it. Don't jinx it.

Isabel *Jinx* it? Come on, Katherine; it's a... what's the word?

Jennifer Inevitability?

Isabel No...

Jennifer Inexorability?

Isabel No...

Jennifer Shoe-in?

Isabel It's a shoe-in.

Katherine But let's not be grabby.

Jennifer Consider the considerable evidence.

Isabel Katherine; just relax. Every lacrosse captain in twenty years has gone on to be Head Girl. That's just the rule.

Jennifer It's tradition.

Isabel You're lacrosse captain; you're Head Girl.

Jennifer That's just the rule.

Isabel That's how it works. Sally Wilson, Amy Glaston –

Jennifer Ruth Davis.

Isabel Alison Gray.

Jennifer Exactly.

Isabel And it's not just that. Everyone knows you're going to be Head Girl. It's just something that everyone knows.

Jennifer Everyone *knows* it.

Isabel Look at the career path. Netball vice-captain in Upper Fourth –

Jennifer / Hockey captain.

Isabel / Hockey captain in Fifth, Netball captain in Fifth, *Caiaphas* editor in Fifth –

Jennifer A year early –

Isabel 10 A-stars, Gold D of E, Five A-levels, Latin a year early, Community Shield, Crossley Cup –

Jennifer Diction Cup, Frenburg Shield.

Isabel And above all you're Katherine Judah. More specifically Katherine Judah daughter of Anthony Judah.

Jennifer Sir Anthony Judah.

Isabel Do you really think after everything he's done for the school they could give it to someone else?

Katherine Well I sometimes think that's why he's doing it.

Isabel So what? He'll get what he wants and you'll get what you want.

Jennifer You're not going to let him down.

Isabel I mean worry about something if you like –

Jennifer Tonight's oration, for example.

Isabel But don't worry about that. Everything's going to be fine.

Katherine Well that's very kind of you to say so.

Jennifer Once the small matter of the speech –

Isabel And the announcement –

Jennifer – is out of the way then from here on it's fun and games till September.

Isabel Just two more weeks of this place –

Jennifer The quad concert tomorrow –

Isabel The garden party –

Jennifer Howett's Pimms reception, Lower v. Upper croquet match –

Isabel Choosing rooms for next term, last night party –

Jennifer Antibes –

Isabel Gloucestershire –

Jennifer Quiet country pubs –

Isabel Watching cricket on the green –

Jennifer Simon –

Isabel First driving lesson –

Jennifer Simon –

Isabel Work experience at Reuters –

Jennifer Simon –

Isabel Yes, alright.

Jennifer Brilliant sunshine both day and night –

Isabel Glorious weeks gliding by –

Jennifer Hang on, haven't done our assignment yet –

Isabel Haven't made it through the reading list –

Jennifer Can it really be September?

Isabel Oh how dreadful the final few days of freedom –

Jennifer Suddenly here we are again –

Isabel Where's it all gone?

Jennifer What's the bloody point?

A pause.

Katherine Now. Girls. Listen. Now obviously Dr Howett appoints the Head Girl –

Isabel Fingers crossed.

Jennifer Done deal.

Katherine – but it's the Head Girl herself who appoints the Deputy Head Girl.

Isabel Correct.

Jennifer Absolutely.

Katherine And there's only one Deputy Head Girl.

Isabel / Of course.

Jennifer / Of course.

Katherine Which of course is slightly difficult, given that there's four of us in the gang.

Jennifer Well… there's us three and there's Hetty.

Isabel But Hetty isn't interested in all that. I mean, she's realistic.

Katherine Well, do we know that?

Jennifer I mean Hetty is lovely –

Isabel Really lovely.

Katherine Of course.

Jennifer Of course she is.

Isabel She's lovely.

Jennifer She's *so* lovely.

Isabel But she's just not…

Katherine *(beat)* Here?

Isabel No…

Jennifer We all like Hetty.

Isabel That's why she's one of us.

Jennifer She's one of us, but at the same time –

Isabel But at the same time she's still not quite / one of us. *(in surprise at their synchronicity)* Hymn sheets!

Jennifer / One of us. *(in surprise at their synchronicity)* Hymn sheets! Don't get me wrong – Hetty is lovely and as good a friend to us as any of us to any of us but she's not quite...

Isabel First rate.

Jennifer Exactly. She's not captain of anything, she doesn't do as well as us in exams –

Isabel She's just an honest tryer, / basically.

Jennifer / Exactly. An honest tryer. On a scholarship.

Isabel And that's not to say anything unpleasant about her.

Jennifer Of course not.

Isabel Although she did refuse to go to Val d'Isere with us.

Katherine She didn't refuse; she couldn't afford it.

Jennifer Yeah, but she was really funny about it.

Katherine Fine, but that still leaves the two of you. For only one position.

A pause.

Isabel Yeah, but Jennifer is...

Jennifer What?

Isabel Nothing.

Jennifer What?

Isabel Nothing, except that…

Jennifer No, come on; / what?

Isabel / No, nothing, I was just going to say that I'm obviously a bit more of a sort of a… sort of a *leader* / than you are, so –

Jennifer / A *leader*? I wouldn't have / said so, Izzy.

Isabel / No, just in some ways, I mean.

Jennifer Well I can't accept that.

Isabel No, OK. I've just… noticed people really respecting me lately.

Jennifer Well so have I. People respect me too –

Isabel I'm sure they do.

Jennifer – but with me it's more a sort of… admiration rather than the ordinary sort of respect that you quite rightly say is all that you ever / inspire.

Isabel / No, no; when I say respect I really mean… more sort of…*worship*, really. I've noticed an awful lot of that lately.

Katherine We shouldn't discuss it unless Hetty's here anyway.

Isabel Come on, Katherine; Hetty knows she's not in the running for deputy.

Katherine I do feel a bit bad there's nothing for her.

Jennifer She wouldn't want anything.

Isabel How about librarian? Head Girl picks that, doesn't she?

Jennifer Yeah.

Isabel Well would you consider giving that to Hetty? She'd like that.

Katherine I'm not so sure that she would, actually.

Jennifer These positions aren't a right, you know.

Isabel She should be grateful she's getting anything.

Katherine Although would you be happy to be librarian?

Isabel What do you mean?

Katherine I mean if... well –

Jennifer I've always thought that Isabel would make a *brilliant* librarian.

Isabel What are you talking about? I've barely read a word since *Stig of the Dump*.

Jennifer Nonsense. You love books.

Isabel Yeah, but it's not about the books, though, is it; it's about the organisational skills – which you've always had in abundance.

Jennifer Well you seem to know an awful lot about what the role requires.

Isabel No; I'm just saying you've always struck me as a good potential librarian.

Jennifer Well I can't retort, I'm afraid; I know so little about the subject.

Isabel Perhaps Hetty *would* be better.

Jennifer Oh she'd be *so* good, wouldn't she.

Isabel She would probably be the best librarian the school's ever had.

Jennifer Seriously, Katherine – give *Hetty* a go as librarian; I don't think she'll let you down.

Isabel You ought to give her something, if you don't mind my suggesting.

Katherine No; I agree.

Isabel I mean she's still one of us.

Katherine Correct.

Isabel But Katherine, our real message is:

Jennifer Appoint who you like.

Isabel Exactly. As you see fit.

Jennifer And we're realistic.

Isabel And once this little hurdle has been cleared –

Jennifer We have the rest of our lives spread out before us.

Isabel Packed with opportunity and success.

Jennifer Picture this: *(she prompts)*

Katherine Well… Head Girl…

Jennifer Of course.

Isabel Of course.

Katherine 5 As at A-level, PPE at Oxford –

Isabel College?

Katherine Corpus / Christi.

Isabel / Corpus Christi.

Jennifer The body of Christ.

Katherine Star First / with Dissertation Prize, PhD at the LSE –

Jennifer / And how about you, Isabel?

Isabel Oh, clearly a leading barrister / at a top Chambers –

Katherine / And you, Jens?

Jennifer Oh, editor of the Times –

Isabel QC –

Jennifer Sunday Times –

Katherine MP –

Jennifer New York Times –

Katherine Minister –

Isabel Judge –

Jennifer Booker Prize –

Isabel Law Lord –

Katherine Cabinet minister –

Jennifer Poet laureate –

Isabel Married to a painter –

Jennifer Doyenne of London society –

Isabel Head of a publishing house –

Katherine City analyst –

Isabel PR guru –

Jennifer War correspondent –

Katherine Governor of the Bank of England –

Isabel Ambassador to Washington –

Jennifer Arms dealer –

Katherine Chairwoman of the Royal Opera House –

Isabel Dubai –

Jennifer Brunei –

Isabel United Nations –

Katherine World Bank –

Isabel House of Lords.

Jennifer Well, girls, until then we'll have to make do with this.

She holds up a slim, ambiguous volume.

Isabel What's 'this'?

Jennifer This is the answer to your Ave Marias, girls. Guess what?

Isabel Oh, not again.

Jennifer Or in this case by, with or from whom?

Isabel Whose is it this time?

Jennifer *(sighs)* Katherine?

Katherine What?

Jennifer Guess whose?

Katherine I really don't know.

Jennifer You don't know.

Katherine Well how could I?

Isabel Exactly.

Katherine / Well it's clearly a diary of some sort.

Isabel / Presumably it's another diary.

Jennifer Correct.

Isabel It could be anyone's.

Jennifer Yes, but think whose you'd most like it to be.

Katherine I don't know.

Jennifer Yes you do.

Isabel We really don't.

Jennifer Well have a think.

Isabel We don't know.

Jennifer Well whose could it be?

Isabel I don't know.

Jennifer Take a guess. *(she 'conducts' their response)*

Katherine / Nicola Slater.

Isabel / Nicola Slater.

Jennifer / Nicola Slater. Bingo.

A pause.

Isabel That's Nicola Slater's diary.

Jennifer Correct.

Isabel You're kidding.

Jennifer *(clicks or 'chucks' with her tongue twice)*

Isabel How..?

Jennifer Don't you worry.

Isabel How did you get it?

Jennifer That's not the issue.

Isabel But how *did* you get it?

Jennifer That's still not the issue.

Isabel You cunning little vixen.

Jennifer Non, non; seulement une enfant parmi les sortilege.

Isabel Where did you find it?

Jennifer She left it in the prep room.

Isabel Oh, the dozy cow.

Katherine No-one should be speaking to that girl.

Isabel Don't worry. No-one is.

Katherine I've said I don't want anyone speaking to her any more.

Isabel No-one is.

Katherine How about the Lower School?

Isabel No-one's speaking to her. I promise you.

Katherine Good.

Isabel Did anyone see you take it?

Jennifer I didn't take it. Well, I have it, obviously, but –

Katherine You stole it.

Jennifer No, I wouldn't go that far.

Isabel Theft is intent to permanently deprive.

Jennifer And I have every intention of returning it.

Isabel In due course.

Jennifer In good time.

Isabel But we've just got to read it first.

Jennifer She'll never know. We'll just have a quick read and put it back.

Isabel She'll never know.

Jennifer No harm done.

Isabel What do you think, Katherine?

Isabel and Jennifer look at Katherine. A pause.

Jennifer This is for your benefit.

Katherine I appreciate that.

Isabel But..?

Katherine I don't know.

Isabel Oh, Katherine! That's not like you.

Jennifer Why on earth not?

Katherine I'm just… jittery and superstitious.

Jennifer You're just worried about the speech.

Katherine Yes.

Isabel And the announcement.

Katherine Yes.

Jennifer But all the more reason to relax and have fun.

Isabel Oh come on! Don't let 'I dare not' wait upon 'I would' like the poor cat i'the adage.

Jennifer That poor cat.

Katherine I don't know. Perhaps we should just put it back.

Jennifer / Oh! *(in disappointment)*

Isabel / Oh! *(in disappointment)* Well, you're the boss.

Katherine It's just a Head Girl should be… benevolent.

Jennifer *(obviously deflated)* Fair enough.

Katherine So perhaps you shouldn't have taken it, Jennifer.

Jennifer Alright.

Isabel But she did.

Katherine I'm not angry.

Jennifer No.

Katherine It was just high spirits.

Jennifer Yes.

Isabel But she's learnt her lesson.

Katherine And now let's move on.

Isabel Yes.

Jennifer OK.

A pause.

Katherine Right: 'A bare strand of hillocks, heaped from ever-shifting sand, matted with thistles and amphibious weeds, Such as from earth's embrace the salt ooze breeds, Is this; an uninhabited sea-side, Which the lone fisher, when his nets are dried, Abandons; and no other object breaks the waste but one dwarf tree and some few stakes broken and unrepaired and – '*(without pause)* OK, OK, let's just have a quick look at it.

Isabel / That's the ticket.

Jennifer / That's the spirit. Ticket.

Isabel Plunge into the wonderful world of Nicola Slater.

Jennifer Release yourself into the sheer magic of Nicola Slater.

Isabel picks up the diary, preparing to read a passage.

Jennifer Oh-oh – wait a second.

Isabel What?

Jennifer That's mine.

Isabel Oh come on; / it's all of ours.

Jennifer / No; I found it, so –

Isabel It belongs to / all of us.

Jennifer / By rights –

Isabel By rights it's all of ours.

Jennifer / Look – I found it.

Isabel / And there's not a court in the land that would disagree.

Katherine Isabel, come on; give it to Jennifer.

Isabel *(an audible sigh)*

Jennifer Thank you.

Isabel OK, Jens, fire away.

Jennifer OK. Here we go.

As Jennifer riffles through the diary Katherine and Isabel make an extended 'Ooh' sound, starting low and increasing in pitch, like spectators watching a bowler run to the crease.

Jennifer Righto! *(she opens the diary at random)* 'It's funny how we use a circle in both our letters and numbers (ie. the letter O and the number zero) but we never use a square. If we did it would be somewhere between a zed and a capital H.'

Isabel What the hell is that? Come on, Jens.

Jennifer That was just a page at random.

Isabel You can do better than that.

Jennifer *Me? I* didn't / write it.

Katherine / This is / ridiculous.

Isabel / Just find something else. Just / find something else.

Jennifer / OK, I'll find / something else.

Katherine / I don't know what you're hoping to find.

Isabel *(Looks at her. Beat.)* Yes you do.

Jennifer *(oblivious)* Right, let's try again. 'Imagine if you will for one moment a huge elephant, much larger than normal, perhaps over twenty feet tall, with great curvy tusks. This elephant is completely covered in lovely thick, white wool like a large sheep. The figment of a crazy imagination? No; this animal actually walked the earth long before you and I were born.'

Isabel Can this girl seriously wonder why she's single?

Katherine We're all single, Isabel.

Isabel Yeah, but… there's *ways* of being single.

Jennifer But you must admit –

Isabel There's no future in dinosaurs.

Jennifer This stuff is pretty unusable.

Isabel Try again.

Jennifer OK. Err… 'Imagine if you will for one moment, a girl, perhaps not unlike your present correspondent; a normal young girl to all intents and purposes – '

Isabel / 'Normal'?!

Jennifer / 'Simply trying to go about her day to day life around the school.'

Isabel / Oh please.

Jennifer / 'The sun may be shining, the birds may be singing high in the treetops but wait! Why isn't this person happy? Doesn't she have everything to live for? What terrible secrets could be burning inside her chest, preventing her from being serene and contented like the woodland idyll that surrounds her, badgers in the undergrowth, squirrels racing after their winter stores, but obvious this poor girl traipses – '

Katherine / She means oblivious.

Jennifer / 'all the heaviness of the world on her – '

Isabel / Resist the obvious jokes, girls.

Jennifer / ' – like a dreadful boulder. But what oh what could it be? Can they not see that I could be just like them – funny and witty and having fun ideas for treats? I just want to run away. I want to flee, to hide away somewhere where I can, if needs be, like an ugly duckling amid the reeds, be still and quiet and unnoticed for weeks at a time, if needs be.'

Isabel Now *that's* more like it. Keep going, Jens.

Jennifer 'Why am I so unpopular?'

Isabel Sorry, is that you asking that, Jens, or is that / the diary?

Jennifer / Sounds a bit like your diary, doesn't it, / Izzy.

Katherine / No, no; keep going. This was going somewhere.

Jennifer 'Why am I' ie. her 'so unpopular' question mark / question mark question mark.

Isabel / Because you're an affront to human dignity, Nicola Slater.

Jennifer 'No-one will talk to me and no-one will look at me and I sort of try to keep my chin up / as if none of it is happening, but – '

Isabel / Sorry, was that 'chin' singular?

Jennifer ' – it's just so cruel and hurtful and I've really done my best to make people like me. At Broomfields I was popular for doing things but when I do those same things here I'm just hated and laughed at. But all I'm doing is the same things that I used to do. I know I don't belong here and I'm not welcome and they make me feel so horrible but all I want to know is Why. If I knew why they hated me it wouldn't be so bad but I don't, so why? Why? Why? Why?'

The others join in the 'Why's and they repeat the word in a crescendo until gradually we become aware the sound has become the 'Rwah!' of crows, one of them possibly singing the Jurassic Park theme underneath etc. – general primitive and sinister mayhem. This eventually ends and Jennifer returns to searching the diary, whereupon she is suddenly arrested by a passage.

Jennifer Bloody hell!

Isabel What is it?

Katherine What?

Jennifer silently shares the diary with the others. They gather round and read in shocked silence. A long pause. Eventually:

Isabel That's not even how you spell it... is it?

Jennifer Yes.

Katherine Can that really be true?

Isabel It must be. It's in the diary.

A pause.

Jennifer What's she doing that for? She'll... get expelled.

Isabel She will do if anyone finds out.

Jennifer She will be expelled.

Isabel She will be.

Katherine But when... how did she... I'm amazed.

Isabel It is...

{**Katherine** / Bloody hell.

{**Jennifer** / Bloody hell.

{**Isabel** / Bloody hell.

They look at each other. The mood has changed.

Isabel What should we do?

Jennifer Well don't look at me. It wasn't my idea.

Isabel *(softly and urgently)* Here's Hetty.

Jennifer What should we do?

Katherine Don't say anything about the diary.

Jennifer No, no, no.

Isabel She'll only get all moral and righteous.

Katherine Well, OK, tell her about the diary if you want but don't show her... everything.

Isabel Right. We'll keep that bit in reserve.

Jennifer OK, quick, here she is; let's just act calm and nice and pleasant.

Isabel No, no; just act normal.

Jennifer Good idea.

Enter Hetty.

Katherine Hello Het-up.

Hetty Hello, girls.

Isabel / Hello Het-up.

Jennifer / Hello Het-up.

Hetty Hello girls.

Katherine Hetty, what have you been up to?

Hetty Nothing.

Jennifer Nothing will come of nothing, Hetty.

Katherine Speak again and mend your words a little.

Hetty Are you ready for the quad concert?

Isabel I will be.

Hetty Have you got anyone coming?

Isabel Well, Mummy said she'll come and I think she really means it but if she does she'll definitely bring Richard and obviously she's only going to come if Daddy *doesn't* come. But Daddy's said he might come and he said if he does come he *might* bring Tatiana but I don't know whether he's actually going to come or not and if he does whether he'll bring Tatiana. But you see if I tell Mummy he might and then he doesn't then I'm left with no-one coming, whereas if I say he definitely isn't coming then they both might turn up and obviously that can't happen. Now to be honest out of Daddy and Mummy I'd rather Daddy came than Mummy but out of Tatiana and Richard I'd rather

Richard came than Tatiana but what I can't work out is would I rather Mummy came even though she definitely will bring Richard who I don't particularly want to come or would I prefer Daddy to come given that he may or may not be bringing Tatiana who I definitely don't want to come at all.

A pause.

Hetty So in the ideal world Tatiana and Richard would stay away –

Isabel Through dysentery.

Hetty And your parents –

Isabel Partnerless and recently bereaved, they would see each other across the candlelit quad, reawakening their old feelings, rush to each other in the interval, fall in love once more, get back together, buy our old house back, record a Christmas Number One…

Jennifer Izzy, you never mentioned this.

Isabel I did, actually.

Jennifer No you didn't.

Isabel Well, I did.

Katherine If you had we'd've rememembered.

Isabel Well *I* remember. You were reading Vanity Fair at the time and asked me to pipe down.

Katherine The magazine or the Thackeray novel?

Hetty Well, listen: good luck, anyway.

Isabel Thanks, Hetty.

Jennifer OK, Hetty; here's fun. Guess who. 'I can, if needs be, like an ugly duckling amid the reeds, be still and quiet and unnoticed for weeks at a time, if needs be.'

Isabel Guess who.

Jennifer Guess who.

Katherine Guess of whom.

Hetty *(beat)* Emily Dickinson?

Isabel Come on, Hetty; context. *Context.*

Hetty Well, it's a diary.

Jennifer But whose?

Isabel We'll give you three guesses.

Hetty *(a brief pause)* Alma Mahler, Virginia Woolf, Sofia Tolstoy.

Jennifer *(beat)* Hetty; look at how it's formatted.

Hetty Some sort of special edition, perhaps?

Jennifer Katherine, surely all the hallmarks of a keen librarian?

Isabel It's Nicola Slater's.

Hetty What?

Jennifer Hey, I'm meant to reveal that. / It's Nicola Slater's.

Hetty / What are you doing with Nicola Slater's diary?

Isabel Don't worry. We're just reading it.

Hetty What made you take that?

Jennifer High spirits?

Hetty I spoke to her this afternoon and –

{**Katherine** / What did you do that for?

{**Isabel** / What did you do that for?

{**Jennifer** / What did you do that for?

Hetty And she's really unhappy.

Isabel In case you hadn't realised no-one's meant to be speaking to her.

Hetty I had noticed that, yes.

Isabel Well there you go then.

Hetty Yes, but that's ridiculous.

Isabel Is it?

Hetty Well isn't it?

Isabel Well what do you think?

Hetty Does that matter?

Isabel I'm sure it does.

Hetty Well what do *you* think?

Isabel I don't think it is ridiculous, no.

Hetty Why on earth not?

Isabel *(shrugs)*

Katherine You've heard the latest thing, have you?

Hetty Well, I'm not sure.

Katherine Now she keeps buying stuff for people.

Hetty Yes, I know.

Isabel Just buying stuff.

Jennifer For no reason.

Katherine She gave Rachel Oldham in 1 and 4 a bicycle.

Hetty Yes. I heard that.

Jennifer (a) she doesn't even hardly know her and (b) it was obviously really second-hand and battered. She must have found it somewhere.

Hetty But 1 and 4 is miles away, that's why most of them have bikes.

Isabel What's your point?

Hetty Well why didn't Rachel Oldham have a bicycle?

Katherine What's that got to do with it? The point is she hardly knows her.

Hetty Well she obviously knew she didn't have a bike.

Isabel But that's no excuse. She's in a different year. It's just really weird.

Katherine Exactly.

Jennifer It's called buying friends.

Isabel Exactly.

Hetty So what did Rachel Oldham say?

Katherine I don't know.

Hetty But is she using it?

Katherine Yeah, I've seen her on it. That's how I know.

Hetty Well there we are. So what's the problem.

Isabel Well I think Rachel Oldham was a bit freaked out by it.

Hetty So why did she accept it then?

Isabel Well I think she didn't know what to do. But it was really weird – someone who doesn't even hardly know you sees you haven't got a bicycle and comes up and just gives you a bicycle. I mean what's she trying to do?

Jennifer Exactly.

Isabel But it's like loads of stuff. You know she buys flowers and puts them in the moabs.

Katherine No, I didn't know that.

Isabel Yes you did – I pointed them out in Cubitt.

Katherine Oh yeah. I didn't know that was her.

Jennifer Well it seems like she sort of tries to do it when no-one's around, like all really cloak and dagger, but I imagine she does it like that only to attract more attention.

Isabel As if anyone cares.

Hetty Well you obviously care.

Jennifer But it's everything, it's everything: it's her whole sense of... self. She was always trying to do stuff like start clubs and –

Isabel Getting people to sign up for things and –

Jennifer Trying to organise outings to museums or whatever. Day-trips.

Isabel But they never come to anything. It's just...

schemes.

Hetty But have you asked yourself why she does this sort of thing?

Katherine Oh don't be so petty, Hetty.

Isabel It's just a cry for help.

Hetty I agree.

Isabel Yeah, but you mean it in a good way.

Jennifer She's obviously just trying to be popular.

Hetty But everyone's trying to be popular, Jens.

Isabel I mean, yeah; normally I get annoyed when people say that life's not a popularity contest like that's a *good* thing, but –

Jennifer But can't Nicola Slater realise that someone like her isn't *meant* to be popular?

Isabel Well you have to bear in mind that this is not a normal girl we're talking about.

Hetty What *does* a normal girl look like, would you say?

Isabel Well, not fat for a start.

Hetty *(pause)* Come on, Izzy.

Isabel I'm just using that as an example. / I mean that's a fact, though. She's obese.

Hetty / But an example of what?

Jennifer She's not *obese*, Isabel, I wouldn't say.

Isabel Anything 20% over recommended body weight is technically obese. You can't tell me she's not that.

Hetty But how does that help us?

Isabel But it's everything; it's the way she looks, it's the way she dresses... I mean she's got to be realistic. I mean if you look like that fine but don't try and be popular as well, *surely*.

Hetty But what's that got to do with us? What she wears is a matter for her.

Isabel But we're the ones who have got to / look at it.

Hetty / I just don't see all that as relevant, I'm afraid.

Isabel Yeah, but you don't deny it, do you.

Hetty It doesn't matter what I think.

Isabel I just want you to admit she's clinically obese and / has no dress sense.

Hetty / I don't admit that. I don't admit that either.

Isabel But it's like saying the sky is blue.

Hetty OK.

Isabel I'm just using that as an example. It just goes to show... she can't make a good decision and her values are weird.

Katherine Come on, Hetty, you've got to admit, she is a little strange.

Hetty She's just trying to make people happy.

Isabel But everyone's just laughing at her.

Jennifer It's sad.

Isabel It *is* sad.

Jennifer But it's true.

Isabel It's so true, I'm afraid.

Jennifer And it seems a bit extreme sometimes that nobody talks to her now and nobody will look her in the eye and no one will get involved with her in any way but…

Isabel That's what Katherine wanted.

Katherine Because that's what it takes.

Isabel It's for the best, I'm afraid.

Jennifer Cruel to be kind.

Isabel Because otherwise how will she learn?

Hetty Well I just think you're being unnecessarily cruel to her.

{**Isabel** / Well it doesn't really matter what you think, does it.

{**Katherine** / Jennifer; do *you* think we're being unnecessarily / cruel to her?

Hetty / No?

Isabel No.

{**Jennifer** / I wouldn't have said so, no.

{**Hetty** / Why's that?

Katherine Well there you go / then; it's not just me.

Isabel / So therefore no-one thinks it's unnecessarily / cruel except you.

Hetty / But it was your / idea to send her to Coventry.

Jennifer / Except Hetty. / Exactly.

Katherine / You didn't object, / though, did you.

Isabel / And that / doesn't count. So effectively… no-one.

Hetty / I didn't think you'd actually do it.

{**Katherine** / Why wouldn't I?

{**Jennifer** / Why would she /not do it?

Hetty / And I certainly didn't / think the whole school would join in.

Jennifer / Effectively everyone / … exactly; the whole school.

Isabel / So it is literally only / you and like I say, your view doesn't matter.

Katherine / Why wouldn't they? Everyone's fed up with her / Attention Seeking Disorder or whatever it is.

Hetty / Why doesn't my view matter?

Isabel Because it's not you / that's going to be Head Girl.

Jennifer / That's exactly what it is, / Katherine.

Hetty / Well actually / it is.

{**Katherine** / Exactly –

{**Isabel** / What?

In the following sentences the two girls say "Head Girl" at precisely the same moment.

{**Hetty** / Actually it is. Howett asked me if I wanted to be Head Girl.

{**Katherine** / Because when you think about it what's

the point of being Head Girl if you can't / prevent these people from swanning about the place as if they –

Isabel / What?

Hetty Howett asked me if I wanted to be Head Girl.

A pause.

Total silence and stillness for perhaps ten seconds, broken suddenly and without warning by a riotous peal of laughter from Jennifer.

Jennifer Sorry.

Another, brief moment of silence.

Katherine Sorry; *what* did you say?

Hetty *(less certain)* He, err… asked me if I wanted to be Head Girl.

Katherine Who?

Jennifer Howett.

Katherine He asked you / to be Head Girl? He asked *you* to be Head Girl?

Jennifer *(to Hetty)* / What did you say? *(as in 'what was your response?')*

Isabel What do you think she said?

Katherine No; what *did* you say?

Jennifer *(to Isabel)* See?

Hetty I said yes.

Pause. Katherine is totally baffled.

Katherine So… *you're* Head Girl.

Hetty Yes.

Katherine Of what?

Hetty Well… the school.

Katherine What school?

Hetty Our school.

Katherine What; *this* school?

Hetty Well, yeah.

Katherine Head Girl of this school.

Hetty Yes.

Katherine The whole school.

Hetty Yes.

Katherine But… what about me?

Hetty How do you mean?

Katherine Well did he not… say anything about me?

Hetty No.

Katherine Did *you* say anything about me?

Hetty Well… no.

Katherine But… my father.

Hetty What about him?

Katherine Why didn't you think of us?

Hetty What do you mean?

Katherine Well, we had plans.

Hetty We all have plans, Katherine.

Isabel Hetty, we've had plenty of conversations about

being Head Girl and you never once mentioned you wanted it.

Hetty Well you never asked.

Isabel She shouldn't have to. You're meant to be a friend.

Hetty Well I am a friend. We'd've still have been friends if Katherine had got it as well.

Katherine But… and don't take this the wrong way –

Hetty Of course not. / I know you're upset.

Katherine / – is I suppose why – I'm not upset.

Hetty / OK.

Katherine / I'm not.

Hetty OK.

Katherine What I don't understand is: Why you?

Hetty I don't know. I think he just thought that…

Isabel I hope you're proud of yourself.

Hetty It wasn't actually my idea.

Jennifer Ah! Now she's passing the buck as well!

Isabel Is that what they teach you at Head Girl school? That's a key / leadership skill, is it?

Jennifer / So does that mean you don't want to be Head Girl, then?

Hetty No.

Katherine No?

Hetty No, I do want to be. I do / want to be.

Katherine / But why? Can you answer that?

Hetty Well… why did you want to be?

Isabel / Ooh!

Jennifer / Ooh!

Katherine It's not that I want to be, Hetty, it's that I'm meant to be.

Jennifer Everyone knows Katherine is meant to be Head Girl and that's why this is a mistake.

Katherine It *is* a mistake, Hetty.

Jennifer You'll be an incongruous laughing stock.

Isabel You're a usurper. An interloper. An anti-pope. This is an inter-regnum. You're fomenting revolt.

Katherine I mean, have you any idea of what you're going to do?

Hetty Umm…

Katherine Have you got absolutely any idea at all what you're going to do at all?

Jennifer As Head Girl?

Isabel As a… would-be adult?

Hetty Well, sort of.

Isabel Answer the / question!

Jennifer / Answer the question! / Answer the question!

Isabel / Answer the question!

Katherine Come on; what are you going to do? What's the big idea? *(pause)* …*Yes*?

Hetty I thought I'd sort of try to change things. Certain things.

Katherine But what from what to what?

Hetty Just to make things a bit more… I've got a list.

Isabel A *list*?

Hetty Just some / ideas, really.

Jennifer / A list of what?

Hetty Just some ideas, really.

Katherine Hetty's got a list, girls. A list! The school is / saved.

Jennifer / Thank God for the / list.

Isabel / Is it Schindler's list? Is it? / Is it?

Jennifer / Is it a list of Jews?

Katherine *(In mock-Germanic tones)* I'm an essential verker. I verk for Hetty Fletcher!

Isabel *(sim.)* I verk in Hetty's factories! / In der factories!

Jennifer *(sim.)* / I am essential! Essential! Nein! Nein!

Katherine So what's on the list, Hetty?

Hetty Umm… *(she searches for it)*

Isabel Oh! She's got it on her!

Katherine Come on! Out with it. Let's hear it.

Isabel *(she chants)* List! List! Hetty's List! / List! List! Hetty's List!

Jennifer / List! List! Hetty's List!

Katherine Shh.

They watch as she prepares to read.

Hetty Umm... just some thoughts, basically. That I did. I sort of... umm... '1.' I, err... I just numbered them / to make it –

Katherine / Come on!

Hetty OK. '1.' I won't bother with the numbers, / actually –

Isabel / Just read the *list*.

Hetty Right. '1.' *(she winces)* 'The School Council will – ' – these are just sort of thoughts, really – 'The School Council will consist of girls from every year in the school.' I thought that was sort of fair. *(she looks at them, uncertain whether to continue)* '2. All girls will be able to vote on the membership of the School Council.' I thought that was sort of... fair. *(she is unconscious that she is repeating herself)* '3. Any girl will be able to set up any club she wishes. She won't need the Head Girl to approve it.' Umm... Shall I..? OK. '5. Girls will be able to request to share studies with a particular friend, and can request to move if things aren't working out.' I just thought, you know... because... well, I just... '6. The school shall be open, honest, hard-working, fair and especially tolerant of minorities. It should be a place where people feel confident and happy and they can all have a fair chance at being liked and valued.' That's sort of it, really.

Katherine And what does all that mean?

Hetty What do you mean?

Katherine Peace and love and happiness. What does all that actually mean?

Hetty Well, just that. Tolerance, you know.

Katherine Right, Hetty, and can you tell me who's seen this list?

Hetty No-one. Hardly anyone. I just went –

Katherine Has Howett seen it?

Hetty Umm... yes, I showed it to him.

Katherine And what did he make of it?

Hetty Err... yes, he liked it. / He liked it, yes. He said...

Katherine / He liked it, did he?

Hetty / Yes.

Katherine / Is that what he said?

Hetty Yes.

Katherine A man of his intellect.

Hetty Yes.

Katherine Well that's brilliant isn't it.

Isabel Hold on a minute. What happened to 4?

Hetty Err... I read 4.

Jennifer No you didn't; you went from 3 to 5.

Hetty Oh.

Katherine Come on. Give us clause 4. *(in sudden, non-sequitured confusion to others)* Clause 4. What's that?

Hetty Umm... '4. A special committee will be set up to

help the problem of…' *(she tries to say the word quickly and inconsequentially)* '… (bullying) in the school / to help girls who are unhappy – '

{**Jennifer** / *Bullying?*

{**Isabel** / *Bullying?*

Hetty ' – or being unfairly treated.'

Katherine *Bullying?*

Isabel But that sort of reads like you think there's bullying going on at the moment.

Hetty Well, do you not think?

Jennifer What do you mean?

Hetty You know, sort of like a bit like the way you sort of treat umm… Nicola Slater.

Jennifer *(sighs frustratedly) That's* not bullying!

Isabel But everyone treats her like that, Hetty.

Hetty Yes, but I think because apparently Katherine said something to her, apparently.

Katherine Oh, she's not still on about that, is she? That was literally one random comment.

Hetty But it was really hurtful.

Isabel To her, maybe.

Katherine But she wasn't even meant to hear it. I mean, I admit I said what she said I said but I certainly didn't say it how she said I said it.

Isabel What?

Jennifer She said she said what she said she said but

not how she said she said it.

Isabel Right.

Jennifer Hetty, Nicola Slater is treated like that because she deserves to be treated like that.

Hetty Just because she's different.

Katherine She *is* different.

Hetty But this is a Catholic school.

Isabel What's that got to do with it?

Hetty Well, because... Nicola Slater's sort of a... don't you see? She's like ostracised, and she's misunderstood, and she's sort of giving away her possessions, and she's, you know... I mean, don't you think that she's sort of... well, sort of a bit like... *Christ* in a way.

{**Katherine** / Christ?

{**Isabel** / Christ?

{**Jennifer** / Christ?

Hetty Well, in a way, yes.

Jennifer Take my theological word for it, Hetty. If Christ comes back he won't be fat and unpopular.

Isabel And if he is perhaps that's why he gets crucified.

Hetty Well you obviously don't agree with me, but –

Katherine But you can't be being serious, Hetty, surely.

Hetty I just think we have a responsibility.

Katherine To Nicola Slater.

Hetty To Nicola Slater.

Katherine Because she's like Jesus.

Hetty No, I'm not saying that, I just think we should be helping people like her, that's what we should be trying to do. The meek and the, you know...

Katherine But that's the Bible, Hetty. You can't take that literally.

Hetty Why not?

Katherine Because it would never work.

Hetty Well I think it would. The king is as the beggar, don't you think?

Isabel But by that logic Nicola *Slater* would be Head Girl.

Hetty Well I have made her my Deputy.

Katherine What have you done? *(a genuine, non-rhetorical question)*

Hetty I asked her to be Deputy Head Girl. *(pause)* And she said yes. *(pause)* And she was... happy.

A pause.

Jennifer *Why?*

Hetty I don't know. I suppose she was surprised.

Jennifer No! Why did you ask her?

Hetty Because... I think Nicola Slater being Deputy Head Girl would say good things about Nicola Slater and good things about this school.

Katherine Hetty. People like us are meant to be in charge. *(she does not include Hetty in this 'us')* That's just… natural.

Hetty But do you not think that Nicola Slater is just as capable as you?

Katherine Well of course I don't. She's just not that sort of person.

Hetty She is.

Katherine Well if she is then everyone is.

Hetty Well maybe everyone *is*.

Isabel Rubbish.

Hetty It's true.

Isabel Rubbish.

Hetty Well I think it *is* true.

Katherine I mean… just look at how she looks. Just look at how she looks.

Hetty What's that got to do with it.

Jennifer If she can't do something better with her hair how can she do something better with the school?

Katherine Well, you know, well done for having a go, Hetty, but come on. It's never going to work.

Hetty Why ever not?

Katherine Just think about it. The school will do as I tell it. I mean effectively –

Jennifer We're already running / the place.

Isabel / We're already running the place.

Katherine We are.

Hetty Yes, but officially –

Katherine Officially doesn't matter, Hetty. Come on; who are people going to listen to? You or me?

Hetty I don't know.

Katherine It's never going to work, Hetty. Look at the House Captains for next year. Cubitt –

Isabel Amanda Wadham.

Katherine Amanda Wadham was netball vice-captain when I was captain. So she's mine. 2 and 3 –

Isabel Sarah Drummond.

Katherine Sarah Drummond. Her father and my father play squash together. So *she's* mine.

Isabel 1 and 4 is / Lizzy Rainer.

Jennifer / Lizzy Rainer.

Hetty Lizzy Rainer is a friend of mine.

Katherine Well that's too bad because she doesn't like you, apparently. And that makes her mine.

Isabel Leighton is Emma Jarvis.

Katherine Now I made Emma's sister prefect when we were at prep school. So she's mine.

Isabel And teams and clubs...

Katherine At least admit *they're* mine, surely.

Jennifer I mean, perhaps some of the B teams, maybe.

Isabel But probably not.

Katherine You see, your total lack of sporting interest

and prowess is going to be a real problem there / I'm afraid.

Jennifer / So that's netball, hockey, lacrosse, swimming, athletics, tennis.

Isabel I'm the riding club.

Jennifer And I'm the debating society.

Katherine Susie Roback is the new *Caiaphas* editor. She's asked me if I want my own column whenever I've got the time, so...

Isabel So what does that leave you with? Maybe about two of the Houses and three of the clubs.

Jennifer And they're mainly like chess club, stamps, the go-out-on-Wednesdays-and-help-the-local-community thing, what is that? In the white minibus?

Isabel Spastics' Surprise or / whatever.

Katherine / So make yourself at home with those but otherwise I think you'll struggle to walk across the quad without everyone laughing behind your back, drawing moustaches on your photo and never sitting with you at lunch. Even the dropkicks won't go near you.

Isabel In fact thinking about it Nicola Slater will probably lend you a bit of credibility. Hetty Fletcher and Nicola Slater. What a team, walking round the school looking like before and after.

Katherine You'll be like that girl in Lower Fourth with one leg longer than the other or whatever's wrong with her.

Jennifer Beverley Watts.

Katherine Now I don't want that and we don't want that –

Isabel / We don't want that.

Jennifer / We really don't want that.

Katherine / – but you've got to be realistic and say that being Head Girl is not for you and you'd rather just be friends with us instead and enjoy life. So why don't you go to Howett and say you've thought about it and you can't be Head Girl any more and perhaps he should give it to someone else. Now will you do that?

Hetty Well, I… I sort of do want to be Head Girl.

Katherine But you've got to be *practical*, Hetty.

Hetty I know. But I still want to do it.

Katherine And that's more important to you than us, is it? Our friendship.

Hetty Well, I sort of would like to have both if I could.

Katherine But this *(gesturing to her)* isn't how friends should treat each other. Trampling on their / feet.

Jennifer / Dreams. Feet.

Katherine So given that you're not interested in being a real friend to us why have you been hanging round with us all these years?

Hetty Well…

Katherine Why? Come on.

Hetty I thought that's what you wanted.

Isabel It's not what we wanted, it's what you wanted.

Jennifer And even you didn't want it, it turns out. You've just been using us.

Isabel You've just been using us to get to the top.

Katherine That's the last time I feel sorry for someone.

Isabel I told you it would be pointless.

Katherine I know.

Isabel I said –

Katherine I know!

Isabel I said it's not worth it, just leave her to her… her…

Jennifer Chess club penpals.

Isabel I said leave her to her… what's it called when they put like dead flowers in between pages of a book?

Jennifer Flower arranging.

Isabel *(Tuts in total disgust. Then to Katherine:)* Like to flatten them.

Katherine Well that's not the point.

Isabel That's what I said. It's pointless.

Jennifer And now that kindness has come back to –

Katherine / Wound us.

Isabel / Betray us.

Jennifer / – has come back to haunt us.

Katherine That one act of pity.

Isabel Like a weed that's grown amid the roses.

Katherine I tell you what she's like; she's like one of those… those things that latch on to you.

Isabel Clams.

Katherine *'Clams'!*

Isabel Yeah; like… limpets. Is that right?

Jennifer She's a limpet. She even sounds like a limpet. A 'lim-pit'. Are you a limpet, Hetty? A little limpet?

Katherine And what are those things, I think they sort of bite you and suck your blood –

Jennifer Bats.

Isabel *(in agreement)* / Bats! *(then, seeing Katherine's reaction)* No, not bats, you moron.

Katherine / And like they used to use them for medical things.

Hetty Leeches.

Katherine Leeches. Thank you. She's like a leech.

Isabel She *is* like a leech, isn't she.

Katherine And I thought I'd take a chance on you, letting you be a part of our gang out of decency and kindness and consideration even though (a) Isabel and Jennifer had profound misgivings, (b) you're not popular with the rest of the school, (c) you don't make much of a contribution –

Isabel (d) Your father works at Waitrose.

Hetty He works for John Lewis.

Jennifer It's the same retail group, Hetty.

Katherine (e) you look pre-pubescent, (f) you got a C in French / GCSE –

Jennifer / (g) You were lapped in the fifteen hundred at the Fourth Form Sports Day.

Isabel (h) You used to think 'fajitas' was pronounced 'fajjitas'.

Katherine (i) When you joined the school you had a purse with a picture of a dog on it that you kept round your neck on a bit of string.

Isabel (j) Someone used the computer after you last year and saw you'd been looking at some sort of anorexic helpline website.

Katherine (k) You cried when we watched the Queen Mother's funeral in Assembly.

Jennifer / (l) –

Isabel / (l) – No, sorry; after you.

Jennifer Thanks. (l) You walked around for about half an hour after chemistry once and you didn't realise you were still wearing your science goggles.

Isabel (m) One time you thought we were laughing at something you said but we were actually laughing at something else.

Katherine (n) Some girls in 2 and 3 hit their ball out of the tennis court and you weren't strong enough to throw it over the fence back to them.

Jennifer (o) We were once talking about dress size 8 and you thought we were talking about Age 8 in children's sizes.

Isabel (p) Sometimes you've got really bad split ends.

Jennifer (q) You were sitting in one of the leather chairs in the common room and when you moved it sounded like you'd farted so you moved again to show it was the chair but that just made it sound like you'd farted twice.

Katherine Where are we?

Isabel R.

Katherine (r) You 'represented' the school on that spelling programme and you didn't know how to spell 'occurring'.

Isabel (s) You didn't understand what we were laughing about when we were reading Macbeth and it says 'Enter Lady Macbeth with a taper'.

Jennifer (t) Kelly Pearce reckoned you once tried to throw away some soiled knickers and then denied they were yours.

Isabel (u) You made a tape for your grandmother at Christmas of you singing carols.

Katherine (v) You believed us when we told you that new girl's name was Sarah Ball-Pawsey and you went up and said 'Hello Sarah'.

Isabel (w) You wrote a poem in calligraphy saying how much you liked us.

Katherine (x) Your mother used to video the Vicar of Dibley and post you the tapes.

Jennifer (y) We can often see quite a bit of hair on your upper lip.

Isabel (z) You're thin but you're the wrong sort of thin.

Katherine *(without the slightest pause)* So even despite all that we decided to welcome you into our gang and help you and do all we could for you.

By now Hetty is evidently close to tears and totally still and silent, perhaps as a defence against external shows of grief.

Jennifer But...

Isabel And this is the thanks we get.

Katherine So on that basis are you *now* prepared to go back to Howett and tell him you don't want to be Head Girl?

Hetty *(after a moment of stillness she silently shakes her head)*

Katherine You still want to be Head Girl?

Hetty *(she similarly nods)*

Jennifer and Isabel begin to boo and jeer, during which Katherine repeats:

Katherine Shame on you! Shame on you! Shame on you!

The booing continues, creating a wall of sound from which the subsequent insults issue.

Katherine Out, out, damned spot!

Jennifer Who will rid us of this meddlesome priest?

Katherine I wouldn't even spit on you, to be honest.

Isabel Oh, I would.

Katherine I wouldn't have to.

Isabel Oh, I would. I'd love to see my spit running down your ugly little face.

Jennifer Your bland little forgettable little face.

Isabel I'd love to see it with the teeth caved in, you on your hands and knees coughing up blood.

Jennifer Your head getting flushed down the toilet.

Isabel Getting kicked in the womb, right in your dead little womb.

Katherine I'll give her this, she's bloody stubborn. You'd have folded by now, Izzy, I know you would for a fact.

Isabel Oh, I'd be admiring her if it didn't make me physically sick just to look at her.

There is a pause. Katherine and perhaps others are visibly frustrated.

Katherine I don't know what to do. I don't know what to do. What are we going to do, Hetty?

Hetty I don't know. I just… want to be Head Girl and try to… can you not just let me?

Katherine Come on, now; now you're really beginning to insult me. *(pause)* I don't know what we're going to do, girls.

Jennifer We seem to have reached something of an impasse.

Pause. They catch their breath, or pace, or say 'hmm' etc.

Isabel Hold on a minute. I think I may have it.

Katherine What?

Isabel I think we can hoist Miss Morality on her own petard.

Katherine How so?

Isabel The diary.

Jennifer What do you mean?

Isabel Well, what we read in the diary.

Katherine Keep going.

Isabel Well, if Howett were to read Nicola Slater's diary she'd be expelled.

Jennifer Yes?

Isabel So if Hetty really is dead set on helping and protecting and all the rest of it then she'll agree to anything to get the diary back.

Jennifer Including renouncing the throne.

Katherine Aha!

Isabel Because she wants to save Nicola Slater a.k.a. our Lord and Saviour.

Jennifer Or does she?

Katherine Girls, I could kiss you.

Isabel Frankly it would be a pleasure.

Katherine So, Het-up. Did you cop the gist of that?

The horns of an ethical dilemma. Can you put your money where your mouth is?

Jennifer Or your lack of money –

Isabel And your moustachioed mouth.

Hetty But what's in the diary?

Katherine Ho, ho! What isn't in the diary? Read it and weep, bird-girl.

Jennifer shows Hetty the relevant section of the diary. She reads.

Katherine Have you read it? Good.

Hetty Is this true?

Isabel It must be. It's in the diary.

Katherine Now if Howett were to ever read that she's going to be expelled and her life will sink without trace. Her one chance is that at least she can say she went to this school but she won't be able to say that if you're Head Girl because if you're Head Girl Howett will see this because I will personally give it to him –

Isabel Or I will.

Katherine – and she'll be expelled and she'll be humiliated and destroyed. *(pause)* You really want to help her? You want the geek to inherit the earth? You want to be decent and fair and all the rest of it? *(pause)* Look at me. Look at me. *Look at me*. I'll give him that diary. I swear I will. I swear to you. *(pause)* So. At the risk of asking it a third time… *Now* will you go to Howett and say you don't want to be Head Girl?

A pause.

Hetty *(perhaps even laughing wearily with relief)* OK, you win.

Katherine I what?

Hetty You win.

Katherine I win.

Hetty If that's what you want, Katherine, you can have it.

Katherine Well, well, well.

Hetty If that's what you want.

Katherine Good girl. You see? Now we can be friends again. That's all it took. So you'll go to Howett?

Hetty Yeah.

Katherine And you'll tell him you've thought about it and you don't want to be Head Girl any more?

Hetty Yes.

Katherine And maybe you'll suggest someone who might be a better choice?

Hetty *(nods)*

Katherine And might that person be me?

Hetty *(nods)*

Katherine Good girl. Now don't cry.

Hetty I won't.

Katherine Don't cry.

Hetty I won't cry.

Katherine There's a good girl. Just think nice thoughts. Can you do that?

Hetty Yes.

Katherine Good. Now. Do you think it's a good idea to still hang round with the three of us?

Hetty *(pause)* No.

Katherine After what you've done?

Hetty No.

Katherine No. You're quite happy to go your own way?

Hetty Yes.

Katherine Back to Nicola Slater. Just say it's all fallen through but at least you've got each other or whatever.

Hetty I'll just... make other plans.

Katherine You'll just make other plans. Exactly. And you don't feel bad about that?

Hetty No. Well... except for... Simon.

Katherine Except for what?

Hetty Simon. My... my brother. He was hoping that Jennifer would sort of spend the summer with us. I know he was really hoping to... I mean like he cancelled soccer summer school so that he could be at home when Jennifer was there but that's OK, I mean I'll tell him and it's probably not too late for him to re-apply so... he should be alright.

Katherine Thanks for that. Now Jennifer, could you give us the diary, please?

Jennifer What's that? *(she genuinely has not heard Katherine)*

Katherine We'll have to hang on to it until Hetty's actually gone to Howett.

Jennifer Oh, yes, right. *(pause)* Although, the thing is... well, maybe we should think a bit more carefully.

Isabel About what?

Jennifer I don't know; don't you think we're being a bit hasty? Why don't we give the diary to Hetty as a matter for her conscience?

Katherine What are you talking about?

Jennifer Just... well, she is Head Girl, and I think we ought to...

Katherine Come on, Jennifer, just give me the diary.

Jennifer I'm sorry, Katherine.

Katherine Just give me the diary, will you.

Jennifer gives the diary to Hetty.

Hetty Thanks, Jennifer.

Katherine Oh! I see.

Jennifer I'm sorry about all this.

Katherine I never thought I'd see the day. Isabel, maybe; I had my doubts about her. But *you*.

Jennifer I'm sorry.

Katherine No you're not.

Jennifer Well I was, but...

Isabel So, that's the end of the gang, is it? Just like that.

Jennifer You've got to think about the future, Izzy.

Isabel The future. Just like that. Brutus.

Jennifer OK.

Isabel Perkin Warbeck. Am I getting close?

Jennifer Not really.

Isabel Marshal Petain.

Jennifer Fair enough.

Isabel The Rosenburgs.

Jennifer What; both of them?

Isabel Lord Haw-Haw.

Jennifer Not actually a traitor. He was Irish.

Isabel Well, he was actually American, but –

Jennifer Carry on.

Isabel Judas.

Jennifer Which one?

Isabel Judas Iscariot.

Jennifer Brilliant.

Katherine And to think I've been sticking up for you, Jennifer.

Jennifer Well, I'm grateful, but I didn't ask you to.

Katherine And had you asked me to I wouldn't have but I did it because I wanted to stick up for you.

Jennifer OK.

Katherine I didn't do it for thanks, Jennifer, / I did it because –

Jennifer / I'm not thanking you.

Katherine No, that's what I'm saying; I *didn't* do it to be thanked.

Jennifer Yeah, I know; you're not going to be.

Katherine Perfect. Because I didn't do it to be thanked –

Jennifer / Brilliant.

Katherine / I did it because I didn't like what literally everybody in the entire school was saying about you.

Jennifer Well done for taking a stand.

Katherine Well don't you even want to know what everyone was saying?

Jennifer Why would I want / to know?

Katherine / You don't even want / to know?

Jennifer / Why would I want to?

Katherine OK. Well, I'll tell you anyway.

Jennifer Fair enough.

Katherine Well I don't want to tell you but it was actually something really cruel to do with your physical appearance.

Jennifer Well what was it?

Katherine I can't say anything, I'm afraid. But thanks for all your years of loyalty, though.

Jennifer That's alright.

Katherine Yeah; thanks very much.

Jennifer That's quite alright.

Katherine Thanks.

Jennifer You're welcome.

Katherine I'm grateful.

Jennifer Yeah; you said.

Katherine Yeah; I am.

Jennifer Brilliant.

Katherine So thanks again.

Jennifer Not at all.

Katherine That's very kind.

Jennifer Don't mention it.

Katherine Very kind.

Jennifer Think nothing of it.

Katherine Just wanted / to say thank you.

Jennifer / I'm sure you'd do the same for me.

Katherine Well, we'll never know now will we. / Will we?

Jennifer / I suppose not.

Katherine We'll never know. And after all my father has done for this school, after all that… And Hetty – *Head Girl* – is on a scholarship. So I'm paying for you to be here. Which sort of makes you our guest in a way, doesn't it.

Hetty I'm sorry that's how you feel, Katherine.

Katherine You just haven't thought this through, have you. Your great social experiment. You think that your Nicola Slaters are going to do well out there? In the big wide world? The average and the unattractive? No? Then don't tell them they are. They've got enough to worry about without you giving them impossible hopes that are going to be shattered at the first of a million hurdles. Don't lie to them, Hetty; at least do them that service. At least tell them where they stand.

Hetty You're not lying to them. You're sort of giving them valuable moments of happiness and pride to help sustain them through difficult times.

Katherine Sure; sounds great but it doesn't work.

Hetty We'll see.

Katherine Thanks, Hetty. Thanks for turning this school into an average school for average people. You know the kind of people I mean. Very nice, very pleasant, much like yourself. But very much... you know; gap year temping, Exeter, Bristol, Durham, Leeds, perhaps then Guildford law school where you meet your husband, or accountancy exams, careful with money, wedding reception at the local rugby club, living an hour and a half from work to have a garden big enough for the children, state school, NHS, packed lunches, holidays in the Lake District, Lib Dem, your husband losing his hair, playing the Lottery, watching Top Gear. Empty nest, perhaps an affair, worried about your pension, retirement job working mornings in the local arts centre. Cancer.

Hetty And what's wrong with that? That's life, isn't it.

Katherine It's not everyone's life, Hetty.

Hetty Yeah, but it's not about that, is it. It's about the stuff in between.

Katherine Like what?

Hetty I don't know; the little things. Little things you don't notice. Long summer evenings on the patio with a bottle of sparkling wine. Love. Duty. You know. Christmas.

Katherine Is that it?

Isabel Always winter, Hetty, and never Christmas.

Katherine You want my prediction?

Jennifer Not really.

Katherine You'll be back here in two days begging forgiveness. You won't last ten minutes without me. You'll be three lepers. Don't worry. You'll be back here in a couple of days when you've had a taste of life outside the firm. And you know what? When you do I'll make a deal. Because that's the kind of person I am.

Hetty Thanks, Katherine.

Isabel Off you go, lesbians. Enjoy each other, won't you. Give my best to Fatso.

Katherine Now get out of my sight.

Jennifer Thanks.

Katherine Yeah.

Isabel And may your God go with you.

Hetty and Jennifer leave. The mood in the room

changes.

Katherine They'll be back. Don't worry. They'll be back. *(pause)* You'll see. They'll come back. *(a very long pause, within which she deflates slightly)* You can clear off as well if you like, Isabel. *(pause)* Izzy? *(Pause. She is not going. The mood alters.)* What am I going to tell, him, Izzy? What am I going to tell him?

Isabel Just tell him… yeah, I see what you mean.

Katherine 'So as we rode we talked, and the swift thought, Winging itself with laughter, lingered not, but flew from brain to brain, – such glee was ours, Charged with light memories of remembered hours, None slow enough for sadness; till we came homeward, which always makes the spirit tame.'

End.

EMBASSYLAND

to Oliver

Characters
in order of appearance

Detective Constable Thomson
Detective Constable Jowett
Alistair Sixsmith
Alan Knowles

Embassyland opened at the Landor Theatre, London on Tuesday 1 November 2005 with the following cast:

Thomson	Adrian Fear
Jowett	Fred Perry
Sixsmith	Robert Linden
Alan	Nathan Griggs

Directed by	Rosie Wilkinson
Designed by	Rebecca Vincent
Stage management	Hannah Ireland
	Marnie Chesterton
	Stuart Griffith

Scene 1

Thomson Look, I don't know if they've said anything.

Jowett Yep, they told me.

Thomson Well hang on; who told you?

Jowett Jarman.

Thomson What did he say?

Jowett Well, I'm not sure I'm supposed to / say anything.

Thomson / No; what did he say? Did he say you had it?

Jowett Well... yeah.

Thomson *(sighs in genuine annoyance at Jarman)* Right, yeah, he was worried it might've... because that was a mistake.

Jowett What are you talking about?

Thomson Yeah, there was a bit of a miscommunication there.

Jowett What the hell / are you talking about?

Thomson / He's sorry about that, I think. Apparently you haven't got it.

Jowett What do you mean I haven't got it?

Thomson Yes; he just meant to say well done... sort of well done anyway.

Jowett What are you / talking about?

Thomson / He said something / a bit ambiguous, I think, and –

Jowett / You're absolutely right he said something; it *wasn't* ambiguous; / he said I had it.

Thomson / Because Jarman spoke to me and he was worried suddenly / looking back that –

Jowett / I don't know what / you're talking about, mate.

Thomson / – it would look like he was saying you'd got it / when actually he was just saying –

Jowett / Yeah, that's exactly what he said.

Thomson / – well done. That it might sound confusing.

Jowett Look, I know what he said. He said well done.

Thomson Yeah, that's what I'm saying he said. Well done. / Despite not getting it.

Jowett / Well there you go then; well done.

Thomson But that doesn't mean you got it, though, / does it.

Jowett / *Fucking hell!* Well why did he say it then?

Thomson It was a mistake. I think he just meant… you know, sort of consolations. I don't think he was thinking.

Jowett But I've already told… oh this is fucking killing. I've already told everyone.

Thomson Well why did you do that?

Jowett Because I was told I'd got it.

Thomson Yeah, but you *weren't*.

Jowett The guy came up to me –

Thomson / Jarman said –

Jowett – / and said / well done and looking forward –

Thomson / I know what he said. But it was a mistake because –

Jowett Well how could he make a mistake like that?

Thomson Because he was just trying to be supportive and nice.

Jowett Oh *fucking hell*. He's really… what the fuck did he do that for?

Thomson He was just trying to help; / he didn't mean anything by it.

Jowett / The moron. What a fucking moron. He's a / fucking dipstick.

Thomson / I think he feels sort of embarrassed / because looking back –

Jowett / *He* feels embarrassed? He hasn't just gone around telling everyone he's been made sergeant.

Thomson But that's what I'm saying; you shouldn't have done that –

Jowett / What do you mean?

Thomson / – until you'd checked.

Jowett *Checked*? Checked with who?

Thomson *(a bit embarrassed)* Well, yeah, ordinarily Jarman, yeah, but / obviously –

Jowett / What a fucking numbnut. What am I going to do now? I've already... oh fucking hell.

Thomson Look, I'm sorry. And I know Jarman's sorry.

Jowett Bloody hell. I've just spent the best part of... *(he sighs angrily)*

Thomson I think everyone's sorry.

Jowett Well who *did* get it then? *(beat)* Oh no, no; you've got to be fucking shitting me.

Thomson Well, that's how it went.

Jowett But why you? *(laughs; so frustrated he is genuinely amused)* Why you?!

Thomson I don't know. I guess...

Jowett I don't understand it.

Thomson OK.

Jowett Can I just say that I just want to say that we both know I scored higher in the exam than you.

Thomson Yes, but that's not the whole thing, is it. That's only part of it.

Jowett I know.

Thomson Well there you are then.

Jowett No, because it's a major part of it and I obviously showed I had potential and then suddenly...

Thomson Yes, but we all had potential it's just that

there was only one sergeant position. So it has to go to –

Jowett The best candidate.

Thomson No, well, no; the candidate... the person who did the best job on the day.

Jowett But that's the whole point – it wasn't just that day.

Thomson I'm not... look, if you want me to say it's unfair I'll say it's unfair but it's always unfair in a way, isn't it. And if you got it and I didn't then that would be unfair too.

Jowett No, I know that. I'm just surprised, that's all.

Thomson Well, there we are.

Jowett It's just fucking... I know it's not your fault.

Thomson I'm not saying it is.

Jowett I know, I'm not saying that. But can they not just take into account... I've got five years on you.

Thomson Doesn't matter.

Jowett Well it matters to me.

Thomson But that's not one of the things they go on.

Jowett *Exactly.* That's why it's unfair.

Thomson No, because how could it be? You can't have... I mean if you were sixty years old –

Jowett I'm just saying it's unfair, that's all.

Thomson Look, your five years are not what it goes

on, OK? That's not my fault. If you don't want to accept the decision then there's nothing *I* can do about it. Why don't you just appeal or something?

Jowett Because I don't want to. I want to get it on merit.

Thomson Yes, but it *went* on merit and you didn't get it.

Jowett Look. Justice was not done. Let's at least agree on that.

Thomson Well, no, I'm sorry, I'm not going to agree on that.

Jowett You honestly think you're a better officer than I am.

Thomson No, I'm not saying that.

Jowett Well in that case justice wasn't done, was it.

Thomson Yeah, but I don't accept that.

Jowett Look, I'm just trying to say… Congratulations.

Thomson No you're not.

Jowett You can take it or you can leave it, mate, but there it is. Congratulations.

Thomson OK. Thanks.

Jowett Yeah. You're welcome.

Thomson Look. I just want to make it clear that this was nothing to do with your… the… incident.

Jowett Wha..? This should have nothing to do with

that.

Thomson It doesn't.

Jowett It's got nothing to do with that.

Thomson Yeah; that's what I'm saying. It's got nothing to do with it.

Jowett Yeah, but you shouldn't have to.

Thomson Well, I just thought you might think –

Jowett Well I wouldn't've ...

Thomson But in case you did.

Jowett That's got nothing to do with work. It's got nothing to do with it.

Thomson Well. It was a work party.

Jowett *(sigh)* Yeah but a work party's not *work*, is it. It's a party.

Thomson Well people –

Jowett / It's a *party*.

Thomson / Well people from work were there.

Jowett Yeah, but it's not *work*, though, is it.

Thomson Well, it sort of is.

Jowett No it's not; it's a party. It's just / a party.

Thomson / Yeah, but people from work were there.

Jowett Doesn't matter.

Thomson Well, it *does*...

Jowett A work party isn't work, that's all I'm saying.

Thomson But there *were* people from work there.

Jowett It's a party.

Thomson Disagree.

Jowett You're the one saying it's nothing to do with it.

Thomson I'm not saying it's nothing to do with work, I'm saying it's nothing to do with the promotion.

Jowett Well how do you know? Five minutes ago we were the same rank.

Thomson We still are.

Jowett Just do me a favour.

Thomson All I'm saying is; in case you thought it was…

Jowett How do you know what the decision is based on? You're just a… fellow applicant.

Thomson I'm just trying to… Look, if everyone was going around talking about me I'd want to know about it and whether –

Jowett Why's everyone talking about me? Why's everyone talking about me?

Thomson They're not. Well, no, I'm saying *if* people were talking –

Jowett Well *are* they?

Thomson No, not really.

Jowett OK. *(pause)* What are they saying?

Thomson I've no idea. I don't know. / I don't know.

Jowett / You must know. How can you know they're talking about me but you don't know what they're saying? / That's impossible, isn't it?

Thomson / No, well, I... OK, well, it's just there's a general... feeling.

Jowett They're just a bunch of fucking gossips.

Thomson I'm not sure that's fair. I mean if someone does something, people tend to talk about it.

Jowett Well, yeah; gossip.

Thomson No, I just think its just... part of what doing something involves.

Jowett Yeah but I didn't even... *fucking hell!* I didn't even do anything. Why can't people mind their own business?

Thomson I don't know. I don't know.

Jowett Look, I'm sorry. This isn't... well, there we are.

Thomson Yes.

Jowett So was it Derek who told you?

Thomson Yes.

Jowett And what did he say?

Thomson Exactly that. Plus... he's just worried about you.

Jowett Why?

Thomson He just thought you might think that it was

because of the party.

Jowett But it's not.

Thomson But it's not. Right.

Jowett Right.

Thomson So just forget about it.

Jowett Yeah, that's the point. I wouldn't *have* to forget about it if you hadn't told me about it.

Thomson I'm just trying to reassure you.

Jowett No, I know, but there's ways of…

Thomson OK, OK. I'm sorry.

Jowett Alright. Thanks.

Thomson Yeah.

Jowett Well did he say anything else?

Thomson No. Other than he told me not to say anything.

Jowett About what?

Thomson The promotion.

Jowett Oh, for goodness sakes! What are you telling me for then?

Thomson Out of fairness. I thought you'd want to know.

Jowett Fucking hell.

Thomson It's not worth worrying about.

Jowett Not for you. You've just got a fifteen grand price hike and your own office for fuck's sake. *(sighs)* I'm sorry, it just really pisses me off.

Thomson I understand.

A pause. Something outside the window catches their eye and they follow its progress silently. The mood changes.

Scene 2

Thomson OK, well, thanks for / *(Sixsmith and Jowett have their conversation sotto voce while Thomson is talking to Alan)* waiting for us, I do appreciate that. I'm most grateful to you for coming in and allowing us to have a bit of a chat; I hope it's not too inconvenient a time and we'll certainly do all we can to speed things up and make things as painless as possible for you.

Sixsmith / John! Congratulations, mate!

Jowett No...

Sixsmith Yeah, I heard from Tony.

Jowett No; I didn't get it.

Sixsmith You're kidding me.

Jowett No, there was a 'mistake'.

Sixsmith Oh, mate. Oh, mate.

Jowett Yeah, that's it.

Sixsmith Well which idiot *did* they give it to?

A pause.

Thomson So have you got everything you need, Alan?

Alan I think Mr Knowles *is* the correct form of address, Officer?

Thomson Of course. Of course.

Alan If we could get these things squared off at the start. You know.

Thomson Absolutely. I'm sorry.

Alan It's just respect, really, isn't it.

Thomson Yes. No, I agree.

Alan Who's the sergeant. *(to Jowett)* Are you the sergeant?

Jowett No. He is.

Alan Well what people tend to forget is that it's policing by consent in this country / and unless the people are happy with –

Jowett / OK, Mr Knowles, / whenever you're –

Alan / Err.. *excuse me*? *(pause)* Excuse me.

Jowett Yeah, I'm just saying if you / want to…

Alan / *Not* a very good start, is it. *(pause)* Is it?

Sixsmith Don't worry, Alan. Don't worry. OK? Now; before we start, don't feel under any pressure to answer any questions and if you've got any questions then just ask, yeah?

Alan Right.

Sixsmith OK?

Alan Yes.

Sixsmith *(to Jowett)* OK, John, we're ready to go, whenever you're ready.

Thomson Thanks, Alistair.

Sixsmith Yeah.

Jowett How's your hand, sir? Is it alright?

Alan Thank you for asking.

Jowett It's alright, is it?

Alan I don't think we need to worry about that.

Jowett No, I'm just asking.

Alan Yes; it's quite alright, thank you.

Jowett Brilliant.

Alan Yes.

Jowett Because it looks like it hurts.

Alan I think we can let me / worry about my hand, officer.

Jowett / That's why I ask, you see.

Alan It's fine. My physical health is a matter for myself, thank you very much.

Jowett Yeah, sorry, I just wanted to / check –

Alan / It's quite alright, thank you.

Jowett Don't want a painkiller or anything?

Sixsmith Err... that's highly inappropriate.

Jowett What? I'm just / asking him whether –

Sixsmith / His health isn't the issue, is it.

Jowett No, I know. I know. I'm just trying to... I was just asking him if he wanted a painkiller.

Alan No, I've already taken one.

Jowett Ah, so it *does* hurt.

Alan No, because I've taken a painkiller.

Jowett Yeah; because it hurts.

Alan No.

Jowett Hmm. Not a very good start, Mr Knowles.

Alan We're not here to talk about my hand, are we.

A pause.

Thomson Maybe. *(pause)* OK. Well, let's start with the job, if we may. How's that all going?

Alan The job is fine, thanks, officer.

Thomson Good. No problems at all?

Alan No; no problems. Just limbering up for a pay award, I think.

Thomson What's that; a promotion?

Alan Well it might be.

Thomson Great.

Alan Thank you. Yes.

Thomson And there's been no… problems there recently.

Alan None whatsoever, officer.

Thomson Brilliant.

Alan Like what, exactly?

Sixsmith No; we don't / need to open that up, Alan.

Thomson / I don't know; anything unusual or strange or anything that sort of sticks in the mind.

Alan No. It's been very busy, I must say.

Thomson Nothing… anecdotal?

Alan No, no.

Jowett *Nothing* that happened to you there recently.

Alan Like I said: No.

Thomson OK. OK. OK.

Alan I hope that's clear.

Thomson Is that clear, Constable?

Jowett Think so, yeah.

Thomson OK. So let's talk a bit about out of work.

Alan Very well.

Jowett Do you own a gun, Alan?

Alan Now hang on.

Jowett OK. *(beat)* Do you own a gun, Alan?

Alan *(sighs petulantly)* I am a member of the Melhurst

Rifle Range so yes, a gun is kept for me there for which I have a licence.

Thomson So how long have you been a member of the club, Alan?

Alan Perhaps a number of years, yes.

Thomson So, what; a couple of years.

Alan Something like that, yes.

Sixsmith If you can't remember, Alan, just say you can't remember.

Alan Thank you, Alistair. Yes; I don't recall exactly, I'm afraid, so I can't help you out there, officers.

Thomson OK. But that big trophy you've got at home; that's from the club, isn't it?

Alan Err… yes. I won that two years a – so yes; it must have been over two years ago that I joined.

Thomson Brilliant. And what was the trophy for?

Alan That was actually the overall… it was for overall best shot of the year. They take into account all your registered shoots over the year, so…

Thomson Brilliant. That takes some doing, yeah?

Alan Well, there are approximately eighty members of the club, so, yes, the, the, the err statistics are against you let's say that.

Thomson Right. Yeah. Good stuff. And what's the name of the guy who runs it?

Alan What, the club?

Thomson Yes.

Sixsmith Sorry; what's the relevance of this?

Thomson Well, you'll / see where we're –

Sixsmith / I can't see how the name / of the owner –

Thomson / Just establishing background. Just establishing background.

Sixsmith *(beat)* Fair enough.

Thomson So. Sorry, Alan. Now can you remember the name of the guy who runs the club?

Alan Err... well, Mr Young is his name, I believe, a young-ish chap.

Thomson Andrew Young, yeah.

Alan You didn't speak to him, did you?

Thomson What do you mean?

Alan No; I was just wondering what this really had to do with anything. I'm just a witness.

Thomson I know, I know.

Alan So, you know; it's not about me, is it? I'm just the witness.

Jowett It's just that you own a gun, Alan, so we have / to just check –

Alan / Yes, but I've told you that it's purely for the club purposes, it's kept at the clubhouse as you know, so quite what –

Thomson Alan, Alan, don't worry. Yes, we spoke to

Andrew / and he said –

Alan / Well you shouldn't have done that. / That was very foolish.

Thomson / I'm not sure, Alan. We spoke to him and he said that you'd actually never been a member of the club.

Alan Err… well, yes, that *is* true, because… but he knows me well.

Thomson He *does* know you well, yes, because apparently the two of you / had a bit of a –

Alan / We had a disagreement, yes, over his unprofessional / approach to –

Thomson / He says you wanted to join but argued over the price and then refused a police check.

Alan That's absolute rubbish.

Thomson Is it?

Alan I did think about joining, yes, but I decided that given the low quality of the facilities it was not worth the membership fee which was, / in my opinion, extortionate.

Thomson / But Alan, why did you say you were a member?

Alan *(beat)* Because… in some ways… I was effectively a member of the club but I just chose not to join at that time.

Thomson Yes, but you weren't a member.

Alan I'm sorry, yes; I got confused. Err... Alistair?

Sixsmith Well I'm confused now too. Sorry, can we just stop for a minute –

Thomson / If you want.

Sixsmith / – while I check to see what he said.

Thomson OK.

Sixsmith OK. Let's get this right. Are you a member?

Alan No.

Sixsmith No.

Alan No.

Sixsmith Right. *(beat)* But you told the officers you were.

Alan I got confused.

Sixsmith OK. That's alright. *(to officers)* Do you want to ask the question again?

Thomson Have you ever been a member of the club, Alan?

Alan No.

Sixsmith So that's cleared that up.

Thomson But why did you say you were, Alan?

Sixsmith He's told you; he was confused.

Alan I was confused.

Thomson But what was confusing, Alan? I asked if you were a member of the club and you said yes.

Alan No. No I didn't.

Thomson You did.

Alan No; that's not quite right.

Thomson You said yes, you said for a couple of years.

Alan No; I was... referring to when I enquired about joining.

Thomson No; we were clear. / We were clear.

Alan / But I didn't understand.

Thomson / If you didn't understand, Alan, why didn't you say so?

Sixsmith / If you didn't understand, Alan, just say you didn't understand.

Alan Yes; that's what I'm doing. I didn't understand.

Sixsmith Well there you go then. He didn't understand.

Thomson OK. Well if I can ask the question –

Alan Yes?

Thomson Were you *ever* a member of the rifle club?

Alan No.

Thomson You weren't.

Alan No I wasn't.

Thomson You were never a member?

Alan No.

Thomson If not of that one then perhaps another?

Alan No.

Jowett Why would you refuse a CRB?

Alan I didn't.

Thomson Yes you did.

Alan No I didn't. I'd have welcomed it.

Thomson Why refuse the check?

Alan I didn't.

Thomson Andrew Young seemed to think you did.

Alan Well he's wrong.

Thomson He's wrong, is he?

Alan He's making all that up.

Thomson Why would he do that?

Sixsmith Come on, that's opinion evidence. My client has made it clear. He's said Mr Young was wrong, that's the end of the matter. *(to Alan)* You've given your answer, there we are, / let's leave it at that.

Thomson / Come on, Alistair; it's a reasonable question.

Alan Well it's not, actually, and my lawyer is right to raise his, err, his, err, his hackles but as it happens Mr Young *was* a rather aggressive young man, not unlike yourselves, I took a dislike to him, he may have done the same and this resulted in bad feelings on both sides.

Thomson All over a straightforward police records check.

Alan But it wasn't *over* the police check.

Thomson Really?

Alan No.

Thomson What, he asked you to do one and you said yes?

Alan No.

Thomson Well there we are then. You refused the check.

Alan No, because he never mentioned it.

Thomson But by law he has to.

Alan Well arrest *him* then.

Thomson Oh, don't worry, Alan; we've already spoken to Andrew Young.

Alan Well I'm not sure what / he said but it's very malicious by the sound of it.

Sixsmith / Ignore that. Ignore that.

Thomson OK. *(pause)* Now how about the trophy.

Alan What about it.

Thomson Well how did you get the trophy?

Alan Well, like I... it was for shooting, basically. Marksmanship. We've been over this.

Thomson But you weren't a member of the club.

Alan Because they were so unreasonable.

Thomson OK, they were unreasonable.

Alan Very unreasonable.

Thomson OK; they were very unreasonable. Now how did you get the trophy.

Alan *(to Sixsmith)* I can just say 'No comment', yeah?

Sixsmith If that's what you want to do.

Alan Well yes, it is, because the line of questioning is highly… objectionable.

Sixsmith Well you say that then.

Thomson Alan. The trophy.

Alan What about it?

Jowett Alan, I've seen it, mate. In your front room. A big almighty trophy with your name on the bottom of it. *Your* name. Who gave it to you?

Alan No-one; it's mine.

Jowett Right, but who gave it to you.

Thomson The club didn't.

Jowett Exactly.

Thomson So who gave it to you.

Sixsmith You don't have to answer if you don't want to, Alan.

Alan Yes, thank you, Alistair.

Thomson Although obviously we'd like you to answer.

Sixsmith But you don't have to.

Thomson Simply because it stops us all wasting our

time and barking up the wrong avenues.

Sixsmith But the fact is he doesn't have to answer.

Thomson No, no; there's no pressure.

Sixsmith Exactly. *(privately to Alan)* Although you are under an obligation to tell the truth / and it could harm your defence if you later say something that you don't say now.

Jowett / Absolutely; if you're really ashamed of who you are, Alan, then by all means hide behind Alistair. That's your right under the law. That's the sort of country we live in / and I think we're all glad about that.

Sixsmith / He's not hiding behind me. He's answering questions perfectly / adequately.

Alan / Yeah; I'm not hiding behind him.

Jowett And it's not for us to pass judgement on that because it's your right.

Alan I'm not hiding behind him.

Thomson Fine. So how did you get the trophy?

Alan It was presented to me by William Forbes & Sons.

Thomson OK.

Jowett Alan, they're an *engravers*.

Alan They are engravers, yes.

Thomson So what; unprompted, they…

Alan No; I commissioned it.

Thomson But *why*, Alan?

Alan I thought I deserved a bit of a treat. Is that a crime?

Thomson / *(beat)* No.

Jowett / *(beat)* No.

Thomson OK, Alan. What else do you like to do with your spare time?

Alan I don't know.

Thomson Watch tv?

Alan Sometimes, of course.

Sixsmith Sorry; where's this going?

Thomson We're just trying to / establish –

Sixsmith / I'll be honest, I don't see the relevance.

Thomson Evidence as to character, Alistair; evidence as to character.

Sixsmith OK.

Thomson OK. Ever watch any videos, Alan?

Alan Sometimes.

Thomson You're a member of the Blockbuster on the High Street, aren't you?

Alan Err… I believe I am, yes.

Thomson OK. Well we've got a list here of the films you've rented from there in the past few months and we'll read it to you now to check if it rings any bells.

Alan Well I'd really rather you didn't.

Thomson Mmm... think we'll do it anyway.

Jowett OK. *(he gives a copy to Sixsmith and reads aloud from his own copy)* 'Patriot Games. Goodfellas. The Magnificent Seven. Seven. Diana – The Death of a Princess. The Boys From Brazil. Princess Diana – A Life in Pictures. Tits & Asses 3. The Nazis – A Warning From History. Baywatch Babes As You've Never Seen Them Before. Jaws. Dances With Wolves. The Tragedy of Charles and Diana. Who Dares Wins. JFK. More Wet Rides. Hitler's Last Army. Stalin. The SAS – Trained to Kill. A Celebration of Royal Weddings. Beauty and the Beast. Ace Ventura Pet Detective. Jenna From All Angles. Lolita. Platoon.'

Thomson Have you got anything to say about that list?

Alan *(pause)* I just want to say I / know what you're trying to do and it's disgusting.

Sixsmith / Don't say anything. Don't say anything.

Jowett It's disgusting, is it?

Alan Absolutely filthy. / You've no right –

Jowett / *We're* filthy? Well, we can talk about rights if you / like because I think you'll find us experts there, but –

Alan / I just mean you've got no business taking everything out of context.

Jowett What context *did* you watch them / in, Alan?

Alan / I've never been treated like this in my life and I'm jolly glad my lawyer is here.

Thomson We're just asking questions, Alan. That's / all we're doing.

Alan / No you're not; you're insinuating… Alistair?

Sixsmith Well I have to say that this sounds a perfectly reasonable list to me.

Jowett You think?

Sixsmith He's perfectly entitled to take out any video available for use in the Blockbuster.

Thomson We're not denying / that, we're –

Sixsmith / Well, you sort of are, / because –

Thomson / No we're not.

Sixsmith Look. These films are available in a, err… retail context, they're commercially available, there's nothing sinister / about them whatsoever.

Thomson / I'm not saying there is. I'm not saying there is. *(pause)* OK, Alan, is there anything about that list you want to talk about? Anything at all?

Alan Actually, yes, thank you, Alistair, I think I will give our friends here a bit of a lesson. *(to Jowett)* No comment.

Jowett Yeah but to be honest, Alan, we've heard it all before. What; you think that's the first time someone's said no comment to me?

Alan I've no comment at this time.

Thomson Nothing at all.

Alan I don't see how this is relevant in any way.

Thomson Really? You don't see a connection.

Alan No. I don't know what you're talking about.

Thomson You can't see a connection.

Alan No.

Thomson Not at all.

Alan *No*. Alright?

Thomson All the Princess Diana stuff?

Alan No comment, officer.

Thomson That's a lot of films about Princess Diana, isn't it?

Alan No comment.

Thomson What's the whole thing with Princess Diana?

Alan Nothing. No comment.

Thomson Come on, Alan; I'm just a bit curious about all the Princess Diana stuff, that's all.

Alan No comment.

Thomson You don't want to help me out?

Alan I can't help you out, officer, since I don't know what you're talking about.

Thomson Well, I'm talking about Princess Diana.

Alan Yes, but I don't know why you're talking about it.

Sixsmith There is a good point there: what's the / relevance –

Alan / I don't know / why they're –

Sixsmith / Wait a second. Wait a second. How's that relevant to the charge?

Thomson We're just trying to establish that he's interested in Princess Diana. *Are* you interested in Princess Diana?

Alan Not really. A bit I suppose.

Thomson Did you like her?

Alan *(peeved) Yes.*

Thomson You liked her?

Alan Yes I did, officer.

Thomson Why was that?

Alan She... she touched me.

Thomson Yeah. A lot of people felt like that. She was very special.

Alan No, I mean she actually touched me. In Ipswich.

Thomson When was that?

Alan When the hospital opened.

Thomson Oh yeah. *(to Jowett)* When *was* that?

Jowett *(shrugs)*

Thomson Yeah, it was quite a while ago now, wasn't it.

Alan 1995.

Thomson And did you speak to her?

Alan Yeah.

Thomson What did you say.

Alan I... conveyed my affection, yes, let's say that.

Thomson But what did you say?

Alan Exactly that.

Thomson What; you said you loved her?

Alan Or words to that effect, officer.

Thomson And what did she say to those words?

Alan I don't think she heard.

Jowett Did you watch her funeral?

Alan No; I had to work.

Jowett You didn't tape it?

Alan No; I didn't have a video then. But I bought a CD of the music and the speeches. And of course I've since bought a VHS recording *of* her funeral.

Jowett Brilliant.

Thomson OK. We'll leave that.

Alan Thank you.

Thomson Why; does it make you worried?

Sixsmith Don't be ridiculous. You've come to the end, let's just leave it. You've said you'll leave it, so just leave it.

Jowett Does it make you worried, Alan?

Alan No.

Thomson Doesn't make you a bit nervous?

Alan No, I just don't see… you said you'll leave it so just leave it.

Thomson *(beat)* OK. Now let's talk about the hand. *(pause)* Can tell us how you hurt your hand, Alan?

Alan It doesn't hurt.

Thomson That's good. How did you hurt it?

Alan No comment.

Sixsmith He just said he didn't hurt it.

Jowett No, he said it didn't hurt.

Thomson Why don't you want to talk about it?

Alan No comment.

Thomson No comment. OK. Do you know *when* you hurt it?

Alan No comment.

Thomson No idea? You don't remember?

Alan No comment.

Thomson It looks like quite a new injury. You really can't remember precisely when?

Alan No comment.

Thomson Now I've an idea you hurt it on Thursday.

Alan No comment.

Thomson Does that sound about right?

Alan No comment.

Thomson OK. Did you hurt it at home?

Alan No comment.

Thomson Right. Did you hurt it before you went to the pub?

Alan No comment.

Thomson Before?

Alan No comment.

Thomson Or after?

Alan No comment.

Thomson How did you get the bandage?

Alan No comment.

Thomson Did you put it on yourself?

Alan No comment.

Thomson Or did someone help you?

Alan No comment.

Thomson Well, Alan, according to the records at St Mark's Hospital you arrived in Casualty at about half-eleven on Thursday night with a large cut across the heel of your hand. Does that ring any bells?

Alan *(he is silent)*

Thomson Now the hospital said that the flesh had been torn, almost like it was bitten. *(pause)* They said it needed six stitches. *(pause)* Now you didn't have the injury when you left the pub. *(pause)* And you left the pub at nine o'clock. *(pause)* And at half-eleven you arrived at St Mark's with the cut. *(pause.)* So I suppose I'm asking: What happened between nine o'clock and half-eleven? *(pause)* That made you get the cut.

Scene 3

Thomson and Jowett are alone now during a break in the questioning.

Thomson Are you going to do this properly or what?

Jowett What? I am. I am doing it properly.

Thomson Have you been drinking?

Jowett Fuck off.

Thomson I'm just asking, mate.

Jowett I haven't been drinking.

Thomson OK, OK. Just asking.

A pause.

Jowett Sorry; can I just ask you… what exactly did you… what are they saying about the party?

Thomson It's not worth worrying about.

Jowett No, I know, / I just –

Thomson / It's not worth worrying about.

Jowett No, but because… I just wondered.

Thomson Well, *you* know what happened.

Jowett Yeah, but that's nothing to do with it. It seems.

Thomson It's not for me to speculate on what happened.

Jowett No; I *know* what happened, that's what I'm saying; I know what happened, I just want to find out what they're saying.

Thomson But it doesn't *matter* what they're saying.

Jowett Well it does to me.

Thomson But it shouldn't.

Jowett Yeah, fine, but it does.

Thomson But if you *know* what happened…

Jowett OK, let me ask you this: if a girl like her walked past would you look at her?

Thomson What's that got to do with it?

Jowett If she got undressed in front of you would you look away? Or would you look? Would you look at her? Catch her eye? Look down her top or up her skirt or whatever?

Thomson What's that got to do with it?

Jowett No; that's just an example. Because when she comes up to me and says… Because it's a slippery slope.

Thomson It's not.

Jowett It *is*. It's like there's some things that everyone does all the time and no-one ever says anything but then as soon as you do something that's kind of similar...

Thomson But it's *not* similar. It's completely different.

Jowett It's *not* completely different. It's *not*.

Thomson Well, it is, because –

Jowett But the point is; I didn't even *do* anything. I didn't fucking do anything. I mean she is attractive, yeah? Let's admit that.

Thomson OK.

Jowett I mean she's beautiful.

Thomson Well that's no excuse.

Jowett No; I'm saying.

Thomson If anything...

Jowett I mean everyone obviously thinks she is.

Thomson Yeah, but that's no excuse.

Jowett I'm just saying why can't people separate the one thing from the other... If other people didn't find her attractive they wouldn't suspect me of... it's all to do with what *they* want, it's just like and now I'm being ostracised and everyone's so... divisive. You know, I walk in and they're all... You know, I've got to explain to my kids that –

Thomson Why say anything to your kids?

Jowett Because they were here. Janet dropped them off early and it was fucking humiliating. I mean if you've got a problem you've got a problem but at least... I mean not in front of the kids, you know; the fucking silent treatment and everything. I had to just say things were difficult at work but it's a fucking low blow, come on.

Thomson I know; I'm not defending that.

Jowett You know; I'm not eating, I'm not sleeping –

Thomson What are you talking about? You've been stuffing your face.

Jowett Yeah, but it's the appetite. I've no appetite any more. And it's like the silent treatment, you know; I walk into the staffroom and it's like fucking tumbleweed. I'm just trying to do my job.

Thomson Fine, but from her perspective –

Jowett Fuck her perspective. Fuck it. She's a liar.

Thomson Why would she lie?

Jowett I don't know. She's just a troublemaker. She's caused a fuck of a lot of problems, that's all I know. She's a bloody menace.

Thomson Now come on. You can't say that.

Jowett That's precisely what I'm talking about. It's the system.

Thomson What is?

Jowett It's fucked.

Thomson No it's not.

Jowett It's fucked.

Thomson No it's not.

Jowett It's fucked.

Thomson OK, it's fucked. Now what? You see?

Jowett But it's like nowadays I won't even get in the lift if there's just a girl on her own in it. You know; there you are, stuck there for thirty seconds and when you get out it's just your word against hers.

Thomson Yeah, but just ignore all that. / Just ignore it.

Jowett / But it's the little things, you know. She says goodbye to everyone but me and I'm like the fucking invisible man. You know; goodbye Darren, goodbye Mike, err... hello? I'm sitting right here you / fucking cunt.

Thomson / Just rise above it, mate. Just rise above it.

Jowett Easier said than done, mate.

Thomson I know, I know.

Jowett But it's like what's the point of her doing all that? What's the point? I didn't fucking do anything and it really pisses me off, it really does. I'm sorry.

Thomson No; *I'm* sorry.

Jowett Yeah, well, so am I.

Scene 4

Thomson So the next thing is the letters, Alan.

Alan No. I won't have any of that bandied about, thank you.

Thomson No?

Alan No; I don't want to talk about them.

Thomson You don't want to talk about the letters?

Alan No.

Thomson But we were doing so well. Why's that?

Alan I don't think they're of significance or relevance.

Thomson We can be the judge of that, Alan, yeah? And I think if you give it a bit of thought you'll agree that they are a bit relevant, aren't they. *(pause)* Now we have had to read some of them.

Alan Why?

Thomson Why? Well, we… we want to try to understand everything to do with… what happened because –

Alan But I don't know what happened.

Thomson Well, we're trying to get a full, like a complete picture of what's happened.

Alan But I've been over all this. I don't know what's happened. I don't know. I told you. I've told you I don't… tell them, Alistair.

Sixsmith Well, let's hear what they have to say.

Alan But I don't want to.

Sixsmith And we can proceed on that basis. We don't have to make a response but we need to listen to what they have to say.

Alan But I didn't *do* anything.

Sixsmith OK, OK.

Alan But all this has got nothing to do with it. / Nothing to do with it.

Sixsmith / Fine, then they'll realise that and move on. Now all this is totally confidential so there's nothing / to worry about –

Alan / No; no; I've got nothing to hide. That's not what I'm / saying.

Sixsmith / No; that's not what I'm saying. I'm just saying that –

Thomson Don't worry. Don't worry. Not to worry. What we'll do is we'll just have a look at one of them now, OK, and see what it says. OK? No-one else is going to see them.

Alan I expressly forbid you to read those letters.

Thomson I understand that. But we have to.

Alan I won't allow it.

Thomson Yes, I know, but I'm afraid we've already read them.

Alan Well you shouldn't have. They're private. Can they do this?

Thomson All you've got to do is listen and then we can have a talk about it.

Alan But I don't wish to discuss them.

Thomson And then hopefully we'll have cleared things up a bit. John, can you…

Jowett *(he reads)* 'My love, I think about you and what we're meant to do. Sometimes it's easy to find someone. I found you and I would find you again because I think I know how you feel. And what you are feeling. 'Fuck' means two things but one you must do and one you mustn't. What do you think? I am so proud of you.' *(he gestures to show completion)*

Thomson You wrote that to her, did you?

Alan I didn't send it.

Thomson We'll get on to that in a minute. Did you write it to her?

Alan I wrote about her, yes.

Thomson Well, it's a bit more than that, isn't it. It's a letter, so you wrote it in order to give to her.

Sixsmith But he didn't give it to her.

Thomson *(to Alan)* Did you?

Alan No I didn't.

Sixsmith Well clearly not.

Thomson What's that?

Sixsmith Well you've got it right there.

Thomson I'm just trying to find out what happened. So you wrote it.

Alan Yes.

Thomson Did you send it?

Alan No. I don't think so.

Sixsmith Is that a no?

Thomson Well, that's not quite –

Sixsmith He clearly means no.

Thomson Well hang on. Why did you say you don't think so?

Alan I didn't send it.

Sixsmith How could he have?

Thomson No, I understand that.

Sixsmith Well there we are, then.

Thomson No, well, we've established that he wrote them.

Sixsmith Right, but he didn't send them.

Thomson Yes, but he wrote them.

Sixsmith Yeah, I know. But he didn't send them.

Thomson Yes, I appreciate that, but he still wrote them.

Sixsmith I know he wrote them, but he didn't send them, did he.

Thomson I know he didn't send them. Goodness.

Sixsmith OK.

A pause.

Thomson OK. Now you have a nickname at work, don't you?

Alan Well, I think, err… yes; I have been given a rather disrespectful name which some people choose to use.

Thomson What is it?

Alan Is this relevant?

Thomson I think so, Alan. What's the nickname?

Alan It's just a rather disrespectful name. It doesn't mean anything.

Thomson OK. *(beat)* What is it?

Alan *(pause)* Bilbo.

Thomson Bilbo?

Alan Yes! I suppose that's my fault now as well, is it?

Thomson And is it just the kids who call you that, or does –

Alan It's just the pupils, yes.

Thomson What; to your face?

Alan No, not really. Well, sometimes.

Thomson They're just having a laugh, yeah?

Alan It's just thoughtless cruelty, that's all.

Thomson Does it upset you?

Alan Well, I wouldn't go that far. I'm aware of it, let's say that.

Thomson And why do you think they call you that?

Alan I really have no idea, officer. Because of the hobbit, perhaps?

Thomson The hobbit.

Alan One can only imagine.

Thomson But you don't look like a hobbit, do you?

Alan Not the one in the film, no.

Thomson No, exactly. So why..?

Alan It's just... something that happens. I don't know why.

Thomson OK, Alan, well I'm not sure if you've read this?

Alan What's 'this'? It looks like *Caiaphas*.

Thomson It looks like what?

Alan *Caiaphas*. It's the school newspaper run by some of the girls.

Thomson Did you read it this week?

Alan No, I must confess I'm not a regular reader.

Jowett *(reads)* 'A plea from this paper. As you all know it has now been three days since Nicola Slater went missing from school and you will have been as saddened as we are. We are becoming increasingly worried by the prospect of what might have happened to her. Nicola was a notable and lively girl who often caught the imagination of the whole school with her individual approach and unique ideas. Our thoughts and prayers are with her and her family at this anxious time and we long for her safe return. Signed Head Girl Katherine Judah and Deputy Head Girl Hetty Fletcher.'

Alan What's your point, officer?

Thomson Well, a whole community's worried, Alan.

Alan I'm not proud of what I've done, officer, but that's life, isn't it.

Thomson But what have you done, Alan?

Alan I haven't done anything.

Thomson Nothing at all.

Alan I didn't do anything, other than what I told you.

Thomson Tell us again.

Alan I've told you.

Thomson Tell us again.

Alan I've told you.

Thomson / Tell us again.

Jowett / Tell us again.

Alan *(sighs loudly)* Look, I told you; I drove past the bus stop, she was there, she was crying, I stopped and asked if she was OK and that was it.

Thomson And she said she was OK.

Alan Yes.

Thomson And you drove on.

Alan Well, I drove off.

Thomson And that was it.

Alan Yes. OK?

Jowett So where is she now, Alan?

Thomson Where is she now, Alan?

Alan How would I know?

Thomson We'll ask the questions, Alan.

Jowett So where is she now?

Alan I've told you; I don't know.

Sixsmith We've been over this.

Thomson No; I know.

Sixsmith We've established he saw her at the bus stop and had a brief / exchange.

Thomson / We're just trying to establish / whether –

Sixsmith / No; you're not; he's been perfectly clear.

Thomson But he's not making a great deal of sense.

Alan But I am.

Thomson Now here's a thing. That night it was very unlikely that she would have been at the bus stop. Because there was a concert at the school and she was playing violin in it.

Alan The violin.

Thomson Yes. Except for some reason she didn't go to the concert.

Alan Why not?

Thomson Exactly. No one knows why not. She was all set for the concert, she'd been rehearsing for weeks and then at the last minute she just doesn't turn up.

Alan She played the violin.

Thomson Indeed she did, Alan. That's not in doubt. What *is* a bit of a mystery, though, is why didn't she turn up to the concert. Can you help us with that?

Alan No.

Thomson Have a good think.

Alan I didn't know there was a concert.

Thomson Really?

Alan I didn't know.

Thomson That's strange because it was going to be quite a big thing. It was a big thing in the school, posters everywhere, you know, posters in the village, you must have seen them; Big End of Term Quad Concert; Mozart, Schumann or whatever, the bits of music they were going to play.

Jowett Schubert.

Thomson Schubert?

Jowett Yeah; the composer's name is Schubert.

Thomson I thought there was a Schumann as well.

Jowett No; it's Schubert.

Thomson *(to Alan)* OK, Alan, so it's quite a big thing and everyone's looking forward to it and then suddenly... where is she?

Alan I don't know. I didn't know there was a concert.

Thomson You didn't know there was a concert.

Alan No.

Thomson Well that's confusing, then, because we understood that you *did* know there was a concert.

Alan No.

Thomson Because someone told us you volunteered for overtime to clear away all the chairs afterwards.

Alan Oh.

Thomson Does that ring any bells?

Alan Maybe.

Thomson Brilliant. Do you know where she is, Alan?

Alan No comment.

Sixsmith Hold on. Do you know where she is?

Alan No.

Sixsmith Well in that case it's no, not no comment.

Thomson Any idea at all?

Alan No comment.

Sixsmith No? Or no comment?

Thomson Do you…

Alan No comment.

Thomson Or don't you…

Alan No comment.

Thomson … know where she is.

Alan I have no comment to make, officer.

Thomson But where would she go?

Alan I don't know.

Thomson And why would she go there?

Alan I really don't know.

Thomson But why would a girl suddenly go missing like that? Doesn't make any sense, does it.

Alan I really don't know where she is or why she's gone.

Jowett Come on, Alan.

Alan What do you mean?

Jowett Where is she.

Alan I don't know.

Jowett Alan? *Where is she.*

Thomson Because it's the *not knowing*, isn't it. I've spoken to her parents. They've spoken to me. Do you know what they said? They said they just want to *know*. That's all they said. Even knowing the worst is better than not knowing anything. Because otherwise…

how can you live? You've got to go through the whole thing of keeping her room as a dust-free shrine, make-up by the bed, unopened post on the chest of drawers *just in case she comes back*; just in case she's still alive, just in case she's still out there. Because if she's been killed, she's been killed and that's the end of it. But when you don't know... that's when she goes on being killed. Because *they don't know*.

Jowett So where is she? *(pause)* Because you'd think she could be anywhere. You ever look out the window on a long car journey – the trees, the forests. Muddy fields. Ditches. Surely a body could stay there for years, hidden away. Stashed. How could anyone ever find it? There's just too much countryside out there. But you see murderers have a phenomenal habit for fucking things up. The forest is so big it ends up like picking lottery numbers – you can't decide so you go for the really obvious ones. What do you choose? How about near that really obvious tree? How about near that gate? You need a reference point. Why? Why do you need to know where it is? No-one knows. They just want to *know*. They feel they have to. So they can sleep at night. But *can* they sleep at night? Because once it's there, it's there. You can't move it. You've got to take your chances, mate. Just sit tight. Just wait. Month after month after month after month and on any given day after the six o'clock news Look East could say 'A man walking his dog in Fenchurst Woods today found what appears to be...' Because all those people and all those dogs and all those courting couples and picnickers and kids larking about, they've lost their football in the undergrowth and the forest is only *so* big and suddenly the probability has flipped the other way and fuck me, it's only a matter of *time*. So what do we do now? What *can* we do now?

Alan I don't know.

Thomson *(to Alan)* Are we going to find evidence of sexual marks on her?

Alan / What?

Sixsmith / Woh-oh-oh! Where did that come from?

Thomson That's a perfectly legitimate / question.

Sixsmith / No it's not; it's pure speculation which my client doesn't have to answer.

Jowett Come on, Alan. Are we going to find evidence of sexual marks on her?

Sixsmith *(to Thomson)* Do *you* think there'll be any evidence of sexual marks?

Thomson Well, I don't know, Alistair.

Sixsmith You don't know.

Thomson Hence the question.

Jowett Alan. Are we going to find evidence of sexual marks on her?

Alan What do you mean?

Thomson Do you really mean that?

Alan I don't know what you mean.

Thomson Really?

Alan Really.

Sixsmith Clearly.

Thomson Any evidence of sexual marks on her?

Alan I don't know.

Thomson So you *do* know what we mean.

Alan I guess.

Thomson So what do you think you understand by sexual marks?

Alan I don't know.

Thomson But you said you did know.

Sixsmith He did not.

Jowett Well, he did.

Sixsmith Wait a minute, wait a minute. You asked my client if he knows what sexual marks were.

Jowett And he said he didn't know whether there'd be any marks or not.

Sixsmith Exactly.

Jowett Yeah, so he knows what they are.

Sixsmith Nonsense.

Jowett He'd have to.

Sixsmith Rubbish.

Jowett To be able to say that.

Sixsmith You're quite wrong.

Thomson Disagree.

Sixsmith Well what do *you* understand by it?

Thomson Never mind that.

Sixsmith Why not?

Thomson *(to Alan)* So you guessed, did you?

Alan Yes.

Thomson OK. What did you guess.

Alan I don't know.

Thomson What sort of marks might they be?

Alan Err… from touching.

Thomson What sort of touching?

Alan I don't know.

Thomson You really don't know?

Alan No.

Jowett Don't you think someone who's watched… *(he briefly checks)* More Wet Rides would know what sort of touching?

Alan I don't know.

Jowett You don't know.

Alan No.

Thomson No, I understand, Alan. I understand how it happened. Because things went too far, didn't they.

Alan No. You're clearly trying to bully me into

admitting something that I didn't do. But I didn't do it.

Thomson Alan, we're talking about sex with a fifteen year old girl.

Alan I don't see what her age has got to do with it.

Thomson Really? Alan; she's fifteen. What's that? Just numbers?

Alan Yeah. Just numbers. *(he laughs)*

Thomson Alan, the girl is missing. Where is she?

Alan I don't know.

Thomson You've no idea?

Alan I've really no idea.

Thomson You really don't know.

Alan I really don't know.

Jowett Alan, look at it from our perspective. This is a fifteen year old schoolgirl who you've obviously had some sort of relationship with, sexual or otherwise. That girl is now missing, having gone missing on a night you admitted seeing her.

Thomson Alan. Come on. Come on. Come on. It all started out pretty innocent, didn't it. She just wanted a lift somewhere. Or she looked like she did. Waiting at the bus stop, tears rolling down her face. There she was. So you give her a lift, she's glad to see you because it's night and this is your big chance, isn't it. It's your big chance.

Alan No, that's not it at all.

Jowett Come on, Alan. You're there, she's sitting next to you but it's not going so well now and it's now or never, isn't it.

Alan No.

Jowett Now or never.

Alan No.

Jowett Now or never. And at last you find the courage to kiss her but she doesn't want to and this makes you embarrassed and angry and then you think... well, what *do* you think? Because you're driving along, you're in charge, she sort of has to do what you want to, doesn't she?

Alan No.

Jowett Really? Alan, I'm trying to help. I'm saying how easy it is. So you drive into Fenchurst Woods. Because you want to spend time with her. You want to persuade her. But she's getting more and more nervous and she resists and then you don't mean to hit her but you're just trying to restrain her, to show that there's nothing to worry about, that it's going to be OK. But when you've hit her... you've sort of crossed that boundary and it's easy to touch her in other ways now.

Alan I never touched her.

Jowett You didn't?

Alan Never. I never hurt her.

Jowett What; you never hurt her or you never touched her?

Alan Both. I didn't hurt her.

Jowett But that's the whole point. You didn't mean to hurt her. And now you're just trying to comfort her. Trying to make her feel better. And then one thing leads to another, doesn't it.

Alan No.

Jowett One thing leads to another, doesn't it.

Alan No.

Jowett Yes it does. Because it gets confusing and everything happens really quickly and before you know where you are, well... where are you?

Alan None of this happened.

Jowett *None* of it happened? Really. I think some of it did, didn't it. Because it's what you always wanted.

Thomson It's in the letters.

Jowett It's in the letters. And there it was. And I think you knew it wouldn't be there again. But by the time you've done it it's too late, isn't it. What were you thinking of? Isn't that what you thought? What were you thinking of? You can't go back. The toothpaste isn't going to go back into the tube.

Alan No.

Jowett No. So what the hell are you going to do now?

Alan I don't know.

Jowett Well, what are the options. You could let her go. But then she'll run home and call the police and you'll go to prison. Or… or what? What's your only chance now?

Alan I don't know.

Jowett *(Trying to speed things up and corner him. With increasing impatience.)* Come on. What's the only thing to do?

Alan I don't know.

Jowett *(annoyed)* Come on. What do you do? What can you do? She's screaming, she's bleeding –

Alan She's not.

Thomson She's not now, no.

Alan Nothing like that happened.

Jowett *Nothing* like that happened?

Thomson Alan, based on this interview we have to make a decision on what recommendation to give the Crown Prosecution Service as to whether they prosecute. Do you understand that?

Alan Yes.

Thomson And all we've got to go on are the answers to our questions that you're giving us or not giving us.

Alan I understand.

Jowett Are we going to find any evidence of sexual marks on her, Alan?

Alan No.

Thomson Any sexual marks?

Alan No comment.

Jowett No *comment*?

Thomson Any sexual marks at all?

Jowett Or no?

Alan I don't know.

Jowett Which is it?

Thomson Any at all?

Alan I don't know.

Thomson Any sexual marks at all.

Alan I don't know.

Jowett Any sexual marks at all.

Alan I don't know.

Thomson Alan, are we going to find any sexual marks on her?

Alan I don't know.

Thomson Or are we not.

Alan I don't know.

Thomson You don't know.

Sixsmith Right. My client has answered that question now.

Thomson Not to our satisfaction.

Sixsmith Not to our satisfaction. Well let's take a look at that. Can we? Now. You haven't got a victim, you haven't got a body, you haven't got a weapon and you haven't got a confession. So you've got nothing to link my client with the charge.

Thomson Well, we've got / a motive.

Sixsmith / No, you've got... that's a circumstantial motive.

Thomson Well we've got a bit more than that, / Alistair.

Sixsmith / No you *haven't.*

Thomson Well, we have.

Sixsmith No –

Thomson Yes; we've got a totally unexplained injury, we've got a, umm... selection of obscene videos and we've got a series of sexually obsessive letters sent to a fifteen year old girl.

Sixsmith Absolute rubbish.

Thomson No it's not. It's not.

Sixsmith Look; it's a minor wound –

Thomson Well, it's an unexplained wound.

Sixsmith But a minor wound.

Thomson But... unexplained.

Sixsmith OK; you've got a series of harmless videos –

Thomson Of a sexually explicit / nature.

Sixsmith / A collection of totally legal / videos –

Thomson / Of a sexually explicit nature.

Sixsmith – available in a mainstream retail / context.

Thomson / But of a sexually explicit nature.

Sixsmith And you've got a series of affectionate letters –

Thomson A series of sexually obsessive / letters.

Sixsmith / Well, affectionate and personal / letters.

Thomson / Come on, Alistair, they're sexually obsessive letters.

Sixsmith You've made your views clear. Fine. I maintain that you've got nothing more substantial than a minor wound, a collection of perfectly normal videos and some affectionate letters and on that basis I'm advising my client to answer no further questions and we'll call it a day on that basis.

A long pause.

Jowett Do you love her, Alan?

Alan *(sighs)* I never spoke to her / and I never touched her.

Sixsmith / Alan, we don't need to say / anything more.

Jowett / That's not what I asked.

Alan I know what you asked.

Jowett So what do you say?

Alan I'm not saying anything.

Sixsmith Exactly.

Jowett But you said you didn't touch her.

Alan Yeah. And you know what? I wish I had.

Jowett / You wish you had?

Sixsmith / Come on now, Alan.

Alan I want to.

Sixsmith I've told you, I'm trying to / help you.

Alan / It's about me now, Alistair.

Sixsmith I don't know what you mean. / Just say no comment.

Alan / It's my turn.

Sixsmith I'm doing my best for you / here, yeah?

Alan / I know, I know, I know.

Sixsmith So you don't have to say anything if / you don't –

Alan / I know what I'm doing.

Sixsmith Yeah, but you don't have to say anything / if you don't want to.

Alan / I know: I don't / have to say anything if I don't want to.

Sixsmith / You don't have to say / anything.

Alan / I understand.

Sixsmith OK.

Alan I understand.

Sixsmith OK! I understand!

Thomson Sorry, can I interrupt here?

Sixsmith Go ahead, *Dave*.

Thomson Alan, you were saying you *wanted* to touch her.

Sixsmith Remember what we said, Alan?

Alan I'm not an idiot, Alistair.

Sixsmith Fine.

Alan I'm not an idiot, you know.

Sixsmith I'm sure you're not.

Alan I'm not.

Sixsmith I'm sure you not.

Alan I can say what I want.

Sixsmith Course you can. Go ahead.

Thomson So you didn't touch her.

Alan No.

Thomson But you wanted to.

Alan Yes.

Jowett Why was that?

Alan For no other reason than pleasure, officer; I'll be honest with you. And I'll be even more honest – I wish I had done exactly what you say I've done. And I'll bet you wished I had as well, yeah? For your own pleasure. Because be honest, officer, that would give you pleasure, wouldn't it. Knowing I'd done that. *(pause)* Wouldn't it. *(pause)* Wouldn't it. *(pause)* Wouldn't it. *(pause)* Wouldn't it.

Jowett So… what? You loved her? Or not. Sorry, Alan, I'm not clear.

Alan I liked that girl. I'll tell you that. She wasn't particularly happy and she wasn't particularly liked. But I liked her. Didn't notice anyone else rushing to help her. But I was there. I bought her presents, I wrote her letters as you know and I took the time to get to know someone who no-one else could be bothered with. When I first saw her… I don't know; I went up to her on some pretext and we just started talking and we walked back together. God knows what we were talking about. Just silly stuff, really; anything. And it was just so… simple. It was the most obvious thing in the world. She was so beautiful, she really was. And there was a match going on on one of the fields and we watched it for a bit and the ground was muddy and she slipped and put her arm out to hold on to me so she didn't fall. And when she touched me… It was like I'd been shot in the chest. And after that I just wanted to see her. That was it. I'd wake up; I wanted to see her. I'd go to work; I'd want to see her. And she felt the same. I know she did.

Thomson But Alan, we've searched her room. Both at the school and at her home. We've checked her email accounts. And there's no evidence that you ever contacted her in any way. No emails; she didn't keep a diary and there's no evidence that she received any letters. The only evidence of letters we've got is between one hundred and two hundred letters like the one we've shown you.

Alan Well there you are, then.

Thomson No; these were all at your house. It looks like you wrote about two hundred letters but didn't send any of them.

Alan But the presents, officer; the presents and treats.

Thomson Yes, but what were they? Because we haven't been able to find anything that looks like it was given to her from a friend or admirer.

Alan Well I don't know about that. They're there somewhere.

Thomson But in all the many times you met and walked together Alan we've not been able to find one person who ever saw the two of you together.

Alan I don't know what you're building up to, officer, but I think I've made myself clear.

Thomson But you haven't. You've repeatedly claimed that you've had a relationship with this girl whereas everything points to the conclusion that you never spoke to her.

Alan Well that's your conclusion.

Jowett But you never even spoke to her.

Alan I did.

Jowett Yeah, but you didn't.

Alan But I did.

Jowett Alan, you never spoke to her.

Alan That's just not true.

Jowett I'm sure you watched her or whatever.

Alan No.

Jowett But you didn't speak to her did you.

Alan I did.

Jowett Did you love her, Alan? Did you? Did you love her? Alan?

Thomson Did you?

Jowett Come on, Alan; did you love her?

Alan *(pause)* Yes. OK? Yes. I loved her.

Jowett Fine. And what does that mean?

Alan Don't you know?

Jowett I just… want to know what you mean by that.

Alan What; do you not know?

Jowett Not personally, no.

Alan Not familiar with love, are you?

Jowett Is that relevant?

Alan I think so.

Jowett I just want to know what you mean by love.

Alan You really don't know.

Jowett No, alright. I don't know.

Alan You've no idea?

Jowett No. *(a long pause)* OK?

Scene 5

Thomson and Jowett are alone again, in another break in the questioning.

Thomson Listen, mate; bloody good going in there.

Jowett Yeah?

Thomson Seriously, mate.

Jowett Thanks, mate.

Thomson Seriously.

Jowett Thanks.

Thomson Yeah; bloody good going.

Jowett Thanks.

Thomson Bloody good.

Jowett Thanks.

A pause.

Thomson I didn't know you were into music.

Jowett No, not really, but I do listen to it on the radio sometimes.

Thomson What; classical music?

Jowett Yeah, you know; Classical FM or some of the other stations sometimes or whatever.

Thomson Yeah, I listen sometimes.

Jowett Are you into it, then?

Thomson No, but funnily enough there was an orchestra in my dream the other night.

Jowett Oh yeah?

Thomson And I've been thinking about it and I can't work it out because I mean in real life I can't even go *(he gestures hitting a single key on a piano three times and approximates the sound)* da-da-da on a piano – I don't know anything about music or anything but in my dream this orchestra was playing all this amazing music and I didn't recognise it and when I woke up I could still remember it for a bit and the thing was it wasn't anything I knew. I'd never heard it before. So when you think about it I must have written it myself. Do you see what I mean? In my dream. It's really weird. And it was like real classical music; you know, the flutes were all going... *(he gestures)* and the *(he mimes a cello or double bass)* you know, they were all playing away, like different things going on at the same time around different bits of the orchestra. But I don't know the first thing about music. So how do you think I came up with that?

Jowett I don't know.

Thomson And more to the point why can't I do it when I'm awake?

Jowett Yeah; if you could you wouldn't be here, I suppose.

Thomson Exactly. I'd be with the London...*(he can't name an ensemble)* whatever.

Jowett Yeah; my dad once woke up to a cooked breakfast he'd made in his sleep.

Thomson Really?

Jowett Yeah; fucking hell; bacon, sausages, fried bread – how'd he do that?

Thomson You can't wake them up when they're like that, though.

Jowett Exactly.

Thomson Yeah.

A pause.

Jowett Look, I'm sorry, I just want to say... well done.

Thomson Thanks.

Jowett No, I mean it. I mean you deserve it.

Thomson No, I appreciate that.

Jowett And, you know, who knows...

Thomson Exactly. I mean, you know, sure, a promotion's a promotion or whatever but at the end of the day work is only work.

Jowett I know.

Thomson Yeah?

Jowett I know what you mean.

Thomson I mean, you know; sure, but still... I mean,

you've got your kids at the weekends...

Jowett I was up Hilvert with them on the day of the storm, actually.

Thomson Bloody hell.

Jowett Yeah, we were out with the kite and it was just blowing up, it was just beginning to really start. You know, we were up the hill and the massiveness of it, you know, the whole place spread out below; it blew right through me and we were looking out over the whole thing and I swear to God the kite was straining like it was about to snap and I was screaming stuff, just shouting for the hell of it and I thought, you know, it was like... *(with real joy) fucking hell!* It was brilliant. It was brilliant.

Scene 6

Back in the interview room.

Thomson Well, well, well, Alan. You know those five teams we've got looking for her? Well, we just got a call from one of them. *(pause)* They've found her. *(pause)* And guess what?

End.

CUMQUATS

to Amabel Ealovega

Characters

in order of appearance

Oscar Rensburg
Douglas Appleford
Lady Margot Milligan
Reverend Peter Marchant
Lady Harriet Schalley
Vivian Manos
Laura Morehouse

Cumquats opened at the Landor Theatre, London on Wednesday 10 November 2004 with the following cast:

Oscar Rensburg	Nathan Griggs
Douglas Appleford	Thomas Rushforth
Lady Margot Milligan	Angela Saul
Rev. Peter Marchant	John Atterbury
Lady Harriet Schalley	Rosie Wilkinson
Vivian Manos	Danielle Urbas
Laura Morehouse	Britten Beaver

Directed by	Adrian Fear
Lighting and sound	Helen Skiera
Stage management	Stuart Griffith
	Philip Thompson
	Marnie Chesterton

Act One

Scene 1

Oscar and Douglas are standing on a balcony. We can hear fireworks etc.

Oscar Perhaps it might be simpler simply to say who's still alive.

Douglas Oh I'm sorry; I thought that was what we *were* doing.

Oscar No, well, righto *(he is trying to mentally rearrange)*... carry on, then.

Douglas Well that's pretty much it, actually.

Oscar You're not serious.

Douglas Err... think so, yes.

Oscar My goodness.

Douglas Hmm.

Oscar How about Kenneth Kennett?

Douglas No.

Oscar When was that?

Douglas *(shrugs)*

Oscar Steadman?

Douglas Somme.

Oscar Forbes?

Douglas Paschendaele.

Oscar How about Hamilton-Baker?

Douglas Err... Verdun.

Oscar Smith?

Douglas Which one?

Oscar EJR.

Douglas Cambrai, I think.

Oscar How about the other one?

Douglas ARL? The Dardanelles.

Oscar *(tuts)* Burgess was at Reims, I know that.

Douglas Yes, Reims.

Oscar Michael de Jersey.

Douglas Somme.

Oscar McCrickard.

Douglas Somme.

Oscar Freddie Delacour.

Douglas Somme.

Oscar Maxwell Snowdon.

Douglas Somme.

Oscar Goodness. Heydon Stokes.

Douglas Somme.

Oscar How about err... oh, what's his name? The umm, the chap... Boodle's, moustache, golf clubs.

Douglas Moylan-Jones.

Oscar Moylan-Jones.

Douglas Verdun.

Oscar Impossible. I've seen him. Since we've been

back, I mean.

Douglas Can't have.

Oscar Err… well, I'm not so sure, you know. At Christmas.

Douglas Well you'll not see him this Christmas, for sure.

Oscar Ho-hum.

Douglas *(beat)* Perhaps it was another ghost.

Oscar Yes, thanks Appleford.

Douglas What? It might have been.

Oscar *(smiling, long-sufferingly)* That was an angel, not a ghost, as well you know.

Douglas What's the difference?

Oscar We don't need to… it's not just me. A good hundred or so people saw it.

Douglas Yes, and conveniently they're all dead.

Oscar That is rather convenient, isn't it. And the papers reported it.

Douglas *(shrugs expansively at the ridiculousness of this comment)*

Oscar I'm not asking you to believe it, Apples, I'm simply telling you / –

Douglas / Again.

Oscar / that I was one of those who saw the angel. An angel of light over the field at Mons.

Douglas An angel of light.

Oscar Yes.

Douglas Hence the theology.

Oscar Hence the theology.

Douglas Good. Because we need more theologians now. Particularly since God is dead.

Oscar You seem to forget I can't be shocked any more.

Douglas Didn't think *that* was shocking.

Oscar I know what I saw, that's all I'm saying.

Douglas And how many can boast that.

Pause.

Oscar Not going to the Spencer's ball are you?

Douglas Not invited, old boy.

Oscar Oh, I'm sorry.

Douglas I'm not. Just a bunch of ducks and drakes. Not my scene, really.

Oscar Very well.

Douglas Will you go?

Oscar I rather thought I might.

Douglas Good luck.

Oscar Yes. Err… Laura Morehouse is going to be there, apparently.

Douglas Even better luck.

Oscar Well, steady on.

Douglas Walking in a dead man's shoes there, aren't you, Renners?

Oscar Yes; I've thought about that.

Douglas Oh, come on; I'm only teasing.

Oscar Which is precisely why I shall not be making any attempt to renew the acquaintance.

Douglas You're not serious.

Oscar Well, I think that's the decent thing to do, don't you?

Douglas *Why?* The chap must have been dead for three years.

Oscar How does that help? I just don't want to... it's just not appropriate under the circumstances.

Douglas Renners, there *are* no circumstances. The circumstances are dead.

Oscar No, well, I'm not sure that that's entirely fair.

Douglas Well I suggest you have a good think.

Oscar I'll think about it.

Douglas That's my advice.

Oscar Yes. *(pause)* You couldn't sock us a smoke could you, Apples? *(he does so)* Ah, that's the ticket.

Douglas *(clears his throat)*

Oscar So how's tricks at the Home Office?

Douglas Hush-hush, old boy.

Oscar You didn't waste any time.

Douglas All their idea, I assure you. Us intelligence men are in short supply, you know.

Oscar Wouldn't have thought there'd've been much use for you at all now.

Douglas That's rich. *(Oscar smiles goodnaturedly)* It's all trade stuff now. Plus everyone who's still got an empire wants to have a slightly bigger empire. There's more spying than ever.

Oscar Well that's a relief. To the spies themselves, I suppose. So what do *you* do?

Douglas I'm sort of an anti-spy.

Oscar Like a spy-catcher.

Douglas Yes, that's it.

Oscar And is that preferable to actually doing the spying?

Douglas It's warm and dry.

Oscar And safe?

Douglas *(beat)* Now I had my aunt have a word with Marchant for you.

Oscar Apples, I specifically asked you not to pull any strings.

Douglas I didn't, I didn't. At least not deliberately. It's not my fault if he dotes on my Aunt is it?

Oscar But you didn't mention anything, did you?

Douglas Oh quite possibly it may have come up by sheer chance that you were looking for a nice, quiet fellowship.

Oscar I certainly hope you didn't put it in those terms.

Douglas Renners, Marchant is pretty gin-soaked at the best of times. Even if I did –

Oscar And you didn't.

Douglas – he wouldn't remember it an hour later.

Oscar I really would have liked to have made it on merit.

Douglas There's time for all that later.

Oscar Yes but it's so unfair. That place rightly belongs to the best applicant.

Douglas Well who's to say... no-one's doing anyone any favours here. It's not like there's a queue – there's only about twelve people left in the country. If anything you're helping them out.

Oscar It just doesn't feel right.

Douglas Look, if you're not up to the job they'll sack you. / They're just giving you a chance, that's all.

Oscar / But I might *not* be up to it.

Douglas Oh, you'll knock them for six. No offence.

Oscar *(pause. he smiles)* That's alright. Actually I did think of going back to cricket. Teaching at the school.

Douglas You can do better than that.

Oscar Obviously not.

Douglas Teaching-wise, I mean.

Pause.

Oscar Douglas, I feel...

Douglas *(still jokey and manly)* Yes.

Oscar I know it is in no way my concern but I feel obliged to say how sorry I am about Ross.

Douglas *(all bonhomie immediately replaced with coldness)* Very well.

Oscar I'm sure it was a dreadful blow to you.

Douglas What makes you say that?

Oscar Well… because… because you were obviously… / obviously…

Douglas / Obviously what?

Oscar Obviously err… / well…

Douglas / What makes you say that?

Oscar Well, simply that the impression I received / was that –

Douglas / Received from whom?

Oscar No; I merely gathered from / my own –

Douglas / Look –

Oscar – observations that / perhaps –

Douglas / Obs… what do you… why would you be observing us?

Oscar Clearly I'm not making myself clear.

Douglas On the contrary, I think –

Oscar Let's just say we'll say no more about it.

Douglas Whatever you say.

Oscar I don't want to intrude.

Douglas You're not intruding.

Oscar No.

Douglas There's nothing to intrude upon.

Oscar No. Quite. I just wanted to say that I was very sorry, that's all.

Douglas So you said.

Oscar Yes.

A long pause, during which Douglas becomes conciliatory. They finish their cigarettes.

Douglas Well, I suppose we better head back indoors. A party's not a party without Captain Rensburg.

Oscar Oh I heard that too.

They turn to leave.

Douglas Listen, thanks for saving my life, Oscar.

Oscar It was my absolute pleasure, Lieutenant.

Scene 2

Margot Ah, yes; my little war heroes. Come in from the cold, that's it.

Douglas Thank you.

Margot Now you all remember Douglas. My favourite nephew, Douglas Appleford. As you see, newly returned and gladly alive.

Marchant Welcome back, Douglas.

Douglas Thank you very much, sir.

Margot And this is his old friend Herr Rensburg,

famous to me from my dear nephew's letters.

Marchant What's this? Forgive and forget, eh?

Oscar Err… no; umm… *Captain* Rensburg of the Coldstream Guards… lately Mr Oscar Rensburg of the Belgravia Rensburgs. I was actually with Douglas in France.

Marchant Goodness. What a stroke of luck. Pretty tough on the old relatives, though, I would have thought.

Oscar Err… no, I don't actually have any German relatives. My great-grandfather came from…

Margot Reverend, come, come, this is the German chap / I was telling you about.

Oscar / (I'm really not German.)

Margot I suggested that perhaps there might be room for him in your college.

Marchant Oh, goodness, yes, of course.

Margot He was all set to be a professional sportsman but the war has put paid to that. He now wants to make his way as a professor, isn't that right, Herr Rensburg?

Oscar Well… yes, I… that's very… well I did mention something to that effect to your nephew.

Marchant And you're a theologian, isn't that right?

Oscar Yes. Eschatology, principally. *(to Margot)* The theological study of the end of the world.

Margot And that's a science, is it?

Douglas Rensburg saw an angel at the Front, / Auntie.

Margot / What?

Oscar *(imploringly)* / Apples!

Marchant / *(oblivious)* You're familiar with the book of Revelation, surely, Lady Milligan.

Margot I've rarely been so disappointed with a book in my life. I was looking for some solid facts, preferably dates.

Oscar We're doing what we can, Lady Milligan.

Marchant Splendid. Well there's always room for a bright young man at Corpus, you know. And any friend of Lady Milligan...

Oscar Goodness, well... that's good to know, I must say.

Margot Herr von Rensburg, I should warn you that Reverend Marchant is an apologist for the Soviets.

Marchant Oh that really is unfair.

Margot On the contrary. I've heard your sermons.

Marchant We really must make a distinction between the Soviet Union and the concept of socialism. I hold no brief for the Soviets, I think that goes without saying. I am, however, convinced that as bold experiments go it is vital and the most likely to yield heaven on earth. If you have two coats give one to him who has none. Is any other country in the world seeking to live by that precept?

Oscar That's a very interesting point, Reverend.

Marchant You think so?

Oscar Oh, yes.

Marchant I think you'll be a real addition to college life, Rensburg.

Oscar I profoundly hope so, sir.

Margot Now you really must tell us all about your adventures, boys. Any anxious moments on the front line?

Douglas *(beat)* Oddly enough none whatsoever, Aunt. Any for you, Rensburg?

Oscar Certainly none that instantly spring to mind, no.

Margot Now now, boys – I / know when my leg is being pulled. I may not have travelled much but I can read the Daily Express you know.

Oscar / Lost a leg, but err… *(quietly, in such a way that 'leg' coincides exactly with Margot's 'leg' – she is oblivious)*

Marchant Captain Rensburg, I see you're wearing the Military Cross.

Oscar Yes, sir.

Marchant May I congratulate you, / young man.

Margot / *(quietly but not intentionally so)* I hear you now / sport a wooden leg. Well done.

Oscar / Thank you, sir. Actually they were pretty much giving them away out there towards the end, you know.

Marchant Surely not.

Margot Where's your Military Cross, Douglas?

Douglas Oh, I turned them down, Aunt. I'm still holding out for something posthumous.

Margot I occasionally feared that I had ruined that boy but I needn't have worried as you can see. He was no stranger to over-privilege in his youth I can tell you but war is a great leveller, it seems. Look at him: not so much as licked a stamp by the time he was sixteen and now a chestful of medals for shooting an entire nation in the head. You don't get *that* at Eton.

Douglas I'm glad the War wasn't totally in vain, then, Auntie.

Marchant No indeed; all those lives nobly given.

Harriet My impression was of them being taken rather than given.

Margot *(to Douglas)* You know Harriet, Lord Shelley's daughter.

Harriet Actually Lord Schalley's daughter, Lady Milligan.

Douglas I'm not sure that I do.

Margot Isn't she a fine figure of a woman?

Douglas Well, it's not for me to say.

Margot Oh, really. Harriet is a 'female writer', Douglas.

Douglas *(shrugs happily yet with confusion)*

Marchant Upon what are you working at the moment, Lady Harriet?

Harriet Well, I'm… I'm finishing an historical examination of the life of Florence Nightingale.

Margot Oh God.

Douglas Aunt Margot, to what on earth could one find to object in Florence Nightingale?

Margot To the character, nothing of which I'm aware. But I know your sort, Lady Harriet. No doubt this so-called book will be nothing more than a thinly-veiled plea for universal suffrage, or the like.

Harriet On the contrary, it simply / explores –

Margot / Silence. My mind's made up. I don't need to be confused with the facts, thank you.

Harriet Would you perhaps be interested in reading a copy, Lady Milligan?

Margot What's it to be? A small, privately published salon book complete with authentic daguerrotypes, dedicated to a member of the royal family, perhaps?

Harriet Which royal family did you have in mind?

Margot *(to Douglas)* Controversial? Oh yes. Yet enchanting? Wait and see, my man. *(to group)* Douglas, tell me, someone was asking me the other day whether you intend to marry now the war is over.

An ugly pause.

Douglas Umm… you never know.

Margot That reminds me. Do you recall a Mr Mortimer Shaw? He was a member of your club, I believe.

Douglas I'm not sure that I do, no.

Margot He was arrested last week in a public convenience in Pimlico.

Douglas Well, I'm very sorry to hear that.

Margot The whole thing was hushed up but suffice it to say: criminal record, sacked from the Bank and disinherited to boot. A life effectively over.

Oscar That's terrible, isn't it.

Margot *(She affixes Oscar with a terrible stare. She then turns to the group.)* You know, when Douglas was very young his mother turned to me and she said 'Margot, dear, there is something wrong with that child. Something wrong, I fear.' *(to Douglas)* You were at the time engaged in some grave, solitary activity perhaps related to the maintaining or expanding of a collection of some sort.

Douglas Coins.

Margot Coins, very well. But I would not countenance such sentiments as these. Wouldn't hear of it. 'Nonsense,' I said. But she wouldn't believe me and bottled him off to boarding school all the same. And then she died, which goes to show just how much *she* knew.

Douglas There we are.

Oscar A telling parable, Lady Milligan.

Margot Now I understand that there is a deal of complexity to your own vie d'amour, Rensburg.

Oscar Err... well... I'm not sure I'd go that far.

Margot You don't need to blush, young man. I'm sure there was no blushing in the trenches.

Oscar Nor here neither, Lady Milligan, I can assure you. It's simply that –

Margot Well, tell the assembled.

Oscar I'd really rather not if that's all the same to you.

Margot Very well. Douglas. Perhaps you would care to give a summary.

Douglas In as much as – ?

Margot Speak! Be brief!

Douglas There's very little to report as I understand it, and what there is barely falls within the realms of romantic love. *(a sympathetic look to Oscar)* It is true that Renners enjoyed a friendship with Miss Laura Morehouse who, like so many others, was very sadly bereaved during the course of the war. Anything beyond that I think is probably a matter for Captain Rensburg.

Margot Captain *whom*?

Douglas Captain –

Oscar *(helpfully, diffidently)* Herr von Rensburg.

Margot Oh, I see.

Douglas So I hope that's cleared the air somewhat.

Margot Perhaps! But this is the way I prefer to look at it. Herr von Rensburg, a young, gloomy German, trapped behind enemy lines –

Oscar *What?!*

Margot – falls ineffably in love with Miss Morehouse, the fiancée of a rich English..? *(appeals to Marchant)*

Marchant Coffee trader?

Margot Cavalry officer. She, too, in turn pines for him but of course their love is doomed. *(beat)* Or is it? One bitterly cold November evening, whilst staggering home after some reckless, front-line binge, our cavalry officer falls beneath –

Douglas Aunt Margot, I'm not sure we can really speculate in this fashion.

Margot The truth must not be silenced. Rensburg, will you confirm?

Oscar Sadly not.

Margot Young man, you may be German /

Oscar / I'm not.

Margot / but perhaps you'll understand this. Those without the gift of sight often have the gift of second sight. I speak in metaphors, of course.

Marchant Beautiful. Teiresias.

Margot I shall say no more.

Oscar As you wish.

Margot Now where were we? Let us return to the game. Whose turn, pray tell?

Harriet I believe it was Professor Marchant's, Lady Milligan.

Margot Let us have you, then, Marchant.

Marchant Yes. Err… If this person were a dance –

Margot & Harriet Had that! Had that!

Marchant Oh yes, of course. Very well. Hmm. Let me think. *(pause)* If this person were a painting they would be in beautiful, rich oils with a gilt frame. Perhaps by Turner or Gainsborough.

Margot Oh how enthralling. And yet how beguiling. Is it me? Is it me?

Marchant Yes, my lady.

Margot It was me! Me again! Oh how thrilling. Oh what fun.

Douglas I can't help noticing that it's you every other round, Auntie.

Margot Well it's better than the game they were playing at the Cameron-Smith's last night. We all had to get together in teams and answer questions about the War. A little too ghoulish for a drawing room quiz if you ask me.

Marchant Rather. Who won?

Margot *(beat)* The *Allies*, Professor Marchant. Even I knew that one.

Scene 3

Marchant It can be a long, slow trudge.

Douglas I'm used to that.

Marchant So why go through it again? There's less mud in Whitehall –

Douglas You think?

Marchant – but a career may still be heavy going. Unless you get a little help.

Douglas Well, spies tend not to give too much help.

Marchant There are plenty of friendly faces around the world if you know where to find them. But consider this. The Soviets have a vast intelligence wing. Imagine if it could be put at your disposal.

Douglas But they're sort of the enemy in a way.

Marchant Are they? Imagine a world in which our resources could be pooled.

Douglas Doesn't that sort of pull the rug under what I'm doing rather?

Marchant Appleford, occasionally one has to be practical. You see, the Soviet Union, for all its faults, is –

Douglas Yes, I know your Soviet views, thank you.

Marchant The Russians may be the enemy but socialism is not.

Douglas Save all that for Rensburg.

Marchant Rensburg is a dreamer.

Douglas And what am I?

Marchant You are an actor.

Douglas What do you mean?

Marchant I think you know what I mean. Saying one thing. Doing another. Gets to be second nature, doesn't it.

Douglas *(no verbal response)*

Marchant All I'm saying is that sometimes a quid pro quo can be… well, just think about it. What would you say if the Soviets shared their lists with you?

Douglas Well that's ridiculous. Why would they do that?

Marchant *(shrugs)*

Douglas There's no way they'd do that.

Marchant But if they did.

Douglas I'd be the most successful agent in the history of the Empire.

Marchant Isn't that appealing?

Douglas But it's not realistic.

Marchant Well of course it wouldn't be something for nothing.

Douglas *(calm but incredulous)* You're suggesting that I give classified British information to the Soviets…

Marchant In exchange for information they have that you need.

Douglas Such as what.

Marchant Information on the Japanese, on the French… on anyone. They'd be quite happy to see you round up a few foreign agents for them. Their enemy's enemies. Doesn't matter to them if they do it or you do it but if you do it you'll make a big splash.

Douglas And all they'd need would be...

Marchant Just the occasional... noisette.

Douglas You realise you're asking me to betray my country, a country I've just spent the best part of –

Marchant I'm not asking you to do anything. I'm simply saying if you're interested in adopting a practical and enlightened –

Douglas I respect you very much, sir; you know that. But the Empire –

Marchant Oh, come on. That sort of thing went out with Rupert Brooke. Those boundaries no longer apply, Appleford.

Douglas Well that's not for us to say, is it. I'm paid on the basis that the boundaries *do* apply.

Marchant Yes, but paid how much? That's no way to support a... yourself.

Douglas Wait a minute. Are you seriously telling me that the Soviets would give me their list *and* pay me into the bargain?

Marchant Just consider this, Appleford. You're how old. You work in this Home Office-SIS set-up for another 35 years, say. You can only hope to be moderately successful at best because let's face it what you do is largely dependent on luck and no-one can be lucky that long. So you're receiving a modest salary and are modestly successful and you bumble along in an average sort of a way.

Douglas We don't know that.

Marchant We don't know that, no. But we do know that with our help your rise could be meteoric. A flawless career, a good deal of money from both camps, a knighthood and who knows…

Douglas Well that would be dependent on my not getting caught.

Marchant But there'll be no one to catch you. You are the spycatcher.

Douglas But they'll know information is being –

Marchant Douglas, you'd be an absolutely vital asset to us. We're not going to lose that for the sake of a momentary advantage. It's in our interests to keep you safe, play for time. We'll use the information simply to provide colour and detail.

Douglas Reverend Marchant, I hacked my way through the trenches for three years for this country.

Marchant And what have *they* done for *you*?

Douglas I'm just not interested.

Marchant You're not interested. Well that's a great shame, Appleford. A great shame.

Douglas Yes. Well I'm sorry about that.

Marchant So am I. Because it puts me in a rather awkward situation.

Douglas Really?

Marchant Yes. You see we weren't sure quite what your response would be and… well, just listen to this.

(he reads) 'Friday last. Mr Appleford leaves 13a Ponsonby Place at just before eight o'clock. He catches a cab to St James's where he enters the Carlton. He is seen playing backgammon and drinking with friends. He leaves the club alone a little after ten whereupon he walks briskly to 101 Greek Street. He remains inside for ten minutes and emerges – '

Douglas *(tuts loudly)*

Marchant ' – with a young man whom we believe to be a Mr William / Forbes of 29 – '

Douglas / What the devil are you / doing?

Marchant / This *is* rather awkward / isn't it.

Douglas / What are you doing?

Marchant This was simply intended to be an innocent demonstration of the level of espionage we could put at your disposal. I had no idea you would / err... visit umm...

Douglas / How do you know who... shame on you. / Shame on you.

Marchant / Do you wish me to... Do you wish me to continue reading?

Douglas *(pause)* What do you think?

Marchant I just want you to think things through, that's all. Will you do that?

Douglas No I will not.

Marchant I'm asking you.

Douglas *(refuses)*

Marchant Douglas, all your difficulties could be... washed away.

Douglas *(still no response)*

Marchant Well, there we are.

Scene 4

(Vivian is reading to Margot)

Vivian 'Then was Nebuchadnezzar full of fury, and the form of his visage was changed against Shadrach, Meshach, and Abed-nego: therefore he spake, and commanded that they should heat the furnace one seven times more than it was wont to be heated.

'And he commanded the most mighty men that were in his army to bind them and to cast them into the burning fiery furnace. And Shadrach, Meshach, and Abed-nego fell down bound into the midst of the fire.

'Then Nebuchadnezzar the king was astonished, and rose up in haste, and spake, and said unto his counsellers, Did not we cast three men bound into the midst of the fire? They answered and said unto the king, True, O king.

'He answered and said, Lo, I see four men loose, walking in the midst of the fire, and they have no hurt.'

Margot Thank you, Vivian, thank you. *(beat)* You may now read from the *other* book.

Vivian closes the Bible and opens a slim, ambiguous volume. She opens her mouth to begin.

Scene 5

Marchant So I couldn't be happier.

Oscar Well, that's my feeling exactly, sir. I'm most grateful to you for accommodating me.

Marchant Nonsense, nonsense. Theology is a little under-represented at present, so it will be a real feather in our cap. I trust you're up with the journals.

Oscar To be honest, sir, my feet have yet to touch the ground since returning from France.

Marchant Of course, of course. Well, I'm sure you'll be up to speed in no time.

Oscar Don't worry about that, sir.

Marchant Good. Well, I do hope you find Corpus life to your liking.

Oscar I don't doubt that I will, sir. Will there be many lecturing duties?

Marchant Would that bother you?

Oscar Quite the reverse.

Marchant Good. Well, it's all hands to the pump, Mr Rensburg, at present. We also have many invitations to lecture overseas. Would that interest you at all?

Oscar Well… as you wish, sir.

Marchant In my experience men of your age are always keen to see the world.

Oscar Right.

Marchant It's not compulsory, old boy; I just thought it might interest you.

Oscar If you'll allow me to speak candidly, sir, I'm not sure.

Marchant That is your privilege.

Oscar It's just that... well, sir, I may... if I were to get married I'm not sure my wife... well, I'd have to see how she would feel about it before committing myself.

Marchant Of course, yes, I remember now; the fiancée of the coffee trader.

Oscar Umm... yes.

Marchant Well, just ask her what she thinks and we'll go from there.

Oscar I should emphasise that this is all... well, I haven't really spoken to her about anything yet, sir.

Marchant Right, I see. Right you are. Well, best of luck.

Oscar Thank you.

Scene 6

Marchant I don't know what you military men thought but I found the minute's silence most moving.

Douglas Rensburg?

Oscar Most moving, yes.

Margot Thank you, boys. When one's dog is destroyed a certain piece of oneself... well, you of all people should understand, Douglas, after the fuss you made when that guinea pig of yours was eaten by the Bainbridge's red setter.

Douglas Auntie, that was twenty-two years ago.

Marchant Have you seen the papers today, Lady Milligan?

Margot I have, although not read them yet.

Marchant There is much about Sir Clifford Crosbie of the War Office.

Margot Oh yes; what happened to him. Didn't he die?

Marchant Well, he was arrested.

Margot It's the same thing.

Oscar *(beat)* Hardly.

Margot In this case, yes. He's to be hanged.

Marchant For spying, I believe. Although I'm sure Douglas could tell us more. Was it not someone in your team who apprehended him?

Douglas I really couldn't say.

Marchant But we may assume it wasn't you.

Douglas As you wish.

Margot Well, better luck next time, Douglas. I do so love a hanging.

Oscar *(beat) Why*?

Margot *(to Marchant)* Now *that* is an impertinence. But I do forget myself. For is not tonight your date with destiny?

Oscar *(genuinely)* I'm sorry, Lady Milligan; are you

addressing me?

Margot Oh, Herr Rensburg, don't play the coy.

Oscar Based on somewhat bitter previous experience I must confess I can suspect to what you are alluding but I fear your comments are rather misplaced.

Margot And tonight?

Oscar Yes, Lady Milligan; the Spencer ball happens to be tonight.

Margot *(to Marchant)* You mark my words, Marchant. This young man is just a hop, skip and a jump away from the aisle.

Marchant Splendid!

Margot Is that allowed at Oxford, Marchant?

Marchant Allowed; yes.

Douglas But encouraged?

Marchant Alas no.

Margot But you must rise above this idle prittle-prattle, von Rensburg. She will, I have no doubt, shortly fall into the egregious spindles that are your arms.

Oscar I really must protest!

Margot Nonsense! It is preordained. *(she points a long finger and goes as if to write on the wall)* 'Eli, eli, lema sabachthani'.

Vivian Madam, I think you'll find 'Mene, mene, tekel parsin'.

Margot I stand corrected.

Oscar At the risk of saying it a third time I really must point out that I am not taking Laura Morehouse there nor following her there, I simply happen to be attending a function to which she too has been invited.

Margot But what a function! Just think! The Devonshires, the Malboroughs, the Rutlands, the Portlands, the Sutherlands. The list is ended. You, young man, will be among their number. And can you dance?

Oscar After dinner, yes, I believe there will be dancing.

Margot No; I mean you specifically.

Oscar Oh, good point.

Marchant You've got him there, Lady Milligan!

Margot Oh that *I* were still young enough to knit.

Douglas Surely to dance, Aunt Margot.

Margot You have your morals, young man, and I have mine. Vivian, transport us if you will! To the fortepiano with you. Something dreamy and listless.

Marchant This is marvellous.

Margot Vivian is a godsend. She cooks, she reads, she... *(pointing to the piano)* strums. And an orphan just like you, Douglas.

Vivian begins to play. As the characters leave just Douglas and Harriet remain.

Harriet Mr Appleford, I'd love to learn more of your spying.

Douglas Well that's sort of against the rules.

Harriet Of course. I'm just saying it sounds fascinating.

Douglas Well it's really not spying at all. It's sort of the opposite of spying. How's Florence Nightingale, anyway?

Harriet I'm beginning to wish she'd never left for the Crimea. Oh that sounds dreadful doesn't it.

Douglas Well I'd be very interested to read it.

Harriet You would?

Douglas When it's finished. I don't actually read much, to be honest.

Harriet Well this may be the book for you, then.

Douglas You never know.

Harriet If you don't read what *do* you do to relax, Mr Appleford?

Douglas *(beat)* I have absolutely no idea.

The music transmutes into an orchestral waltz and we are suddenly in the ballroom.

Scene 7

Laura is sitting alone at the beginning of this scene. Oscar sees her, stalls momentarily, and presses on.

Oscar Miss Morehouse. What a pleasant surprise.

Laura Ah, Mr Rensburg.

Oscar I didn't know you were invited.

Laura A clerical error, I believe.

A pause.

Oscar Are you well?

Laura Yes, thank you, Mr Rensburg.

Oscar Splendid.

Laura And you? All well, I trust?

Oscar Oh yes; quite well, thank you.

Laura Oh good. I am glad.

Oscar Good.

A pause.

Laura Quite well, you say?

Oscar Yes, that's right.

Laura 'Quite' in the sense of absolutely, or in the sense of reasonably?

Oscar I'd have to say absolutely.

Laura Oh good.

Oscar Yes, all running smoothly.

Laura I am glad. And what is your occupation now? Have you returned to your books?

Oscar Yes, that's right. I'm at Oxford.

Laura And it's theology, is that not right?

Oscar Yes, that's right. I'm at Oxford.

Laura Yes.

Oscar And still teaching, Miss Morehouse?

Laura Oh yes, in fact I suppose this week saw the

unconscious intersection of our spheres in that I am encouraging the children to embroider biblical texts onto cushions.

Oscar Oh that *is* good news. And what is the text?

Laura Promise you won't laugh?

Oscar Miss Morehouse, those Biblical jokes have not withstood the test of time.

Laura Very well. 'Jesus himself stood in the midst of them and saith unto them Peace be with you. But they were affrighted and supposed that they had seen a ghost.'

Oscar Rather heavy for a cushion, isn't it?

Laura It wasn't my first choice. But we rather seem to be running out of stuff we haven't embroidered yet. And it's the perfect number of letters to fit round the outside.

Oscar Well, I'm sure it's all to the good.

Laura Oh yes, certainly. Next month we are to go up to Scotland and I am to teach them to draw.

Oscar Rather ambitious, isn't it? For how long do you intend being away?

Laura Well, just pointing out that the sky meets the earth at the horizon will be a step in the right direction, I think.

Oscar Yes, indeed. You know when I think of governesses I tend to picture rather stern, elderly ladies in pince-nez who delight in rapping one's knuckles.

Laura Yes, well, that's our reputation.

Oscar Whereas in fact, of course, you're... very different from that.

Laura A little different, perhaps.

Oscar And in fact very... err... very... err... very beautiful. In certain ways. So many have said.

Laura Thank you very much, Mr Rensburg. I certainly seem to have no shortage of unsuitable suitors.

Oscar Oh, how dreadful of them.

Laura They're very sweet but they do cluster round one so at the most inopportune moments with flowers, fruits. Rabbits. Chickens, sometimes.

Oscar I can imagine.

Laura Yes; they're always there, muttering sweetmeats in the corner.

A pause.

Oscar Look, I know things have been rather tough for you.

Laura Have they?

Oscar Oh yes.

Laura Perhaps a long time ago.

Oscar Of course.

Laura Three years.

Oscar Well, the heart is not a clock.

Laura No. No.

Oscar But all the same…

Laura I'm glad you're back, Oscar.

Oscar Yes. Me too.

Laura Yes. Me too.

A pause.

Oscar But I'm forgetting my manners. Surely you would care for a drink.

Laura Oh, no, not for me. But don't let that prevent you.

Oscar I'm rather keen for a glass of wine if truth be told.

Laura Oh, they have it all here. Red. White. Blue. I heard Lady Spencer say they've brought up a crate of eighty-year-old port tonight that Queen Victoria gave them twenty years ago.

Oscar Goodness.

Laura Although whether that means she gave them eighty-year-old port twenty years ago and it's now a century old or twenty years ago she gave them sixty-year-old port I don't know.

Oscar Tricky.

Laura Care to risk it, anyway? Or would you rather dance first?

Oscar Goodness. Well, goodness. I err…

Laura It's entirely up to you. I'm simply suggesting, not recommending.

Oscar The truth is that I would love to but I'm not convinced I… I'm slightly impoverished in certain ways.

Laura Oh Mr Rensburg, that needn't hold us back. We once danced before the war did we not?

Oscar We did. I seem to recall having two left feet on that occasion.

Laura Well I'm assuming that that is no longer the case?

Oscar *(smiles shyly and happily)* Very well, Miss Morehouse.

They hold each other and prepare to dance as the music swells. The instant they begin to dance, however, all music and sounds of the ballroom are gone – instead we hear the sounds of shells raining down on them and rifle and machine-gun fire. They dance oblivious, slightly awkwardly at first but with increasing confidence and elegance. We gradually become aware that the music is returned but it is now crackly and gramophonic.

Scene 8

Oscar is alone in his study. He is reading, perhaps. Enter Douglas.

Oscar Apples! What on earth are *you* doing here? *(pause)* What is it? *(pause)* What? Come on; what?

Douglas *(sighs)* Renners, there's been the most dreadful accident. Umm… They were… they telegrammed the club because they didn't know where you'd be and… so

I came straight up here. They were... up in Scotland. One of Laura's pupils, some young boy, got into difficulties in the lake... *loch*... and the thing is that Laura of course tried to save him being the sort of person she is... Was.

Oscar What are you talking about, Apples?

Douglas Umm... yes; she obviously did her best to help the little chap but in fact she herself got into difficulties and... well, it's...

Oscar *(pause)* What?

Douglas I'm really sorry, Renners, but Laura's dead.

Oscar Don't be ridiculous. She's in Scotland.

Douglas Yes; that's right. Scotland. She err... she drowned. Like I... like I said.

Oscar No? You don't understand. I saw her last week. At the ball. I told you.

Douglas Yes, well that's what I'm... yes; this happened yesterday.

Oscar But it can't have.

Douglas Well, they... I think it has, you know.

Oscar But I got a letter from her today.

Douglas Yes.

Oscar So... *today*. Do you not see? Today.

Douglas Yes, but in order for that to arrive...

Oscar And she says in the letter she's going / to Aberdeen on Friday.

Douglas / Oscar, just think: *In order for the letter to arrive today* it must have been / posted a couple of days ago, ie. before –

Oscar / And today's only Thursday. So, you know... tomorrow.

Douglas Oscar, she sent the letter a couple of days ago.

Oscar But I don't understand. I don't understand. We were meant to...

Douglas Renners, look... *(he sighs)* I'm sorry.

Oscar This isn't... she's up in Scotland, Apples.

Douglas I'm so sorry.

Oscar *(An almighty sigh. He winces and looks away.)*

Douglas Well what I'll do is I'll wait downstairs and whenever you're ready if you want to... Right. *(Pause. He turns to leave and turns back.)* The boy also drowned, by the way. He drowned too. Which when you think about it sort of...

He leaves.

Scene 9

Margot This is a tragedy. A real tragedy. But one must be practical. What do we have here? A young man thwarted by dreadful circumstances, so tragic one cannot even refer to them. But we must put such sorrows to one side.

Oscar Lady Milligan, I really must protest.

Margot Silence! It is hardly your place to protest now,

is it? *(a genuine question)* But dwell not! For that is behind us. And in front of us? Marriage. No! *(perhaps holding up a hand to imaginary protest)* No, no. Hear me out. To smooth over. To start afresh. To close this sorry chapter of your youth. And I refuse to blame you, despite everything. You are what you are. But we may work to change that. Still. Always positive. We must look on the bright side. And things could have been a good deal worse. Had Reverend Marchant not interceded in the matter before it reached the magistrate –

Douglas Aunt Margot, I'm sorry but I refuse point blank to get married, least of all to Harriet Schalley.

Margot I always wanted something a little better for you, I admit. A minor royal, a duchess, perhaps, even the daughter of an oil tycoon. However. A writer may be only one up from an aviatrix but any port in a storm, n'est-ce pas?

Douglas N'est-ce pas.

Margot For let us consider what a marriage is. A social contract? Perhaps. A convenient route through life? Perhaps. A loving, caring union of body and soul? Not necessarily.

Douglas I will not give in to this kind of rot, Auntie. I'm sorry.

Margot Douglas, dear boy, listen to me. I speak to you now not only as your legal guardian but also as the trustee of the Appleford Estate and thereby the conduit of your sizeable and no doubt much relied-upon per diem.

Douglas So it's come to this, has it?

Margot Oh, no melodrama, please. Back me up here, von Rensburg.

Oscar I'm... I'm not so sure I can, Lady Milligan.

Margot But you promised!

Oscar I'm not sure I did, you know.

Margot Think of your career, besides all else. Think of us. You simply cannot continue your life in its current illegal and immoral vein. Just think. This is the perfect solution to our problems and our problems may very well soon be out of control. But I am realistic, Douglas. The leopard does not change her spots overnight. I know you will need to occasionally wet your beak a little. And that's fine. But now, with discretion, you will be perfectly safe. We have an alibi for you.

Douglas I will not ever discuss this with you again and I would be most grateful if you would take these words as the final ever spoken on the subject. There was an unfortunate mistake, yes, but that's all it was and I will not, not, be cajoled into marriage with a total stranger for the sake of your social standing. This is the most disgusting blackmail and I will not give into it. Permit me also to observe how unnecessary it is for you to broach this unhelpful subject in front of others.

Margot It's Reverend Marchant you should be thanking, not me. If it weren't for him you'd be in jail now, you selfish little boy, and how he arranged otherwise I'll never know. You are considerably in his debt, I think.

Douglas Goodnight, Aunt.

Margot Good night.

He leaves.

You swore to help me, Rensburg.

Oscar With respect, Lady Milligan, I did no such thing.

Margot 'Peradventure you will be enticed, and we shall prevail against you, and we shall take our revenge on you.' God's words, not mine.

Oscar Jeremiah 20 verse 20.

Margot I won't forget this bromidic little incident, Rensburg. Mark my words.

Blackout. A montage of bells, first mournful, then celebratory, finally rather sinister.

Act Two

Scene 1

Marchant This is good, Appleford. This is very good.

Douglas Is it?

Marchant Yes; I'm most grateful to you.

Douglas Well, I'm glad that this is what's required. It was actually very easy.

Marchant And no-one noticed anything?

Douglas I was a civil servant in a civil service building. What is there to be noticed?

Marchant Appleford, I don't want you to feel uneasy about this.

Douglas That's exactly how I feel.

Marchant Nonsense.

Douglas Well… I do.

Marchant Well, there's no need.

Douglas Sir, I have to tell you I'm having second thoughts.

Marchant Come on, Appleford. It's a bit late for that, isn't it?

Douglas Well that's sort of why they're called *second* thoughts, isn't it.

Marchant But we have an agreement.

Douglas Yes sir, but… look, they asked me if I wanted a secondment to Delhi.

Marchant What?

Douglas Well it came up, sir, and I rather thought…

Marchant You thought you might take it.

Douglas I thought about it.

Marchant Even though…

Douglas Well I thought it might… and then you could always find another…

Marchant Appleford, you're not thinking.

Douglas Well I think I *am*.

Marchant No, no. No-one wins with you in India.

Douglas It's just I'm uneasy about this as you know, and I –

Marchant You're jumpy.

Douglas A little.

Marchant Just a little jumpy.

Douglas A little jumpy.

Marchant Yes. You'll settle down.

Douglas That's what I'm afraid of.

Marchant Nonsense.

Douglas Sir, we know what happens to spies, / and I fear...

Marchant / You must never dwell on that.

Douglas Well one is tempted, for the simple reason that –

Marchant Appleford, it's not possible you could ever

be implicated. If things ever get tight – and they won't – but if they did, well, *then* is the time to get abroad for a bit until things blow over. But not now.

Douglas To be candid, Sir, I think I wanted to run away.

Marchant But you mustn't. We've spent a long time trying to get someone in your position on our side. And we want to keep you where you are.

Douglas I'm sorry, Sir.

Marchant No; I'm glad you came to me. Thank you for your honesty.

Douglas No.

Marchant I travelled a good deal as a young man. With the Church. I wanted to see the world, like you. But let me tell you. There's a small village on the uppermost tip of Cyprus called Apostolos Andreas. It's still there; much unchanged, I believe. Beautiful. Just a few daubed houses basking in the sun, one or two fishers drying their nets in the late afternoon, you know the sort of thing. Hidden from tourist and native alike. Almost entirely surrounded by the Med, like a peninsula. Totally isolated. I was there for six months – this must be twenty-odd years ago now – and between you and me had the total run of the place. In such places, Appleford, the Englishman is worshipped. Almost as a god. But after a while… well, there's no challenge, there's… nothing there. No newspapers, no club, no-one with whom to play chess. One is sort of confronted with a terrible blank. The most beautiful place in the world and I've never been so happy to get back to London. It was dark, it was raining, and of course twenty yards from Paddington I had my pocket picked, but...

Douglas I'm sorry to hear that.

Marchant Well, no harm done. But I'm simply saying your time is best spent here, do you not think?

Douglas You may be right.

Marchant And of course you have family duties.

Douglas Well, I think Margot's health is still pretty robust, don't you? Despite the occasional complaint.

Marchant I actually meant your wife.

Douglas Oh.

Marchant Does she enjoy London?

Douglas Err… yes, I think she does.

Marchant So why were you thinking of leaving?

Douglas Actually perhaps she doesn't.

Marchant Well, you know best.

Scene 2

Harriet What's the matter?

Douglas I'm sorry?

Harriet What's the matter?

Douglas Why, nothing.

Harriet Nothing?

Douglas No; nothing at all.

Harriet You seem somewhat subdued.

Douglas No, no.

Harriet A little gloomy, perhaps.

Douglas Not at all.

Harriet Not troubled in any way?

Douglas Simply trying to concentrate, my dear.

Harriet Upon what?

Douglas Oh, nothing.

Harriet *(pause)* It's not the house, is it? That's bothering you?

Douglas Why on earth would it be the house?

Harriet Well, I don't know. The walls are rather thin and sometimes –

Douglas Oh are they? I hadn't noticed.

Harriet – sometimes it can be difficult to relax with all the commotion next door.

Douglas I can assure you I have never noticed anything from next door, commotion or otherwise.

Harriet Very well.

Douglas Yes.

Harriet Well, if there's anything I can help you with.

Douglas No, I don't think so.

Harriet Righto.

Douglas That's very kind, though.

Harriet Oh, thank you. *(pause)* Do you not think that you might be working a little too hard?

Douglas I wouldn't say that; no. We have to pay the bills, my dear.

Harriet Last night I came downstairs very late and you were still poring over all your papers.

Douglas Well, I have to make sure I'm on top of everything.

Harriet I'm surprised they even let you take such a large volume of documents from the office.

Douglas No, no, no, no, no. Perfectly normal. Perfectly normal.

Harriet Oh good. *(pause)* What are you reading?

Douglas Oh, just something to lift my spirits a little.

Harriet Oh I am glad. What is it?

Douglas The Bible.

Harriet Oh; which part?

Douglas The massacre of the innocents.

Scene 3

Vivian Oh, it's wonderful.

Oscar You think so?

Vivian Oh yes; wonderful.

Oscar Really?

Vivian I thought it was brilliant.

Oscar You're most kind, Vivian.

Vivian Not at all, no. *You're* very kind to let me hear it before the rest of the world.

Oscar Well, it won't exactly be the world. And I somehow doubt that the fellows of Corpus Christi College are going to be as enthusiastic an audience as yourself.

Vivian Well they're just silly then.

Oscar That's not society's view, rightly or wrongly. But I am most grateful to you. I couldn't think who else to ask, and since Lady Milligan didn't need you this afternoon...

Vivian It's certainly better than listening to myself read aloud.

Oscar Now, is there anything you'd *change*? Anything that perhaps could have been clearer?

Vivian Oh no. I thought the whole thing beautifully clear.

Oscar In that case perhaps there might be some areas that are too... lowbrow and populist.

Vivian On the contrary; it was erudite and challenging.

Oscar So, on balance...

Vivian Brimful of wonderful ideas. It was like sitting under a waterfall.

Oscar Oh that is good. I wanted to use this as an opportunity to... so often the public lectures one hears are so dry and fusty –

Vivian Well yours isn't like that at all.

Oscar I want to say something that everyone can understand, that touches the listeners. Changes their outlook on things, makes them act differently.

Vivian I thought it very beautiful.

Oscar Thank you, Vivian.

Vivian No, thank you Professor.

Oscar No, I'm just a… just a Mister, really. A junior Fellow. But tomorrow is my big chance, I think. If I can impress some of the dons then… well, who knows.

Vivian I'm sure that it will make a great impression.

Oscar Oh, we shall see. *(smiles)* Were you educated back at home, Vivian?

Vivian My mother taught me English, which is all the education one needs, really.

Oscar Lady Milligan mentioned you were an orphan. I had no idea. I'm very sorry.

Vivian I did know my mother. She died when I was ten.

Oscar And how about your father?

Vivian No. But my mother told me of him. *She* learnt English from *him*.

Oscar And what did he do?

Pause.

Vivian Sir, can I say how sorry I am about your lady friend.

Oscar Laura.

Vivian Yes, Laura. We were all devastated to hear.

Oscar Oh, I do hope not.

Vivian Well, I was.

Oscar Thank you, Vivian.

Vivian It must be very difficult for you.

Oscar A second amputation is never as tough as the first. Or is that the other way round?

Vivian I understand you used to be quite a cricketer.

Oscar That seems a long time ago.

Vivian *Were* you good?

Oscar Err... I could have been. Ever follow the game?

Vivian Never, Mr Rensburg.

Oscar Well that's a great shame. I used to think it was one of the most beautiful things in the world.

Vivian Is it because of your injury that you can't play now?

Oscar *(trying to suppress a laugh)* You really don't know much about the game do you, Vivian?

Vivian Nothing. Well; bats and balls, obviously.

Oscar Stumps? Pads? Silly mid-on? Deep cover?

Vivian You've lost me now. *(shrugs)* Well, fingers crossed for tomorrow night, anyway.

Oscar Goodness. Yes.

Vivian Perhaps we might shake hands.

Oscar Oh yes; a good luck shake. A sensible idea. *(they shake)* Good luck!

Vivian Good luck!

Oscar Amen.

Scene 4

We hear jeering and bombs dropping.

Oscar Perhaps an apology? How about that?

Marchant My dear boy, I'm not sure that that would be an appropriate step.

Oscar I do feel terrible, sir. Perhaps if I wrote to the Dean.

Marchant Oh let's not disturb *him* for heaven's sakes.

Oscar Oh dear.

Marchant The assembled were hoping for a forensic analysis of the two extant versions of the text. Some I believe were expecting the lecture itself to be in Greek.

Oscar I think perhaps that I misunderstood the needs of the audience.

Marchant Rensburg, I'd go a little further than that. You simply cannot stand up in front of an academic community like that and talk in bald terms about death and angels and what have you.

Oscar But that's what we're... surely we can't avoid talking in those terms. We're theologians.

Marchant But never forget your manners. We're not trying to give these people a vision of heaven or hell.

We're trying to expound our views of the historical context of the New Testament writings. I'm quite certain at one point you told them to love their neighbour.

Oscar Well, isn't that sort of standard?

Marchant But it's just not appropriate.

Oscar But I thought that... given the insights that... I just thought...

Marchant Rensburg, you defended your country and you're a war hero and as such you should be rightly proud.

Oscar Oh, I'm not interested in all *that*.

Marchant And I'm sure all types of things happened or seemed to happen out there but certain matters are best left outside the lecture theatre.

Oscar I see that now.

Marchant Well, I wonder if you do. To speak frankly, Rensburg, I don't think I've ever seen a lecture deteriorate into such an unquestionable laughing stock in thirty years.

Oscar It was shocking, wasn't it.

Marchant Now academics can be as boorish as rugby players, I'll be the first to admit that, and are not necessarily any better judges of quality.

Oscar Well, that's very good of you.

Marchant But sadly they rule the roost.

Oscar The chap from New Caledonia liked it. Taylor.

He shook my hand.

Marchant Well that's *one*, but… the point is what the Master says goes.

Oscar But the Master wasn't there.

Marchant Alas bad news travels with some speed.

Oscar Oh dear.

Marchant Yes; I received a letter from him this morning, I'm afraid.

Oscar Oh goodness. Not concerning the lecture, I trust?

Marchant I'm afraid so. The rather sad thing is that one of the things he mentions is… well of course he's in a very difficult position but… he says that you are to be relieved of all lecturing duties.

Oscar But I've already… oh, come on. Look, I've already… *(an angry sigh)*

Marchant Yes, I'm terribly sorry about this.

Oscar Well how about a second chance?

Marchant That is not what's proposed, I'm afraid.

Oscar What happened to being forgiven not seven times but seventy times seven?

Marchant Oh please don't drag the Bible into this.

Oscar *(he gestures his incredulity and frustration)* Sir, you're making an error. We could be on the brink of something new here. A popular theology, sir, that changes people's lives.

Marchant Don't get me wrong, Rensburg; I admire

you. Really I do. And I wish I had your faith. But this is not Speakers' Corner. This is an Oxford college and they are the Senior Common Room. In my experience these things are best changed slowly.

Oscar But it looks like I shan't be changing them at all now.

Marchant We don't know that.

Oscar But what shall I do?

Marchant There are plenty of things a mind such as yours can be set upon in a place such as this.

Oscar Such as?

Marchant Oh, many, many things.

Oscar Such as what?

Marchant Oh, any number of things.

Oscar Yes, but what?

Marchant / Well, I couldn't say.

Oscar / Sir, I must keep lecturing; I feel this very strongly.

Marchant Rensburg, you have something very special. And I don't want to see you lose that. But perhaps this is not the environment to best see you flourish.

Oscar Sir, I wish to keep lecturing.

Marchant And I'm saying that's not possible in this college. Now I'm offering you something else, something with perhaps slightly fewer responsibilities. Whether or not you take up the offer is a matter for you.

Scene 5

Douglas How is he?

Harriet He's asleep. *(pause)* I'm sleepy too.

Douglas Yes.

A pause.

Harriet You know, he has your nose.

Douglas Oh, I was wondering where that went.

Harriet Will you be needing it back? It rather suits him.

Douglas *(he forces a smile)*

A pause.

Harriet Did I mention the Campions accidentally left their sandwiches here before setting out this morning?

Douglas No?

Harriet I wrapped them up and sent them ahead. They should have them by now. Still fresh, I hope.

Douglas Oh, well done, Harriet.

Harriet Just trying to help them out. *(pause)* You've made me very happy, Douglas.

Douglas I think *he's* made you very happy.

Harriet In any case I'm very happy.

Douglas I'm glad.

Harriet *(pause)* I wish… Douglas, I think sometimes a

thing may not be good but good may come of it.

Douglas Do you. Do you.

Harriet And you know I wonder how one might fathom whether that makes it worthwhile. And indeed who is to say, finally.

Douglas Who indeed.

Harriet But I wish *you* were... complete and happy and –

Douglas But none of us is these things. None of us.

Harriet And to look at your son and to feel –

Douglas Now come on.

Harriet But do you not see? To be able to enjoy / what it is that –

We hear unmistakable sex through the wall.

Douglas / To what? I'm sorry?

Harriet To enjoy... well, I don't know how to say it, really. Certain things are a shame, that's all.

Douglas Harriet, we have so much for which we may be grateful if we so wish. You choose to be grateful. That is your choice.

Harriet Yes. Yes, I know. Very well. I just wanted to say –

Douglas I know.

Harriet I'm... thank you. Thank you, Douglas.

Douglas That's quite alright. There's no need to –

Harriet Thank you.

She touches him and he starts, whether through surprise or revulsion. She, too, therefore, starts.

Douglas There's... there's no need to...
From the next scene we hear 'For he's a jolly good fellow...'

Scene 6

They finish singing and are happy and expectant, even Douglas. It's Christmas.

Margot Douglas, I couldn't be happier.

Oscar One thousand congratulations, old boy.

Margot Look at him! Douglas, I do wish your mother were alive to share my pride.

Douglas Oh, it's really nothing, you know.

Margot How dare you? You're the most successful little boy in the country now.

Douglas Well, I wouldn't go that far.

Margot There's a glow to your cheeks, my man. That's what promotion does for you.

Douglas Auntie, it's freezing out there and the brandy is very good.

Margot Oh, I'm so thrilled. Herr von Rensburg, will you join me in my unending hymn of praise?

Oscar I have to say that I can't think of a single piece of news that could make me happier.

Douglas Well, thank you all very much.

Margot Mrs Appleford! Are you the power behind the throne?

Harriet Not at all. I didn't even know until Oscar's 'well done' telegram came through.

Margot Oh, you're a secretive little chap, aren't you! *(to Harriet)* You must be very proud.

Harriet Very proud.

Marchant Congratulations, Douglas. *(this moment is almost chilling – it is something of a reminder – and it curdles the atmosphere, at least between Marchant and Douglas)*

Douglas *(pause)* Thank you, Reverend Marchant.

Marchant Well done.

Douglas *(beat)* Thank you.

Margot Marchant! Have you ever heard of such a dazzling rise?

Marchant I suspect not. Tell me, Douglas, what will your new duties require of you?

Douglas *(coolly)* Well I'm not sure I'm at liberty to discuss.

Margot Oh, come on, Douglas. Everyone knows you're the Empire's number one spycatcher. There's no secret to that.

Douglas Well it's not quite as... well it's very boring but essentially I'm now head of strategy instead of a small area of operations.

Margot What does this mean?

Oscar Presumably Douglas is now the leader of some sort of division.

Douglas Yes, that's pretty much right.

Margot Goodness! Over how many men do you hold sway?

Douglas Eighty-five men, Auntie.

Margot Eighty-five men, honest and true.

Douglas Yes.

Marchant How do you know they are honest and true?

Douglas *(he gestures)*

Marchant How can you be sure?

Douglas *(sighs in embarrassment and exasperation)*

Marchant Would, say, a traitor in your organisation be more safe or less safe now that you head a division?

Douglas There is no traitor.

Marchant But if there were.

Douglas There is no traitor.

Marchant But if there were.

Douglas *(silence)*

Marchant Safer? Or not?

A pause.

Oscar Apples, tell us exactly what happened. How were you told? Were you called into the chief's office?

Douglas Well…

Oscar I'll bet he sat you down and poured you a drink

and offered you / a cigar and said –

Douglas / Can you all just shut up about it? Just shut up –

Harriet / Douglas?

Douglas / – the lot of you.

He leaves.

Margot Marchant! Go after him! Redeem the poor lamb.

Marchant Very well.

Margot You see? All the hallmarks of the common cold!

Marchant catches up with him in the hall. They are alone.

Douglas Someone has filed a report about me.

Marchant About *you*?

Douglas About me.

Marchant How?

Douglas Well they don't know it's about me but it's about the documents.

Marchant How the hell did you manage that?

Douglas I didn't do anything.

Marchant They went over your head?

Douglas No; well, it's more difficult now I'm… I'm no longer first on the scene of the crime as it were.

Marchant What do you mean?

Douglas Up till now I'd assess the threats and pass on

my findings. So no-one would know about things that I decided were not important. I would just overlook them and not report them. Sort of hide them away.

Marchant Such as this.

Douglas Such as this, yes, but now I... I thought it would be easier as I got higher up but in fact I just can't control eighty-five free-thinking people. At some point someone's going to discover something.

Marchant So have they discovered something or not.

Douglas No.

Marchant No.

Douglas No, but an inconsistency has been flagged.

Marchant What does that mean?

Douglas It means that someone has discovered something but they don't know what it is.

Marchant So what happens next?

Douglas Nothing, unless something happens again.

Marchant So what do we do?

Douglas We just have to be more careful.

Marchant Well how do we do that? Can't you just order them off it?

Douglas No, I have clearance to add to the warning but not dismiss it.

Marchant Well can't you just...

Douglas Sir, potentially it's only a matter of time before... who knows what might be found. I *must* have left a trail somewhere.

Marchant We don't know that.

Douglas Sir, I *must* have *somewhere*, and if there's the slightest indication that the Soviets are acting on –

Marchant Let me worry about that.

Douglas Why?!

Marchant Just trust me.

Douglas Sir, I'm in an impossible situation. Even if I do nothing I'm doomed.

Marchant We don't know that.

Douglas Sir, we do know that at any moment one of my men could raise a second flag. And at any moment the Soviets could carry out any small act that would show they're receiving information from us. In either case a full scale investigation will commence and it's only a matter of time... Meanwhile I just have to sit here waiting for one of these eventualities to happen.

Marchant Just stay calm. Neither of these things may happen.

Douglas *(sighs in impatience)* Well, *neither* of them may happen, but equally one or both of them might.

Marchant Just don't think about it. Go home and have a drink.

Douglas How's that going to help?

Marchant Just get drunk. Isn't that what you like?

Douglas Sir, that is not going to solve the problem.

Marchant Yes, but you won't know that.

Douglas *(pause)* Is that it?

Marchant I'm sorry, Appleford.

Disgusted, Douglas leaves.

Scene 7

Harriet So you have everything you need?

Oscar Oh yes. Yes, thank you.

Harriet Do you use dental paste?

Oscar I do, yes. I have all my paraphernalia with me.

Harriet Oh, well done. I do hope you sleep soundly.

Oscar I'm sure I will. And chapel is at eight?

Harriet Umm… not sure. Sorry, I really should know.

Oscar That's quite all right. I might get there for half past seven just in case.

Harriet Very good. Well, I'll leave you to it. If you need anything simply shout up the stairs.

Oscar Oh, I'm sure everything will be fine.

Harriet I hope so.

Oscar Harriet, I'm most grateful to you for letting me stay over.

Harriet Nonsense, the snow's so bad. I'm quite certain the trains aren't running.

Oscar Thank you. *(pause)* Listen… do you think Douglas is alright?

Harriet Oh, I'm sure.

Oscar He just doesn't seem very well.

Harriet I think he's just exhausted.

Oscar You don't think he may be drinking a little too much?

Harriet Yes, but... what can I do?

Oscar I see. I do hope they don't work him too hard in his new position.

Harriet How are things in your new position?

Oscar Oh, wonderful, yes. It's quite a journey for me back here –

Harriet I can imagine.

Oscar – but they are so keen to learn. Frankly that was less true at Oxford.

Harriet Well. I'm happy for you.

Oscar Thanks Harriet.

Harriet Goodnight, Oscar

Oscar Good night Harriet.

Harriet leaves. Oscar is left alone for some time. He sits studiously and rather cutely on his bed and reads. Eventually he puts his book down and extinguishes the light. We are in darkness for some time before hearing the bombs start up. We hear Oscar call out uncertainly as he fumbles for the light. When the light is turned on we see him sitting upright in bed with Douglas now in the room.

Oscar Goodness! Douglas! You gave me quite a fright!

Everything under control? *(pause)* I thought you'd be out like a light. *(pause)* Having trouble sleeping, eh? *(pause)* Or perhaps a funny dream? Is that it?

Douglas *(pause)* Do you remember… that Easter when we were sort of herded into that little chapel and the raid started outside and…

Oscar Yes. I remember that.

Douglas And it's funny. What the brain remembers. Because I don't recall the sermon or anything, I just recall the music and thinking that after months of trying to avoid it it would have been just the time to die… you know, all the singing and the bombs and everything and it was all so… straightforward and it all fitted together for once. It was really beautiful.

Oscar Yes. Yes, it was.

Douglas That hymn was the most perfect sound I've ever heard. *(he tries to hear it)* Just a bunch of idiots like us singing and we didn't have a clue but it was like the sound was falling from the skies, and the mortars sort of just fitted into that and the organ and everything and I suddenly realised that everything was… good, you know; all those chaps were a decent bunch and that chaplain was a nice enough fellow and… it was like that for a moment or so and I then I sort of lost it again and I got irritated and annoyed and realised my feet were still wet and all the rest of it. But I think about that a lot, you know.

Oscar I sometimes wish I'd been killed too, Apples.

Douglas Yes. I understand, old boy. *(There is some slight physical touch; an affectionate ruffle of the hair* *or a squeeze of the hand or a pat on the back. After a pause one of them begins humming the hymn 'Dear Lord and Father of Mankind'. It's very quiet and it's not clear whether he even realises he's humming it. In similar fashion the other joins in and they sit there, humming together.)* Times are changing, Oscar.

Scene 8

Marchant But I don't understand it. I simply don't understand it.

Oscar Let me start by saying I think you are entirely justified in being angry.

Marchant I'm not angry.

Oscar But were you to be you'd be entirely justified. What I did was completely foolish. I know I got the job thanks to your intercession and I did not intend to let you down.

Marchant So why did you do it, then?

Oscar Sir, I thought I could trust them. At least... to be honest I have to admit that the whole issue of trust simply did not occur to me.

Marchant But did you not think..?

Oscar It really didn't cross my mind for a moment that they might err... abuse that trust. But let us not forget the unseen pressures under which they may be working.

Marchant Rensburg, forget about that. You chose to leave Oxford because you wanted to lecture and despite misgivings I respected that.

Oscar And I respected *that*, sir.

Marchant Yes, but look; through my good offices you got a respectable job at a respectable university and now through your good offices their library is now twelve volumes short and they'll never see those books again.

Oscar Oh, we don't know that, sir. We could always try to find them in the town and ask for them back.

Marchant But that's the point. They weren't even students.

Oscar Well, I thought that made it all the more important to ensure that they encountered ideas and literature, sir. These men work in mines all day. What chance do they have in there?

Marchant Rensburg, do you not see? They didn't take those books because they wanted to read them; they took them in order to sell them, no doubt to buy drink.

Oscar But we can't say that for sure, surely.

Marchant Did they really look like they were theologians to you?

Oscar I wonder if we look like theologians to them.

Marchant No doubt they were very glad to chance across your ilk.

Oscar Sir, they really seemed interested in what I was saying. I was so happy they turned up to the lecture. I really thought I'd made an impression on them.

Marchant Well you obviously made some kind of impression.

Oscar Oh, how could I have been so stupid?

Marchant Rensburg, come on. You're not stupid. You are in many ways highly intelligent, I think.

Oscar Thank you, sir.

Marchant But you just don't think in the way that others think, I think, and I think that's why you struggle.

Oscar Oh.

Marchant But that's potentially a strength.

Oscar Oh good.

Marchant I can't blame you, indeed I don't think anyone blames you.

Oscar Thank you. That is most merciful.

Marchant You see, there you go again. 'That's very *kind*'. That would do. You don't need to bring mercy into it. It's just manners. Just manners.

Oscar Well thank you anyway.

Marchant But you do understand that I can't have them writing to me in these terms.

Oscar No, of course. That really wasn't my idea.

Marchant I'm sure, but the fact remains that your university has in financial terms sustained a great loss and they have turned to me as your guarantor.

Oscar Sir, I forbid you to pay that fine. I... please, sir. I must pay my way.

Marchant I'm very glad you say that, because I'm simply in no position to assist.

Oscar No, of course not. I'm sorry they even wrote to you.

Marchant Well. We're in agreement. And do you have the ninety pounds?

Oscar *Ninety*?! Oh for goodness sakes! How am I.... can they not appreciate that an honest mistake will happen once in a while?

Marchant Those books must be paid for, Rensburg.

Oscar But that's practically a year's wages, sir. Can't they just… I must say I think they're being a little spiteful, don't you?

Marchant I'm not sure that's fair. You took the books –

Oscar Well I *took* them, yes, but I didn't… *take* them.

Marchant That's not a distinction they recognise, I'm afraid.

Oscar *(sighs)* Well I'm just going to have to pay. I'm not doing very well, am I.

Marchant Nonsense. You're just unlucky. You're a good man, Rensburg.

Oscar With respect, sir, I've noticed that people keep saying that to me and I've no idea what it means.

Marchant Well, it means… well, it's difficult to say, really.

Oscar Perhaps it doesn't mean very much.

Marchant Oh I wouldn't go quite that far. Now listen, this is a bit awkward and I don't know how to tell you so I'll just read it to you. The letter also says the following.

Scene 9

Vivian Oh I'm sure you're brilliant at it.

Oscar I wouldn't say that. But I do love it. They're all so sweet.

Vivian But what do they make of your theology?

Oscar Who knows. Christ spoke in parables and now so shall I.

Vivian And are the children well behaved and attentive?

Oscar No. They behave dreadfully, the poor things.

Vivian Why? What do they do?

Oscar Oh, most of it is pretty harmless stuff, you know. A bit of innocent name-calling and so forth.

Vivian What do they call you?

Oscar Oh, nothing, nothing. And it's not particularly cruel. If it weren't my leg it would be something much worse, I'm sure.

Vivian Oscar, I do wish they weren't so beastly to you.

Oscar Not at all. I love them very much. It's all high spirits. A bit of shouting, wandering around... throwing things – I'm sure I did much worse as a child. But I can,

I hope, give them a bit of the attention and love that they're missing and perhaps... well, who knows.

Vivian Must you always look on the bright side?

Oscar But there is much that's very positive about it.

Vivian Well, I think it's very brave of you.

Oscar *(gestures)*

Vivian And do you get to eat meals at the school?

Oscar Unfortunately not. I'm learning to cook in my rooms but it's slow progress, I'm afraid.

Vivian I hope you're not starving.

Oscar No, no, not at all. I can make a few things now without reference books.

Vivian You mean recipe books.

Oscar Yes. It's a useful skill to have, you know.

Vivian You're lucky. I eat with Lady Milligan but never could get used to her tastes. Swan in particular is a very oily meat.

Oscar How are you faring with *Bleak House*, by the way?

Vivian I sense she doesn't like it so I skip quite a lot of paragraphs.

Oscar Oh that's a shame.

Vivian For her, yes. I read them silently to myself whilst speaking the following paragraph out loud. It's a trick I learnt.

Oscar Goodness.

Vivian Yes.

Oscar I understand that you have this Sunday off, and with this in mind I have successfully managed to take this Sunday off too in exchange for working... well, the point being I was minded to suggest a jaunt of some description.

Vivian Oh, Oscar, I'm sorry. It's not *this* Sunday I have off.

Oscar Oh no!

Vivian I'm sorry. I don't... perhaps I got confused.

Oscar No; I'm sure it was I who was confused.

Vivian Then I must have been confusing. I'm so sorry, Oscar.

Oscar That's quite alright.

Vivian *(pause)* What did you have in mind for us to do?

Oscar Well, it was sort of going to be a surprise, actually.

Vivian Well, perhaps you could surprise me now.

Oscar We thought... I thought we could visit the bandstand, where there have apparently been some very fine ensembles of late. And of course the zoological gardens are well worth seeing, I understand. Have you ever seen an elephant, Vivian?

Vivian Yes.

Oscar Oh yes, of course. Well, this one's a real

specimen by all accounts.

Vivian And where would you take me for tea?

Oscar Oh, well for tea I thought perhaps a picnic.

Vivian Well that would be a real treat.

Oscar Yes, it certainly would.

Vivian And what would be in the hamper?

Oscar Oh, probably some bread and butter.

Vivian Come on, Oscar, buck up. This is meant to be a treat. How about a pudding?

Oscar Bread and butter pudding?

Vivian I suppose so. But how about queen-of-puddings, seed-cake, home-made jams, champagne and sponge fingers?

Oscar Very well.

Vivian Muffins, meringues, tongue, eggs, brown sherry, tinned crab, cucumber, radishes. Lime juice.

Oscar Well that's what we would have done.

Vivian And I would have enjoyed it greatly.

Oscar As would I.

Vivian We could then have strolled home.

Oscar Yes.

Vivian Arm in arm.

Scene 10

Douglas But why now?

Marchant Because we need it.

Douglas Are you not happy with what I'm giving you?

Marchant Yes but you're not giving us as much as we're giving you, are you.

Douglas Well that's not the point. The –

Marchant / Well that *is* the point.

Douglas / – point is that... the point is that I'm giving you what you ask me to give you.

Marchant But we need more now. And if anything you should be in a position to give us more.

Douglas Sir, you know full well that the department's suspicions have been raised. Now, I've interceded and I'm happy to do that but there's only so long I can hold off a larger investigation.

Marchant But did you not tell them –

Douglas Doesn't matter what I told them. The fact is I am effectively in charge of catching a spy and that spy is myself.

Marchant But that's perfect. He cannot be caught.

Douglas *(exasperated)* No it's *not* perfect sir, for the simple reason that at some point I'm going to need to give them something.

Marchant You should be worrying about giving us something.

Douglas I don't think you're taking me seriously. I'm in a corner here.

Marchant Appleford. We need you to do this.

Douglas Too big, sir. It's too big.

Marchant Perhaps I should be the judge of that.

Douglas Well I'm telling you sir we can't get away with it.

Marchant Can't or won't?

Douglas Sir, we can't.

Marchant We need it.

Douglas Yes.

Marchant We need it.

Douglas Yes but I'm saying it cannot be done.

Marchant Yes, I'm saying we need it.

Douglas Yes, I appreciate that but… very well, you don't believe me; fine. But ask someone else, if there is anyone else –

Marchant There isn't anyone else.

Douglas – which I doubt… well there you go then. And they'll say the same thing. Because it cannot be done. Not without…

Marchant Aha! So it can be done!

Douglas No, it cannot be done. At least, not without… well, everything will be out in the open. And that's going to kill the whole enterprise.

Marchant Not necessarily.

Douglas Sir; *necessarily*. It cannot but be the case.

Marchant Appleford, answer me this. We've been

helping you out for eight years now.

Douglas Well that's one way of looking at it.

Marchant And in all that time have you ever been suspected? Ever?

Douglas *(pause)* No.

Marchant Well don't you think a little trust may be in order?

Douglas Sir, if I steal what you're asking me to steal I will be in mortal danger. They'll know it's me. I cannot take that kind of information. They'll come after me. And then they'll come after you.

Marchant Wait, wait, wait. What if they don't come after you?

Douglas They will.

Marchant Yes, but what if they don't.

Douglas They will.

Marchant Yes, but what if they don't? You'd no longer seek to implicate me, surely.

Douglas Well, how could I?

Marchant Exactly.

Douglas Without –

Marchant Precisely.

Douglas But they're going to come after me.

Marchant Not if they go after someone else.

Douglas What do you... who else?

Marchant Does it matter?

Douglas Well, of course, because…

Marchant Just think.

Douglas I am thinking.

Marchant Well think out loud.

Douglas A crime is committed.

Marchant Yes.

Douglas The crime is investigated.

Marchant Undoubtedly.

Douglas I am suspected.

Marchant Yes.

Douglas *(pause)* Well now what?

Marchant Well go on.

Douglas I am suspected.

Marchant Yes.

Douglas And arrested?

Marchant No…

Douglas …*Briefly* suspected?

Marchant Exactly.

Douglas Because…

Marchant Because here's where our decoy comes in.

Douglas Our *decoy*?

Marchant Of course.

Douglas But who is he?

Marchant Does it matter?

Douglas Well yes because they're going to swear blind they don't know what we're talking about.

Marchant But they may not be believed.

Douglas Why on earth not?

Marchant Douglas, I think you underestimate your position in life. Look around and you'll see you're a figure of some standing. Not just in the intelligence community but in society. Have you not noticed that?

Douglas I'm not sure.

Marchant There's a lot of light on you. And the chances are that society will believe whatever you say.

Douglas Sir, that won't be enough.

Marchant Which is why you must start featherbedding now. It's surely a matter of a morning's work to prepare a false paper trail. Take a few access documents, botch a forgery of your pass... just fabricate a bit of evidence. Easily done.

Douglas Are you quite sure?

Marchant But you must also try to clean yourself up a bit. People are beginning to express dismay at your drinking.

Douglas At my drinking what?

Marchant Appleford, come on.

Douglas What people?

Marchant People who matter.

Douglas And in what way does it affect them?

Marchant I'm simply saying it doesn't help that you're seemingly making some sort of vague exhibition of yourself. You're drawing attention to yourself.

Douglas Well not deliberately.

Marchant Freud might disagree.

Douglas I thought he was bunk.

Marchant Well, so he is, but I fear that we are being unwise.

Douglas I'd say drinking is a lot safer than what you're proposing.

Marchant But is it as advantageous I wonder?

Douglas Look, I'm not going to prejudice or jeopardise, don't worry about that.

Marchant Good. So now we just need our sacrificial lamb.

Douglas Yes.

Marchant But you must trust me, Douglas. People will believe whatever you tell them. That's your reward in a way.

Douglas Well that just makes it all the more tragic, don't you think?

Marchant I'm no expert, Appleford.

Scene 11

Douglas I should be at home but… I've been drinking.

Oscar Well. Any joy?

Douglas *(sighs)* Rensburg, are you happy, would you say?

Oscar Am I what?

Douglas Happy? Roughly, I mean.

Oscar I've absolutely no idea. Why? Are you?

Douglas I rather fear not.

Oscar Oh. Oh, dear. I'm sorry about that.

Douglas Well there we are.

Oscar Anything I can do to help?

Douglas No, I don't think so.

Oscar Oh.

Douglas I'm just under a terrible strain at the moment, Renners.

Oscar Yes, I'm sure you are.

Douglas Renners... I'm... in difficulties.

Oscar Oh, goodness. Care to talk about it?

Douglas Everything's a bit of a mess, actually.

Oscar But what is the matter? Can you not tell me?

Douglas It's gone a bit beyond all that.

Oscar Well it's not too late, is it?

Douglas Probably.

Oscar That's just not fair. It's too late for *me*. Did you ever think about that? *(pointing to his leg)* It's too late for this, isn't it. As ridiculous as it sounds all I ever wanted was to thwack a cricket ball around. As simple and straightforward as that. And I genuinely believed that if I could do that for eight hours a day every summer with a winter in the nets I'd be happy. That's all I wanted. And I didn't get it. But we just have to battle on. And you have Harriet and Thomas. They rely on you and love you and you all support each other. Now I know things seem rather difficult but I can't help you unless you tell me what the problem is.

Douglas Do you know what they do to spies, Rensburg?

Oscar Well, sort of, yes.

Douglas What do they do?

Oscar They generally hang them, don't they?

Douglas What they do is they rush them. Do you know what that means? The chap knows he's going to be hanged that day but he doesn't know precisely when and suddenly out of nowhere these four fellows rush in at break-neck speed and they put a hood on him just like that and drag him to the next room where there's a gallows but he doesn't know it and in about twenty seconds he's hanging there.

Oscar Well that's barbarous, don't you think?

Douglas I do now. *(a dreadful sigh)*

Oscar *(after a decent pause)* I expect you're just tired.

Douglas *(laughs ironically)* Yes, yes; that's it. Just tired.

Oscar You must be very tired indeed.

Douglas Yes, that's it, Rensburg.

Oscar You better get home. Do you have any Sedebrol

in the house?

Douglas Oh, perhaps, perhaps.

Oscar Well I'd advise you to seek it out. It's very good.

Douglas Yes.

Oscar A hot whisky, even, given the circumstances, might be appropriate.

Douglas Whisky, yes.

Oscar Or a warm, milk-based drink such as a cocoa, perhaps.

Douglas Yes, it's just... I have to tell you, Renners... *(He dissolves into anguished tears. They last and eventually fade. Silence for a bit.)*

Oscar *(pause,* totally *ignoring the mood)* Lettuce, I understand, is very soporiphic if you're interested in giving it a try.

Douglas Thanks, Rensburg.

Oscar But do take something that'll send you right off.

Douglas Yes.

Scene 12

Harriet Where have you been?

Douglas I'm sorry.

Harriet Yes. Where have you been?

Douglas Where have I been? I've been at work.

Harriet You're telling me you've been at work.

Douglas Correct.

Harriet You smell like a distillers.

Douglas I had to have a drink. I forget why.

Harriet *(a peeved sigh)*

Douglas Look, I'm sorry. I forgot… I genuinely forgot it was today.

Harriet How did you manage that?

Douglas I just got confused, that's all. Cannot a man be confused?

Harriet Well I think you're deliberately confused.

Douglas Can you not just relent briefly?

Harriet Never mind. Thomas understands. I told him you'd be here for his next birthday. Or perhaps I shouldn't have.

Douglas Well I'm here now.

Harriet Well it's a bit late now, isn't it. They're all gone and he's in bed.

Douglas I'm sorry. I don't know what else to say.

Harriet Needless to say there doesn't appear to be a big box wrapped in bows under your arm either.

Douglas Oh no; that's too far. I *did* get him a present. If Selfridges chooses not to deliver it on time then I can hardly take the blame on their behalf.

Harriet And what was the present?

Douglas In what way?

Harriet Come on; what was it?

Douglas A... a surprise. From the toy department.

Harriet And all the while your son is in tears, of / course, but that –

Douglas / He is not in tears. He is not in tears.

Harriet How would you know?

Douglas Listen, I've to be honest pretty much had enough of this. / I would rather –

Harriet / You've had enough of this? How dare you? I've been up to my eyes in blancmange for two days whilst you've been doing God knows what.

Douglas I've told you what I've been doing.

Harriet Would it kill you even to read to him once in a while?

Douglas No, but it would certainly bore me.

Harriet You're just a fraud.

Douglas I'm what?

Harriet You don't fool me.

Douglas A fraud? Everyone's a fraud; hadn't you noticed?

Harriet Not really, no.

Douglas Just... look; I'm doing my best.

Harriet Everyone's doing their best. Not everyone gets a medal.

Douglas I don't expect you to understand since you've no idea the pressure I'm under.

Harriet I've no idea because you never tell me. You

never discuss it. You never discuss anything. You never actually *speak*.

Douglas Well if I felt you might be interested / I might be –

Harriet / It just amazes me that you can do so much harm simply by saying so little.

Douglas All I want is for you to occasionally leave me alone. Just –

Harriet Leave you..? All I *do* is leave you alone, ostensibly out of / consideration for –

Douglas / You see? You make it impossible / for me to –

Harriet / Douglas, you're drunk all the time. All the time. The doctors have said you shouldn't drink so much.

Douglas They also say you shouldn't stand bolt upright in a wet trench for two years but sometimes needs must, I'm afraid.

Harriet Oh don't play that card / with me.

Douglas / Didn't notice anyone rushing to help me then.

Harriet Is the War always going to be your excuse?

Douglas *Excuse*?!

Harriet I'm sick of you and your ugliness. Do you not see how you're ruining Thomas.

Douglas Rubbish.

Harriet You're ruining him.

Douglas Absolute rubbish.

Harriet Did you know he's in trouble for bullying other children at school.

Douglas Yes, I read the letter.

Harriet You read the letter? That's it?

Douglas No, I...

Harriet Well what do you propose to do about it.

Douglas Nothing. Nothing.

Harriet Nothing?

Douglas Look, we'll just send him to another school if it makes you happier.

Harriet How's that going to help?

Douglas I don't know. He'll be a new boy. He won't be able to bully.

Harriet But don't you see?

Douglas If anything they'll bully him.

Harriet But he learns it from you. He just copies you. That's all he knows.

Douglas I will not listen to you.

Harriet You're ruining us all.

Douglas I will not listen to you.

Harriet You're ruining us. Something's happening in my head. Do you not care about that?

Douglas What are you talking about?

Harriet I don't know. Something's… I don't know.

Douglas Well stop scratching away at your books then.

Harriet Do you not care about anything?

Douglas And you call me a fraud.

Harriet You are a fraud.

Douglas At least I don't parade myself as some sort of intellectual.

Harriet But I *don't*.

Douglas Oh come on.

Harriet Have you read any of my books?

Douglas I don't read.

Harriet Oh but I think you do.

Douglas I don't have time.

Harriet Are you sure?

Douglas I'm telling you.

Harriet But this is your book, is it not? *(by now she is at the shelf and is brandishing a volume)*

Douglas What the… leave that alone!

Harriet Is it interesting? *(she looks at the title and reads it aloud)* Is it interesting?

Douglas Leave that alone. It's not –

Harriet Look! Look! *(She shakes it open and crowds of male photos spill onto the floor. Perhaps in his panic Douglas vainly tries to scoop them up.)*

Douglas What are you doing?

Harriet What am *I* doing?! Look at yourself. Look at yourself. Just look.

Douglas I didn't know. They were… that's Oscar's book, I think.

Harriet *(a gasp) That's* what's disgusting *(his remark)*, not this *(the photos)*.

Douglas Please, just…

Harriet Why can you not talk to me about this?

Douglas Please, just don't tell anyone. Don't tell anyone. I'm asking you.

Harriet But according to you these are Oscar's.

Douglas No no no – please, just, please. Don't make me crawl through the mud. Please don't mention this. Please. Don't ever mention it. It's destroying me.

Harriet Well it's destroying me too, Douglas.

Douglas Look, I promise… just don't tell anyone about me. I can't…

Harriet I want to help you. I really do. Don't you see?

Douglas Please.

Harriet Why don't you trust me?

Douglas I'm sorry.

Harriet Why don't you trust me?

Douglas I'm sorry.

A certain calmness is restored.

Harriet I was simply asking if you'd read my Boer

book.

Douglas You know I haven't. Why.

Harriet It might be of interest. It might even help you.

Douglas Why? Is it about… this?

Harriet No. *(beat)* It's about spies.

Scene 13

The salon of Lady Milligan is no longer a happy or vibrant place. The assembled sit or stand there in silence, occasionally distracting themselves. A grandfather clock ticks loudly and seems to dominate the room. Marchant is reading the newspaper.

Margot Any amusing deaths recently?

Marchant Lord Sidbury shot himself in India.

Margot Oh no.

Marchant Yes, the peacock farm failed. Too hot, apparently.

Margot Those poor birds. A decent enough man, although suffered from some sort of curvature of the spine.

Marchant I believe some poor chap walked straight into the Thames from Embankment Pier in the fog last week.

Margot Wonderful. The fog really has been appalling, hasn't it.

Marchant Very bad, yes. *(pause)* Some unfortunate individual managed to mangle themselves in their own printing press.

Margot Oh why are men such asses?

Marchant Well, it could have been a woman, could it not?

Margot Marchant, what would a woman be doing with a printing press?

Marchant Touché.

Margot *(pause)* Still writing are you, Harriet?

Harriet A little, Lady Milligan.

Margot A little ain't enough, baby.

Marchant But your last publication was well received, was it not?

Harriet Generally, yes.

Margot But why such slow progress? Writer's blank?

Harriet I find it difficult to… reconcile with my family life.

Margot Well, I wish to encourage you in your hobby. If I should die I want you to have the Queen Anne bureau.

Harriet *If*, Lady Milligan?

Margot No Douglas again?

Harriet He's at home. He's looking after Thomas.

Margot But I thought Jennifer was looking after Thomas.

Harriet Oh yes. I think actually Douglas is working.

Margot On a Sunday.

Harriet Yes, he works very hard.

Marchant 'The Lord thy God hath blessed thee in all the works of thy hand.'

Margot I would have thought 'Thou shalt observe the Sabbath and keep it holy' might have been closer to the mark.

Marchant I believe the good Lord's precedent is that of the man who must pull his neighbour's donkey from the well.

Margot Well as long as someone is keeping our island safe from... from what, exactly?

Marchant The threat is over-rated. Mis-conceived, even.

Harriet You consider it mis-conceived, do you, Reverend?

Marchant Well, yes, my issue is not with those who try to discover secrets but those who seek to withhold them in the first place.

Harriet Oh I'm quite familiar with your views, Reverend.

Marchant You are? How so?

Harriet *(she shrugs ambiguously)*

Margot Herr von Rensburg, perhaps you can clear up a small mystery for me.

Oscar I shall do my best.

Margot Last week you were sighted at Marylebone

station standing on some sort of box and giving out leaflets.

Oscar No mystery, my lady. I spend much of my free time in such a manner.

Marchant Rensburg is a true priest; you mark my words – he is bringing about more social change through that soap box than a hundred Russian spies.

Oscar That's not my intention at all, sir.

Marchant But you wish to see a new heaven and a new earth and the first heaven and the first earth pass away?

Oscar This is all in the pamphlets.

Margot Oh for shame. Such promise. Did he have promise?

Marchant In so many ways, my lady.

Margot So what *is* your vocation, exactly, Herr von Rensburg? Not a cricketer with your wooden leg, not an academic. I even seem to recall your wife dying.

Oscar Well, she wasn't my wife, Lady Milligan.

Marchant This world is not Rensburg's home. He is in it but not of it.

Margot Is that why you now associate with servants?

Oscar *(pause)* I... try to associate with everyone. We're all servants of a type.

Margot I'm not even going to ignore that. Vivian, the Old Testament, quickly. The room is polluted. *(whilst Vivian prepares the book Margot continues)* Rensburg, take my advice. Be more like Douglas. Husband, father, senior civil servant. Now *that's* a successful young man. Dwell on his example. *(she sniffs to Vivian)* Commence.

Vivian 'Before the angels lay down, the men of Sodom compassed the house round, both old and young, and they called unto Lot, and said unto him, Where are the men which came in to thee this night? bring them out unto us, that we may know them.'

Margot Err… I mean the New Testament. Come on, girl; quickly.

Vivian 'Now when the even was come, he sat down with the twelve. And as they did eat, he said, Verily I say unto you, that one of you shall betray me. And they were exceeding sorrowful, and began every one of them to say unto him, Lord is it I? And he answered and said, He that dippeth his hand with me in the dish, the same shall betray me…'

Her voice has begun to slow and slur and become weird and incomprehensible. We notice that Lady Milligan is falling asleep. All others present – Vivian, Marchant, Harriet and Oscar – are suddenly a string quartet and strike up a lively Beethoven theme with mimed instruments. Vivian then prods Lady Milligan awake with the end of her bow. The reading is instantly resumed.

'The Son of Man goeth as it is written of him: but woe unto that man by whom He is betrayed. Amen.'

Margot Amen. Thank you, Vivian.

Marchant Mrs Appleford, just to pick up on something at which you hinted earlier.

Harriet Yes?

Marchant I'm just curious. Douglas doesn't ever discuss his work with you, does he?

Harriet Oh no, Reverend Marchant. No, no.

Marchant I see. Thank you.

Harriet *(pause)* He doesn't have to.

Oscar and Vivian are alone now.

Vivian Do you really believe that there will be a new heaven and a new earth? And that the old one will pass away?

Oscar Yes. At least, I believe I believe.

Vivian I marvel at your faith, Oscar. I wish I had it.

Oscar I always imagined, ever since I was a little boy, that what happens to you when you die is what you most wanted to happen to you whilst you were alive. The things you could never do which you felt you were meant to do.

Vivian And what does the Bible say to that?

Oscar Well... the kingdom of God is rather topsy-turvy. Everything's back to front. He who is first shall be last, the meek shall inherit the earth. Don't you think that the cripple may walk?

Vivian I'm sure he may run.

Oscar We shall see, Vivian. We shall see. And everything that we want, that we secretly want, may be given us.

Vivian We shall see.

Oscar *(pause)* Sometimes when I can't sleep I lie there in the darkness and I try to lose touch of where I am by imagining myself in another room, perhaps the room I used to have as a child. I try to picture the walls around me as they would have been and the furniture and where the window is. And after a while the imagined room seems to be the real one.

They embrace chastely for a long time.

Act Three

Scene 1

Oscar Apples! My God, you look dreadful! Are you alright?

Douglas Rensburg I've seen your lover.

Oscar What on earth are you talking about?

Douglas I saw her today. Well, last night. I've been up all night.

Oscar Apples, you're drunk. *(said happily or resignedly, not critically)*

Douglas I'm not drunk. But I have been drinking.

Oscar I don't doubt it. Now what on earth are you babbling about, old boy?

Douglas Rensburg you will never believe me but frankly I don't care because it's true. I saw her.

Oscar Well, I'm entirely prepared to believe you, old boy, but you're going to need to make yourself a good deal clearer.

Douglas I'm sorry but I can't be any clearer. I saw your lover. Last night.

Oscar But I don't *have* a lover, Apples.

Douglas Yes you do. Laura Morehouse.

Pause. The whole mood changes.

Oscar Laura? *(pause)* Where?

Douglas Alright. It's late. It's gone midnight. Still in the office. Chuck it – couldn't be bothered. I leave. A few drinks later. Tight as an owl. Few more drinks and cat the whole lot up there and then on the pavement. Not very thrilling. Anyway. But now I can think, you see. Clear as a bell. So I grab a cab down to Soho. A private cinema I go to. Yes; that's right. A disgusting little place for disgusting little people like me to watch disgusting things. Does that shock you, by the way?

Oscar Oh, no; not in the slightest.

Douglas I was looking for a catamite. Ha!

Oscar Do go on, Apples.

Douglas Very well. So I'm there and I'm sitting at my table and all the drinks and the smoke and everything and looking around and getting a feel for the evening but then all of a sudden I'm looking up at the screen and I suddenly see… *Laura*. On the screen. It's an image of Laura. But it's not part of the film. It's like the film is going on almost in the background and there she is; this… *image* is just standing there, looking at me. And her clothes are soaking wet. And it's as if it's not part of anything but just being projected onto… it's like it's there, staring at me. And I can't believe it. I don't… and I look round and people are just carrying on as normal and no-one's any the wiser or they haven't seen it so I stand up and I put my hand out, I don't know why, I just put my hand out and of course people are telling me to sit back down and yelling because I'm blacking out the film but I look and I can still see her even though she should be blacked out by me… by my shadow. My silhouette. She's still there, she's still just… standing there looking at me. And that's what happened.

Oscar Apples. What are you talking about?

Douglas As I stand here now, that's what happened. I don't know. I don't know. But she was there.

Scene 2

This scene melts from the previous one – we see Oscar alone, staring, and we hear the projector whirring. We hear also the inevitable sounds of the film. Perhaps we also hear Duke Ellington's Caravan being played.

Scene 3

Vivian Are you sure?

Oscar *(Nods and smiles. They embrace, perhaps.)*

Vivian So you were right. Everything is upside down and back to front. Just like you said.

Oscar But I never thought... Vivian, this is a miracle. It's a miracle. You must believe me.

Vivian I do.

Oscar It changes everything.

Vivian Will it change... will it change *us*?

Oscar What do you mean? No, no, of course not. But... I don't know what it means.

Vivian I grew up in a little village called Apostolos Andreas. At the topmost tip of Cyprus. It's so secluded and no real progressive ideas ever penetrated and everyone had all these superstitions. My mother thought that when you see the ghost of someone you love it means that you are soon to die. They can't rest, you see, until you do.

Oscar And did your father's ghost appear to her?

Vivian No, and it was when she was ill that she told me this. So she didn't know whether it meant he was still alive or whether it meant she would survive the illness.

Oscar I'm just a little scared, Vivian, if truth be told.

Vivian Yes. I am too.

Oscar Please… don't be scared. Don't be scared. You're not an orphan any more.

Vivian Thank you.

Oscar And I'm sure your father is safe, wherever he is.

Vivian Thank you.

Oscar *(he touches or holds her face)* Do you think you take after him?

Vivian I hope not. My mother always thought he was a spy.

Scene 4

The salon. Lady Milligan, Vivian and Harriet are present. Off-stage we hear Thomas reading to himself: 'This is the pig. He lives in the sty. And what does the pig say? He says "Oink-oink" This is the sheep. She lives in the pen. And what does the sheep say? She says

"Baa baa".' The story continues quietly in the background along these lines.

Douglas Oscar! All well?

Oscar Appleford, you're right. You're right. She's there.

Douglas I'm sorry?

Oscar She's there. I saw her.

Douglas Alright, Renners, just calm down.

Oscar *(agreeing)* 'Just calm down'. Yes.

Douglas Yes. Now what are you talking about?

Oscar What..? At the cinema.

Douglas The..?

Oscar The cinema.

Douglas The cinema. What cinema?

Oscar Well, the... I don't know; you know – the one... she's there, man, she's there. She's up on the screen.

Douglas Right. Who's there? Who's on the screen.

Oscar Douglas? *(a slight, embarrassed pause)* Laura.

Douglas *Laura?* What...;

Oscar Yes; just like you said. Just like you said.

Douglas Rensburg, are you alright?

Oscar But listen. When I returned it was boarded up. The cinema had gone. It's gone now. So together we've got to try to –

Douglas Look, what on earth are you talking about?

Oscar About this morning. What you said.

Douglas What?

Oscar Douglas, did we not have a conversation just this morning about the cinema in Soho?

Douglas No. I don't think I've seen you all week, have I?

Oscar What do you mean? You drove to Whitechapel this morning. We were in my rooms this morning. Just this morning.

Douglas But why would I drive over to Whitechapel?

Oscar Well, to tell me what you'd seen, of course.

Douglas But I haven't seen anything. I've been in the office all day.

Oscar Impossible. Impossible.

Douglas Rensburg, I haven't seen you for some time. Certainly not today. I've been working all day. Anyone at the office would tell you that.

Oscar Look, it was just… this morning and you told me you'd seen Laura.

Douglas Are you talking about Laura Morehouse?

Oscar Yes, of course, just as you said.

Douglas I'm sorry but I don't know what you're talking about.

Oscar Yes you do; yes you do. You said you saw Laura on the cinema screen. And you were right.

Douglas What cinema?

Oscar The cinema where you said you met people to

do disgusting things. You said –

Douglas *What?*

Oscar No, that's what you said. You said you were looking for a catamite –

Douglas What did you say? *(beat. In fear)* Look, I don't know what the hell you're talking about. *(to others)* I've no idea / what he's talking about.

Oscar / This is impossible. You told me you'd seen Laura. *(to others)* You've got to believe me. We saw Laura. Really we did.

Douglas Look, I've never been to any cinema.

Oscar Well, I'm just saying / that I have to –

Douglas / I'm not one of those. I'm not one of those, dammit. You hear me?

Oscar Douglas, it's perfectly alright / with me...

Douglas / You're obsessed with trying to find me out.

Oscar What? I'm not interested in all that. The real issue is... so where were you that night?

Douglas I was – don't speak to me in those terms. You're not a policeman.

Oscar The real issue is that we both saw Laura. Vivian. You / believe me don't you.

Margot / Oh no! / Don't involve my staff for the Lord's sake.

Oscar / Vivian? I told... You told me... you said that it was true, didn't you.

A pause. All look to her.

Vivian I'm… I'm not sure.

Oscar *(he visibly gives up)*

Margot Oh, I've waited a long time for this. You shall leave my house and never return.

As he leaves he stops and stares at Vivian. We hear once more the boy reading: 'This is the cockerel. He lives on the roost. And what does the cockerel say? He says "Cock-a-doodle-do. Cock-a-doodle-do."'

Scene 5

Marchant I thought Oscar was a friend of yours.

Douglas Sir, he's out to destroy me.

Marchant Pick anyone. / But not him.

Douglas / 'Anyone'? There is no anyone. I mean who?

Marchant Douglas, I won't have you involving Rensburg in all this.

Douglas It's him or me.

Marchant Pick someone else.

Douglas There's no time. I know for a fact the papers will print it tomorrow. And at that point I will have perhaps six hours before someone is formally questioning me.

Marchant You're quite sure?

Douglas No one will be above suspicion, and I'm the most obvious culprit.

Marchant Do not involve Oscar.

Douglas Sir, we just *don't have time.* We don't have… do you understand? I've just committed a major larceny.

Marchant Well let's have a think.

Douglas No, sir. Listen to me. Tomorrow they're going to come to me and I'm going to tell them that Rensburg has been borrowing my pass and I knew it but I didn't think anything of it because… sir, I've already forged the documents… it's a fait accompli.

Marchant I'm asking you to leave him alone. Appleford, this man has the DSO. He has the Military Cross. He was a Cambridge Blue for rowing. He was a Harrow Blood for rugby. Could have batted for England. He is the most decent and moral man I've ever met. Now I want you to go away and think about that. We're all as bad as each other but don't mix Rensburg up in this, surely. Because he's different.

Douglas All I need from you is a guarantee that you will not cause trouble.

Marchant Sadly I don't respond well at all to that sort of tone. I may be his sole protector but given the position you're in I'm all the protection he needs. Nothing is going to happen to that man. Not while I'm alive.

Douglas Rensburg is as good as a traitor and he's as good as doomed.

Marchant If you so much as mention his name during your interrogation I will produce sufficient evidence implicating you in this to wipe you off the face of the earth. You take the rest of the night to think about that.

Douglas Will do.

Marchant Good.

Douglas Reverend Marchant, thank you very much. Aunt Margot sends her regards, by the way, and hopes that you will be able to visit her tonight.

Marchant Of course. How is her health?

Douglas Not good, sir.

Marchant I'm very sorry to hear that. I shall be there shortly.

Douglas Very well.

Marchant is leaving but turns back briefly.

Marchant Just remember this. If you give them Rensburg's name… I'll give them yours.

Scene 8

Margot Dear Douglas came round at the weekend and helped me from my sickbed to my deathbed.

Marchant Oh come, come, Lady Milligan. I don't think matters are so grave yet.

Margot I can feel it, Marchant, I can feel it. The lifeblood is draining. I have worked my whole life for this moment.

Marchant But your mind is still as alert as ever, God be praised.

Margot Nonsense. This morning I felt so flustered and distant that I was unable even to recall my telephone number.

Marchant Oh, there's no shame in that. I'm always forgetting mine.

Margot *(to Vivian)* What is it, again?

Vivian One, Madam.

Margot Oh yes. You see? We are near the end. But I have no fear. Just regret.

Marchant Don't consider yourself alone in all this, Lady Milligan. We are all here for you.

Margot Thank you. Thank you. Thank you. I shall now take my leave of you if I may. Do I sleep or do I wake?

A long pause. Margot reaches her hand out and grasps Marchant's.

Margot Peter.

Marchant Margot.

Margot *(pause. weakly)* I think 'Lady Milligan' may be preferred.

Scene 9

Vivian suddenly bursts into tears.

Vivian *(through tears)* I'm sorry. I'm sorry.

Marchant No, no; that's it – cry it all out. That's it.

Vivian I'm sorry, I'm sorry. I promised I wouldn't make a fuss.

Marchant That's alright, that's alright. We're all worried about her.

Vivian No, it's not that.

Marchant Well what on earth is the matter?

A pause.

Vivian Sir, I am expecting a child.

An allmighty pause.

Marchant Who's? *(pause)* Not Rensburg's?

Vivian No, sir.

Marchant How can you be so sure?

Vivian It can't be, sir. We've never…

Marchant You're not serious.

Vivian Yes, sir.

Marchant Oh God. Well can't you just say it's his?

Vivian Sir, I don't… I'm not sure I can do that.

Marchant Oh for God's sake, girl. What were you thinking of?

Vivian Sir, I'm… I don't know what to do for the best.

Marchant But how could you be so *stupid*?

Vivian What do you mean, sir?

Marchant You know damn well what I mean. Stupid.

Vivian But sir –

Marchant Stupid. Just stupid. You hear me?

Vivian I'm sorry sir.

Marchant This is a real mess. A real mess. *(he sighs)* Could you not have warned me?

Vivian What do you mean?

Marchant Well couldn't you?

Vivian *Warned* you, sir? But don't you think this was somewhat inevitable given...

Marchant Do not refer to that. Not to me, not to anyone else. Is that clear?

Vivian But perhaps Lady Milligan. She –

Marchant Oh, so now you're selfish as well, is that it? Can you not see the woman is dying?

Vivian Yes, I'm sorry, it's just that I don't know to whom I may turn.

Marchant *(he is taking out money and throwing at her)* This is all I've got. That's all I've got. Do you understand?

Vivian But what should I do?

Marchant *(sighs exasperatedly)* Look, have you not got a family you can go to?

Vivian No, sir. My mother is dead.

Marchant Well what of your father?

Vivian *(she shakes her head)*

Marchant Well then, surely some childhood friend for God's sake.

Vivian Yes; I suppose there still must be people I know in Apostolos Andreas.

Marchant Yes, can you not... *what did you say?!*

Scene 10

Douglas and Harriet stand before the coffin.

Harriet Poor old Margot.

A pause.

Douglas Yes.

Harriet This is a real tragedy.

Douglas Hmm.

Oscar Poor old Margot. I know it sounds strange, given her age, but she had such plans. Although one wonders...

Eventually enter Margot, who stands in the doorway. Sure enough she looks like death.

Margot Is that you, Douglas?

Douglas Auntie! Permit me to assist you.

Margot Very well. Welcome to the sepulchre.

He assists her.

Harriet Lady Margot, please accept my deepest condolences at this terrible time.

Margot Very well, Mrs Appleford.

Harriet Professor Marchant was a good and decent man and his death is a profound loss.

Margot That's very kind of you to say so.

Douglas Was there much suffering, Auntie?

Margot To my knowledge none.

Harriet It's just so senseless.

Margot Well, no one lacks a good reason for suicide.

Douglas No indeed.

A pause.

Harriet And still no news of Vivian?

Margot No; upped and left without a moment's notice. Took the family silver into the bargain. When sorrows come, they come not single spies but in battalions. *(they stand before the coffin)* Marchant left a good number of papers by his bed. Would they be of any interest to you?

Douglas They would be of much interest to me. Thank you.

Margot *(pause)* Well, my dear family. Some rise by sin and some by virtue fall.

Douglas That remains to be seen, Auntie.

Scene 11

Oscar Douglas, I'm leaving. I'm leaving the country. There was a chap called Taylor from New Caledonia who heard my Corpus lecture when he was here on research leave and he seemed to admire it. Anyway, he's just been made professor out there and has offered me a fellowship. It's perfect – I can still do the pamphlets but I can lecture and perhaps write a book. They've been very kind to me. So I sail on Friday. So I thought I'd come round to... say goodbye. And just make sure everything is... *(pause)* Yes; New Caledonia. A very beautiful part of the world by all accounts. Almond trees in blossom, toucans, cumquats. Crocodiles amid the mangroves. I understand they have a bridge there, an old wooden bridge over a remarkable green lagoon from which one can see one thousand species of plant. One thousand. Can you imagine? *(pause)* Listen, Apples. I also want to apologise. About... about the cinema. I hope you can forgive me. I didn't mean to make things difficult for you. I promise I'll not mention it again. I thought what we saw... what I saw would change everything. But I realise... it's a sign. That's all it is. It's just a sign of what we already know. And what we know is that love comes first. And I forgot that and sort of trampled all over you. And I know you're right not to trust me but that's partly why... well, look, I'll be on the other side of the world in a month's time so I doubt I could do much harm to you there. Laura's gone, Vivian's gone... you and I seem to have... it's just a chance to start again.

Douglas Did you read about the spy?

Oscar Yes, yes I did. It's in all the papers.

Douglas An inside job.

Oscar So they say, yes. Do you think you'll be able to find him?

Douglas Yes, I know who he is.

Oscar Oh, brilliant. That's brilliant. So has he been apprehended yet?

Douglas Not quite, no.

Oscar But you've told the authorities?

Douglas Oh yes.

Oscar Oh, well, well done. That is good news.

Douglas *(he nods)*

Oscar And was the spy someone you knew?

Douglas Yes. It was me.

Oscar *(pause)* What?

Douglas Yes.

Oscar *(pause)* But... hold on. Hold on... You're the spy. You're the spy. I don't understand.

Douglas It's reasonably simple.

Oscar Oh God, Douglas. And you turned yourself in?

Douglas No. I told them it was you. Because otherwise I'll hang.

They stare at each other until Douglas, collapsing somewhat, clumsily reaches out to Oscar. At this point the scales and arpeggios from next door's piano become a halting rendition of 'Dear Lord and Father of Mankind'. The two demi-embrace and Douglas buries his face in Oscar's chest, crying silently and shaking. Oscar quietly says 'There there, there there...' and kisses the top of his head fondly. The two shuffle awkwardly, unconscious that it appears they are dancing to the music which is coming through the wall. The music continues throughout the next scene but is transmuted into a choir.

Scene 12

Voice-over '...and all in all you have shown scant regard for your innate obligations as a British subject. Oscar Rensburg, you have, in the most chilling way conceivable, seen fit to turn your back on all the many opportunities that life has given you. I am grateful for the steadfast testimony of Sir Douglas Appleford of the Home Office who at no point has flinched in his patriotic duty in this deeply distasteful matter. I am relieved at least that you had the good grace not to deny the charges; perhaps the one decent act you have ever committed. However, given the severity of the crime and the persistent manner in which it was carried out over many years, I have no hesitation whatsoever in refusing your counsel's request for clemency and I sentence you to be taken from here to a place of execution where you will be hanged by the neck and I wish to note for the record that rarely have I witnessed such an impossibly perfect day as we bid farewell to McCanlis who has carried his bat for a well-placed 44 – a beautiful batsman but unfortunately for us left-handed. So once again the deeds of our national side are being discussed up and down the country and now of course Rensburg is up and he's strolling confidently, serene and totally unbowed by the prospect of the Australian bowlers. Last Test of course we saw Rensburg playing some really bright cricket showing a much welcome return to form and the conditions should prove ideal for him here today. Irvine battling splendidly all the while here this morning but I'm sure he is appreciating the arrival of new blood and Rensburg now looking every inch the player as he prepares himself… and now we have Wallis up to the crease and my goodness! Rensburg finds it and it really didn't look like a hit, more a kind of forward push and the ball pitches straight out of the ground, I repeat straight out of the ground and of course the crowd absolutely loves it and I must say I don't think I've seen anything like that from a first stroke since Frank Mann hit a ball from Robson for Middlesex versus Somerset ten or twelve years ago. And a wonderful, cheery grin from Rensburg, modest to a fault but perhaps the faintest suggestion of "Yes; there you go…"'

Throughout this the crowd noise has increased but now both crowd and commentator fade away and we become aware of nothing but the crackle and hiss of the gramophone. The men have been dancing throughout this scene until we can no longer see them.

BLACK SOAP

to Marcus Alcock

Characters
in order of appearance

Alec McConnolly (Mac)
Secretary of State for Trade and Industry

Angus Kettley
Director of Strategic Planning, DTI

Michael Mason
head of a PR company

Jonathan Baxter
Director of Communications, DTI

David Hobbs
Minister for Trade and Investment

Dennis Flattery
a lawyer

Will Simpson
Director of Communications, 10 Downing Street

The majority of the action takes place late one evening at the Department of Trade and Industry, with other scenes taking place in the previous month and in the six months that follow it.

Black Soap opened at the Landor Theatre, London on Tuesday 4 November 2003 with the following cast:

McConnolly	Patrick Bird
Kettley	Fred Perry
Mason	Simon Edwards
Baxter	Tim Scragg
Hobbs	John Lucey
Flattery	Nathan Griggs
Simpson	Breandan O'Connor

Directed by	Adrian Fear
Lighting by	Daniela Baker
Stage management	Stuart Griffith
	Marnie Chesterton
	Dave Harding

Scene 1

Mac What else?

Kettley OK.

Mac Yeah, look, I've got Cabinet tomorrow and they're going to want something more substantial than five to ten years.

Kettley Fine. Tell them five.

Mac Yeah.

Kettley This is just our opinion.

Mac OK.

Kettley I mean –

Mac Alright.

Kettley Fine.

Mac I've got literally one hour. If that. It's my youngest's end of term concert tonight, and... *(he gives an explanatory shrug)*

Kettley Of course.

Mac She's very nervous. She has a little solo bit, so...

Kettley I'm sure it will be wonderful. Now tomorrow morning is the press call for the prize so we're just going along at about ten, so please pop down for the photos if you can.

Mac Fine. No problem.

Kettley The prize is going to a girl called Rachel Langford.

Mac OK. Well I'll try to make it.

Kettley It's just an easy hit. Just a really nice little photo opportunity and it'll play very well for the Department. She's new, she's a girl, you know…

Mac Yes, I'll err… look, I'm going to give it a miss. Tomorrow is just too –

Kettley Well we could just get the photographer to do it right here. You'd only need to look up from your desk.

Mac Yeah, look, I just haven't got time, I'm sorry.

Kettley Fair enough.

Mac OK.

Kettley And err… last but not least: Michael Mason is here to see you.

Mac What?

Kettley Yes, I thought you'd like that.

Mac What does *he* want?

Kettley He says it's to do with UBC.

Mac Are you sure?

Kettley So he said. Now what does a man like Michael Mason have to do with UBC?

Mac The merger decision is due in two weeks.

Kettley Two weeks today.

Mac OK.

Kettley Yeah.

A pause.

Mac Well, I'll see him, I guess, and see what he says.

Kettley OK.

Mac Right.

Kettley OK.

Mac Good.

Kettley Best of luck, sir. For the concert.

Mac Sure. Yeah.

Scene 2

Mason Don't shoot the messenger, Mr McConnolly. *(pause)* I said, Don't shoot the messenger.

Mac Yes. No.

Mason I'm just the messenger.

Mac Yes.

Mason We don't make this stuff up.

Mac No.

Mason Links in the chain, do you see?

Mac *(Clears his throat.)*

Mason We're links in the chain.

Mac Right.

Mason I do have some advice for you, though, Secretary of State.

Mac Oh yes?

Mason Got to choose your scandal carefully.

Mac Yes.

Mason You understand?

Mac Generally speaking we don't have much choice.

Mason *(an ambiguous gesture)*

Mac I said we don't tend to have much choice.

Mason Well, that depends on your timing. You've just got to stay ahead of the curve, that's all.

Mac Hmm.

Mason Sorry?

Mac Yes. Yes.

Mason Which do you prefer, by the way; Secretary of State or Mr McConnolly?

Mac Oh, please, just call me Alec.

Mason I'll call you Secretary of State.

Mac OK.

Mason You see, I don't insist on all these formal titles, unlike yourself. Just plain Mr Mason for me, or Michael if you like. If you must. I don't insist on them because I don't believe in them, you see. But it's a free country, you know; you can put on all the fancy graces you like, just as long as you still remember to show us some respect. OK? *(pause)* The press may not be articulate, mate, but they do have the loudest voice.

Scene 3

The two phone conversations that begin this scene take place simultaneously. They also end together.

Baxter /*(on phone)* Principally because there's a lot of issues at stake here, a lot of issues involved here and so I think the strategy he's adopting is simply one of... no, no, not wait and see per se, not wait and see; it's more a case of just not doing anything until we're absolutely sure we know what we're doing ... No, *(laughs)* I don't mind you asking but you know as well as I do we're not saying anything about that until we've spoken to everyone involved and we know what the story is... OK, until we know what the *truth* is, yes *(shakes his head to Angus)*... Simply because as you know, well, the phoney war is over, let's say that *(laughs)*, and if the gloves are off we've got to be sure that we don't... Look; you know this, I know this – it's awkward, it's just really awkward, it really is, and let's keep our powder dry until... it's not a question of trust, that's the *policy*... that *is* the policy, and there's no sense in... Well, when we said that we had no idea that things would get a little more... we've been surprised by events, somewhat, surprised by events here, *(laughs)* yes, and no doubt I *will* say it again before *(his pager beeps)* Ope! Here it is now. Yeah, I'm going to have to read it and ring you back, Charlie. OK, sure, OK, sure. *(he hangs up)*

Kettley /*(on phone)* No, no; I'm not *saying* that, I'm not *saying* that. I'm just... I'm saying *if* it happens we have to know what to do if... if it actually *happens*... Right, well we just don't know, do we... You know, it doesn't make any difference to me – I can only tell you what I know and until we know any different then what else can I tell you? I mean what *can* I tell you? Do you see what I mean? Look… no, I'm not getting irritated, I'm purely telling you that I can't help you… You can do that because that's your privilege but I'll tell you now he's just going to tell you exactly what *I'm* telling you… Which is we don't know but when we do know we'll tell you… Because we will… Because we *will… (suddenly)* No no no no no, because everyone's gonna ring and I can't be taking a call from you every five… *(he makes laconic eye-contact with Baxter and rolls his eyes)* Fine, fine… Look, and by the way I know you don't believe this but we're actually on the same side, believe it or not, so we're actually on the same side, so… OK, fair enough, fair enough *(his pager beeps simultaneously with Baxter's)* Hey, this is it I'll speak to you later. *(he hangs up)*

Both take out their pagers and prepare to read.

Kettley *(sighs heavily and clears his throat)* Talk about a… *(shakes his head and tuts)*

Both are now reading the message.

My God did you get this?

Baxter *(nods)*

Kettley Oh my God oh my God – Two eighty-eight… what's that..?

Baxter Err... majority of twelve. Majority of / twelve.

Kettley / Fucking hell. *(sighs)* Two eighty-eight, two seven six with 95. Gee.

Baxter Well –

Kettley Well, it got through, well that's something.

Baxter *(laughs sadly)*

Kettley But I mean hardly, I mean *barely* and what's / the deal with –

Baxter / Ninety-... just under a hundred abstentions.

Kettley *(snorts)* Yeah, those are the guys that really get me, do you know what I mean? Some nerve. I mean it's as if they don't see it's the same thing as voting *against*; it's the same *thing* / I mean you're still –

Baxter / They may's well vote against.

Kettley Right, I mean what difference does it make? I mean it either gets through or it doesn't, so every vote away is one off –

Baxter Well, it's sort of a way of making an honourable –

Kettley Do me a favour. They just haven't got the guts, that's all, just the lot of them and don't tell me they don't know what they're doing because they do –

Baxter No; I agree. / I *do* agree.

Kettley / And this stuff is nothing to do with Hobbs.

Baxter No.

Kettley Absolutely. The vote tonight had absolutely nothing to do with Hobbs.

Baxter No.

Kettley No. But everyone thinks yeah, let's use it as a

protest vote to – *(his phone rings)* Hey, yeah, John, I'll ring you right back. *(to Baxter again)* You know; let's just wreck everything that they've been working on.

Baxter Yeah.

Kettley And it's like suddenly everything's everything to do with Hobbs. It's not, / it's *not*, –

Baxter / And it's not even us, I mean the DTI; it's *Health*.

Kettley Yeah; it's not his paper, it's not his *epartment* for Christ's sakes, it's not –

Baxter So they're basically looking / to do out –

Kettley / So the government's basically trying to reform the health service and shorten waiting lists and these guys are basically trying to get back at us, despite the fact that... So well done guys and too bad you didn't make it.

Baxter I mean they're just shooting themselves in the foot.

Kettley Right.

Baxter I don't necessarily mind them making some kind of protest, or objecting in some way –

Kettley Well –

Baxter But the system's...

Kettley It's so fucking *clumsy* –

Baxter It *is*, and so now this, which is nothing to do with the DTI –

Kettley They have to take it out on...

Baxter Yes.

Kettley But they're actually missing the bigger picture, believe it or not because –

Baxter Until we get –

Kettley They don't realise that this could still be turned around and it's happened in the past and it'll happen again but they don't realise that, they just don't *think* about it in that way, despite all we've said, despite all we've done for them and they haven't got the vision they haven't got the *backbone* to say OK yes or to at least, I mean – and they think they're thinking about their futures –

Baxter Well I think for some of them –

Kettley Their, *Their* futures. Do you see what I mean? I mean –

Baxter Well.

Kettley It's basically just a bunch of guys ripping each other off / –

Baxter / And women.

Kettley / – because they were all born yesterday, because they've all played the numbers game and they make the calculation and if / we're gonna go down –

Baxter / It's just basically a case of do they take a principled stand –

Kettley / And we're not necessarily *going* to and that's not just me saying that, that's the voice of experience here as well, by a *long* shot, and I'd respect their principled stand a lot more –

Baxter Right, but even so it doesn't take much –

Kettley Yeah, it doesn't take anything.

Baxter It hardly takes anything –

Kettley And suddenly they're scuttling away –

Baxter I agree.

Kettley Scuttling away with their tails between their legs.

Baxter And meanwhile...

Kettley Right. And we're left to run the thing –

Baxter Yes; we're left / running the show –

Kettley / Picking up the pieces I mean but the whole thing is stupid.

Baxter It is.

Kettley I mean it's pathetic. *(sighs)* I mean this is how buggered their logic is when you think about it: Here's the government – *their* government – trying to push through a *health* reform, which we know for a fact they're all in favour of in principle, but just because there happens to be rumours flying around about Hobbs – Minister for Trade, Minister for *Trade* – do you see what I mean? –

Baxter Yes.

Kettley – They think great, let's block the reforms to show they're fed up with all the Trade stuff. It's a vote on the hospitals, so let's take it out on the Minister for Trade. It's pathetic.

Baxter Right, but when you actually *look* at the Trade

stuff –

Kettley Exactly.

Baxter It just shouldn't have been that controversial.

Kettley No.

Baxter I mean when you look at it what's there to...

Kettley Well, it's the accumulation of –

Baxter Sure, yeah, but even so. I mean let's look at it. The FirstCom and UBC merger was approved on, err, on Wednesday –

Kettley And frankly there wasn't really that much wrong with that decision.

Baxter Well no, no; not compared with the reaction we got for it / certainly.

Kettley / There really wasn't that much wrong with it.

Baxter No, not in itself, no, but I think the context was...

Kettley It was just the media going on about the media. That's all they talk about. It was just because they were media companies.

Baxter OK, well, I guess, but also the whole thing about oh there they go again hopping into bed with big business and it's all –

Kettley Right, but that's just not the case.

Baxter No, of course not. I mean you could put forward a perfectly sound argument for approving that merger –

Kettley Which is what we did.

Baxter Sure; two big media companies –

Kettley Two media companies, not the biggest in the world.

Baxter Two media companies, not the biggest in the world, although certainly the biggest in… well, I agree, it just shouldn't have been that controversial a decision. I mean we've seen worse, *surely*.

Kettley I know I have.

Baxter But it just went down really badly.

Kettley Yeah, basically we didn't anticipate the reaction. I think that's where we went wrong. I mean the press hated it, industry hated it –

Baxter Yes. Yes. But in fairness we had no way of knowing it'd be so… so vitriolic.

Kettley Right. And then the whole Hobbs thing. The merger was fine compared to the Hobbs thing.

Baxter Well, it's –

Kettley *(laughs)* Yeah. Four days in and suddenly –

Baxter In swoops the Observer.

Kettley In comes the Observer, front page splash, shock horror, and it all blows up all over Hobbs.

Baxter And we just can't do enough.

Kettley We just haven't been able to get our side across, we haven't been proactive; we're not making a dent in this story, because… and the vote tonight it's just pathetic. I mean can't they see it's *really* not helping. And meanwhile we should be taking the initiative, not just huddling here dodging calls from all and sundry. I mean do they *want* the press? Do they actually *want* the press? *Do* they?

Baxter Yeah, of course.

Kettley Because we're not going to get them, we're not going to get them. And meanwhile of course where *is* Hobbs?

Baxter Well he's on his way so we'll just take him through it and see what he says, poor chap.

Kettley *(tuts and rolls his eyes)*

Baxter Right, but –

Kettley Anyone would think he was the innocent –

Baxter Well, we don't *know* that. We don't *know* that. We don't know whether he's innocent or not, we ought to be very clear on that.

Kettley Ah come on. We know.

Baxter That's just not fair and it's also not accurate / by the way.

Kettley / I'm not in.. I'm not interested in fair and accurate. I'm interested in instinct and perception. What do I instinctively think? That he *did* it. What is the perception? That he *did* it. So… I mean he effectively did do it. *Effectively*.

Baxter Yes, but that's why we have the legal process, that's why we have enquiries and –

Kettley Yeah, sure look at the legal process, go through all that but there's no time. The public needs to make up its mind *now*. Because that's what counts, and that's what they'll remember. And the legal process has got nothing to do with it. You're found guilty, you raise the stakes, you appeal, oh, you're innocent again, oh no, hang on, or is it *them* who's appealing, and you know, so where does it stop? And how long does it take? Basically if you're accused of something you did it. OK? Because people like it simple. Plus they can never remember how it ends. Were they found guilty or not guilty in the end? Be honest: it's a struggle to remember, isn't it? We just remember they were accused. That's all we remember.

Baxter That's what we have to deal with, and / that's why it's so important –

Kettley / Look, I'm not making any judgement on this, I'm not making any judgement on this, I'm just making the point that there's a lot of this already out there, and whatever is already out there is finally going to be a lot more important than what no one knows about yet, because it's *already out there*. Do you see what I mean?

Baxter *(sighs)* Well, let's just see what he says.

Kettley Sure, let's see what he says.

A pause.

Baxter Do you want a Coke?

Kettley Yeah; cheers, Baxter.

Baxter leaves momentarily, we hear two clunks of a vending machine and he returns. Sweat is rolling down the cans and we realise how thirsty the two men are.

They open their cans and drink in silence for a moment. The mood changes.

Kettley You know I'm not saying he did it. You know that, don't you.

Baxter Yes. I know. I know that.

Kettley Because, sure, we don't know. And sometimes I look at it and I agree. And sometimes I don't know what to think.

Baxter Well, we'll see what he says.

Kettley Yeah, right.

Baxter Well, we'll see.

Kettley OK, well how about the papers? What've we got?

Baxter About what we were expecting, frankly.

Kettley That good?

Baxter Yeah; No real –

Kettley OK, take me through them.

Baxter OK. *(he begins to produce faxed covers from his folder)*

Kettley Ha! Here we go. *(said with genuine relish)*

Baxter OK. Err.. FT: Time is up for Hobbs.

Kettley Fuck Gareth Davies-Cole.

Baxter Right. The Times: Minister for Trade in Free Fall.

Kettley Fuck William Redfern.

Baxter Telegraph: Too Little Too Late – McConnolly Attempts to Staunch the Flow.

Kettley Fuck Sir Andrew Lindner.

Baxter Independent: Doomed, exclamation mark.

Kettley Fuck Susan Stoporopholous that fucking illiterate Turkish deigo.

Baxter Daily Mail: Why the sleaze has got to stop.

Kettley Fuck Jonathan Eades that fucking hypocrite.

Baxter Err… The Sun: Out For The Count.

Kettley Fuck Dominic Weidenbrook.

Baxter You mean as replaced / by Jane Gooch?

Kettley / Fuck Jane Gooch and fuck Dominic Weidenbrook who's retained as World Affairs Editor.

Baxter And The Guardian: The wages of spin.

Kettley Fuck Chris Day. Do I tell *him* how to do *his* job?

Baxter Well, technically yes.

Kettley *(sighs)* OK, well, they're gonna say what they're gonna say, we knew to expect that. There's not much we can do about that now. That's just another… collateral…

Baxter *(looking at papers still, or referring back to them)* Oh, err, there may be life on Mars, by the way.

Kettley *(a 'so what' shrug)*

Baxter Other than that…

Kettley You see, we're not making a dent. Not a *dent*.

This guy's on a one-way ticket and I don't think he realises, I really don't think he does and I'm not sure you realise it either.

Baxter No; I realise it, yes.

Kettley And meanwhile do you know where McConnolly was all day?

Baxter Well; he's been at a funeral.

Kettley Right, a funeral. And don't get me wrong, I admire it, and it plays very well, and if he means it so much the better, but this is without question the biggest crisis we've ever seen and we *really* need him in London I mean we *really do*. And I'm not being cruel and obviously to those involved it's a tragedy or whatever but she was only a researcher I mean she only answered the fucking phones and it's not like he'd even *met* her and we have a *real crisis* here.

Baxter We should have just sent someone, I mean surely Jackson could have gone.

Kettley That's what I told him, I said Jackson should go but he said ah he was Secretary of State and he wanted to represent the Department and I think maybe he went to the same college as her *father* or something because they wrote to him, or he wrote to them, I don't know.

Baxter Oh, OK. I didn't know that.

Kettley I may have made that up. So he makes the great gesture – you know, noble man in the midst of his eye teeth takes time out for the human touch or whatever and none of the wankers even reported it. I mean you saw the papers.

Baxter Yes I did.

Kettley So a total waste of time. They didn't go near it. Couldn't have been less interested.

Baxter No.

Kettley So we lose a day, we don't *gain* anything and we're back where we started only it's a lot worse, it's a lot worse, just like what we said – I mean we told him, it's not like – and meanwhile it's only a matter of time before –

Baxter Yes; I agree.

Scene 4

Enter Hobbs and Flattery. This is technically the same scene; there is no break or pause.

Kettley *(sighs)* It's only a matter of time and of course we're expected to work miracles here but no can do. No can do. I mean *with what*? Hello David. Do come in.

Hobbs Angus. Hello John.

Baxter Hi David.

Kettley *(pointing to Flattery and looking questioningly)* Err..?

Hobbs Yes, this is my lawyer Dennis Flattery.

Kettley Now, David, come come, what's this? This is just meant to be a friendly, err..

Baxter An off the record chat.

Kettley A chance to clear the air.

Hobbs Yes, I appreciate that, but / I've been advised –

Flattery / My client is merely / exercising his –

Kettley / Oh *please*, just call him David for / God's sake. You're not trying to pass your Bar Finals now.

Flattery / With respect…

Baxter *(to Flattery, by way of placatory explanation)* We don't call him Minister, it's all very…

Kettley OK, well, my point is just we don't mind you being here and of course no-one's disputing your right I'm just telling you now it's just a… there's nothing contentious here, it's just a… fact-finding –

Flattery Nevertheless, if it's alright / with you –

Kettley / I've *said* it's alright with you. Umm, with me.

Flattery Good.

Hobbs Now, first off I have to tell you… I'm advised to tell you that I am under no obligation to resign and any threats or unreasonable / behaviour will be construed as –

Kettley / Woh-oh-oh; hang about, lad.

Baxter David, now no-one's –

Flattery In all fairness I think my client / should be –

Kettley *(to Flattery)* / Look, you're making things far more difficult than / they need to be.

Flattery / For you, perhaps. For / you, maybe.

Kettley / You're making things difficult for all of us, because –

Flattery Look, we can be as inf –

Kettley Excuse me.

Flattery No; –

Kettley Yes; –

Flattery Look, –

Kettley No; –

Hobbs Listen.

Kettley Err –

Hobbs Listen. *(pause)* OK? Now. None of this is any reflection on anything, but we've all got our interests and we need to protect ourselves and safeguard... because it doesn't need me to tell you this is an extremely awkward and subtle situation / here –

Kettley / Well I'm not sure –

Baxter OK, yes, we understand. And of course, –

Hobbs And I'm certainly not going to apologise for having my lawyer with me because as far as I'm concerned that's just basic common sense –

Baxter I agree.

Hobbs And any of you would do the same if you were in the same...

Flattery So look, everything here is on / the record –

Baxter / We're all above board, here, Mr Flattery, please... just try to understand that we're kind of all in this together and it's a question of what can we do to help, because of course none of this reflects well on any of us, so...

Hobbs Yes, I understand.

Flattery OK.

Kettley Right.

Baxter Yeah.

Kettley OK, well, David, let's err let's start with the basics; as you know your brokers, BN&D, bought two million pounds worth of shares in FirstCom the day before FirstCom's merger with UBC was announced, the merger having been approved by us here at the DTI. Now BN&D runs your blind trust for you, so obviously you can't contact them in any way anyway, but as you know a story ran in the Observer on Sunday which included a claim that someone had alleged that you *did* contact them and you used your insider knowledge about the merger and you instructed them to buy the shares on your behalf, knowing that they'd shoot up in value the next day. OK? Now, what's your err... wha-what do you say to that?

Scene 5

Flashback. Hobbs and Flattery now alone before the meeting.

Hobbs Finally Dennis we have to face up to the fact that at this meeting they could do anything up to and including demanding my resignation.

Flattery They can demand it David but they're not going to get it.

Hobbs And we know this because..?

Flattery You didn't authorise the buying of the shares, so therefore they can't prove you did authorise the buying of the shares, so therefore they can't fire you.

Hobbs Them firing me is not the same thing as them demanding my resignation. And it's not just that. I mean we could be talking about *prison*.

Flattery David, you're not going to prison. You are *not* going to prison. You're... almost certainly not gonna go to prison. I personally / guarantee that.

Hobbs / That's tremendous.

Flattery So just don't resign. How difficult can that be?

Hobbs You don't know Angus Kettley, you don't know the culture there. I mean they really run the Department, they really do, effectively.

Flattery I'm sorry, but I can't believe a Minster of State can be ordered around by anyone / other than – other than McConnolly.

Hobbs / No, I'm not saying they *order* anyone around.

Flattery I mean, you have a structure.

Hobbs Yes of course, but it's a bit more subtle than that. I mean they're so… you know; they've got McConnolly's ear, they really… they're kind of enforcers, basically.

Flattery Well none of that should make any difference.

You didn't break the law, and therefore they can't sack you.

Hobbs But my worry is that they *want* to, and they have a funny way of... they just exert a very odd sort of pressure.

Flattery Listen, David, just don't worry about it. That's why I'm here; you've got your lawyer – sure, they won't like that but that's life. I can keep a proper record of what's said, I can just basically ensure that your rights are protected.

Hobbs Yeah. Well, we'll see what happens. You're a good man, Dennis.

Flattery Thanks.

Hobbs OK.

Flattery Look, well, we have the statement.

Hobbs Yes.

Flattery Do you still want to use it?

Hobbs I guess so. I mean we don't have a lot of choice.

Flattery I think we should use it.

Hobbs OK, well let's use it. But we'll see what Kettley and Baxter say.

Flattery They can say what they like, David. It makes no odds.

Hobbs OK, well, we'll see.

Scene 6

We now return to the meeting of scenes 3 and 4.

Kettley What's your err.. wha– what do you say to that?

Hobbs It's not true.

Kettley It's not true.

Hobbs That's right.

Flattery No advice was given from the Minister to his broker, no shares were bought at his behest, no –

Baxter So how do you explain the story? How do you explain the source?

Hobbs I really couldn't... it's not for me to...

Baxter But it's a little unfortunate, don't you think?

Hobbs Well, it's bloody unfortunate, yes. That's why we're here.

Baxter Yes, but David, those rumours must have come from somewhere.

Hobbs Well?

Baxter So?

Hobbs So what?

Kettley Look, David, this is all really unpleasant and no-one's saying otherwise but you have to look at it from our perspective.

Hobbs Frankly no. I'm really not interested in your perspective; I'm interested in the fact that there are untrue allegations being flung around about this

Department which is also your Department by the way, / and you're paid to sort –

Kettley / No, no, no; the allegations aren't about the Department, David, they're about you.

Hobbs Look; you're paid to deal with this kind of thing, I'm paid to encourage free trade, to –

Kettley Oh come on.

Hobbs No; –

Kettley Oh come on.

Hobbs Well, look –

Kettley No, you look; if that is my job then you're not making it any easier.

Hobbs So?

Kettley Well, OK if it is my job –

Hobbs It is.

Kettley Yes, I'm saying if it *is* my job –

Hobbs It *is* your job.

Kettley OK, it's my job and I'm paid to sort it out any way I see fit, whatever's for the good of the / Department...

Flattery / Is that a threat, Mr Kettley?

Kettley *(peeved)* It's not a *threat*, for goodness' sake; it's just a... reflection of the way things are. That's all it is.

Flattery Well you're quite mistaken, Mr Kettley. You serve at the behest of the Department, which is to say –

Kettley Look; I know my business, alright? Don't tell me / what it is I am or I'm not –

Flattery / Which is to say whatever McConnolly tells you to do, OK?

Kettley OK, yes; fine, but look, I know my mandate, alright? and I'm here to tell you it's pretty fucking broad.

Baxter Look, the point being obviously things are in a bit of a crisis, and we need to know exactly what happened –

Flattery If anything.

Baxter OK, if anything.

Hobbs Yeah.

Baxter And plus what it is you're going to say.

Flattery If anything.

Baxter Well, actually no; something has to be said, something does have to be said, and I'd go so far as to say something has to be said before tomorrow ie. tonight.

Kettley Because this is as far as it can go, realistically, and so...

Hobbs *(sighs loudly)*

Kettley Yes, it's no good... look, you're in this mess, it's got nothing to do with me; this isn't personal, David, surely you can see that and that we're on the same side and we're all trying to... look.

Hobbs So what do you propose we do.

Kettley I have to be honest here and say if you bought the shares then please for God's sake tell us now.

Hobbs Look, I've *told* you.

Kettley Because we need to... OK, look, the point is we want to help you but we can't if you don't tell us what the / story is.

Hobbs / I've told – I've told you what the story is. I've told you what the story is. I didn't authorise the purchase of any shares in anything, not in FirstCom, not in UBC, not in anything.

Flattery I think we've been quite clear on this.

Baxter But how do you explain the leak?

Flattery It's not a leak, it's a groundless allegation.

Baxter So how do you explain the groundless allegation?

Flattery It's not for us to explain groundless allegations.

Baxter I'm not saying it is, I'm not saying it is, I'm just saying look, the rumour is out there… and err, we need to know why.

Hobbs So why come to me? I really couldn't tell you where the story came from or why it was made, / or –

Kettley / We just want to be sure that you're being straight with us.

Flattery Right; I'm going to put a stop to this. This is going nowhere. We've been perfectly clear on this – no shares were requested, no tip-off was given –

Kettley But the fact remains mate that David's broker bought the shares. How do you explain that?

Flattery Were shares bought? Yes. But that's just a coincidence. These people buy / shares every day.

Kettley / I'm not paid to simply accept coincidences, Mr Flattery.

Flattery They happen, Mr Kettley, they do happen, believe it or not, like it or not.

Baxter But can you not see how weak an argument that is, sir? I mean just look at it. You're telling me by *sheer* coincidence… I mean I'm not saying it's *not* a coincidence, I'm just saying look at how it looks. I mean look at how it *looks*. Because the word on the street was that the merger would *not* go through.

Kettley So it doesn't look good, does it. I mean your broker bets the other way, / you know.

Flattery / How it looks is neither here nor there. We've told you the truth.

Kettley But it just *doesn't look good*, does it. By sheer coincidence he bets the other way.

Flattery Have you any idea how many shares were bought and sold on that day in that company?

Kettley No, cos I'm not interested in that.

Flattery Well, perhaps you should be, because circum/stantially –

Kettley / I don't care if everyone in the country put their shirt on it, alright?, the point is no-one knew the merger would go through. No-one except the committee, and you're the only guy in the committee who bought shares.

Flattery Err?! He did *not* buy shares; the firm did.

Kettley *(genuinely)* OK, I'm sorry, I'm sorry. His brokers. The firm at large, then, whatever.

Flattery Did the Minister know the merger would go through? Yes. Did he instruct his broker to that effect? No. Is he therefore guilty? No.

Kettley I'm sorry, you just haven't come up with a believable explanation.

Flattery Not our job.

Kettley Don't be daft.

Hobbs I'm telling you it's just a coincidence.

Kettley A coincidence.

Flattery It's just a coincidence.

Kettley And are you going to make a statement to that effect?

Flattery We have a statement, yes.

Kettley But are you going to use it.

Flattery Well, that's a matter for us.

Kettley Not while he's in his job it's not (no offence, David).

Hobbs / None taken.

Flattery / Look, this is a simple matter between David and m / – if he's –

Kettley / We have to approve that statement; we have

to see it, we have to approve it, we have to –

Flattery Surely the only person who David might have to run it past as a courtesy is McConnolly.

Kettley As far as you're concerned, mate, I *am* Mac. / That's the mandate.

Flattery / Well, we'll see what he says about that.

Kettley Sure, go ahead. Go to his office and see how interested he is.

Baxter The point being this. What are you going to say?

Kettley And when are you going to say it?

A pause.

Baxter Would it be possible to hear the statement now, perhaps?

Flattery looks at Hobbs, Hobbs gives him the nod.

Flattery This is just a draft.

Kettley & Baxter Sure.

Flattery 'Despite their totally defamatory nature, allegations continue to be made concerning the Minister for Trade and Investment. The Minister wishes to make clear that at no time has he acted improperly and specifically he wishes to refute the allegation that he authorised the purchase of shares using privileged information. It must be noted that no formal investigation appears to be forthcoming at this time, which further underlines the spurious nature of the rumours. The Minister is fully confident that this statement will lay the matter to rest, but if it does not he wishes to assure the authorities that he will co-operate in any way necessary in order to clear his name and that of the Department for Trade and Industry. Furthermore any party continuing to report these defamatory allegations will be subject to the full measure of civil law for attempting to smear an innocent man's reputation.'

A pause.

Kettley OK. So you're saying –

Hobbs Yes.

Kettley You're saying you didn't authorise the purchase of shares –

Hobbs That's correct.

Kettley In either of the companies involved in the merger.

Hobbs Or of any other company.

Kettley Or of any other company.

Hobbs No.

Flattery That's what we're saying.

Kettley OK.

Hobbs At no time have I discussed shares with my broker, –

Kettley OK.

Hobbs – and at no time have I divulged privileged information to anyone outside the circulation list.

Kettley OK.

Hobbs That's right.

Kettley So did you or did you not authorise the purchase of shares?

Hobbs No I did not.

Kettley Did you *suggest*..?

Hobbs No I did not.

Kettley Did you in any way disseminate the informa/tion that –

Hobbs / No. No I did not.

Kettley To anyone? Anyone at all?

Hobbs No I did not.

Kettley Did you tell your wife?

Hobbs No I did not.

Kettley And did you –

Flattery Angus, I think David has been reasonably clear on this.

Kettley Sure, I'm just trying to get it clear in my own mind.

Flattery We've been *over* this.

Kettley Yes, –

Flattery You've heard the statement.

Kettley No, I know –

Flattery And frankly –

Kettley Yes, look, this is just a taste of... I just want to make sure we're all clear and all our stories add up. OK?

Flattery gestures questioningly to Hobbs. Hobbs shrugs and agrees.

Kettley So you didn't tell your broker to buy the shares?

Hobbs No.

Kettley And you never mentioned to anyone that the merger was going to be approved?

Hobbs That's right.

Kettley And you never said anything to anyone.

Hobbs That's right.

Kettley OK.

A pause.

Baxter And you had no contact with the broker of any kind?

Hobbs *(a very subtle start and confusion)* Umm? *(he looks questioningly at Flattery)*

Scene 7

Flashback. Hobbs and Flattery are now alone once more, as if before the meeting.

Hobbs And what do we do if they ask if I spoke to the broker in any way?

Flattery My advice is we should deny it.

Hobbs Sure?

Flattery Well, they don't need to know that do they? There's no advantage in telling them that. None at all.

Hobbs No, of course, but do you not think that if we levelled with Kettley and –

Flattery You'd be mad to trust those guys; *mad*. Stuff'em. Why help *them* out?

Hobbs Don't you think we might be helping ourselves out?

Flattery Look, by the sounds of it all those guys want is for you to produce enough rope to hang yourself with. Don't give in to them.

Hobbs Right, but if it comes out later –

Flattery What's going to come out? That you spoke to another human being on a totally innocuous –

Hobbs Dennis, we both know it's not as straightforward as that.

Flattery But we can *make* it as straightforward as that. Should you wish it.

Hobbs But we can't. We *can't*. It's going to be tough to beat these guys. And you have to admit it just isn't going to look that good.

Flattery Because...

Hobbs Because of the favours thing, because of the protocol, because of the rules, basically.

Flattery Right, right, but you've got to put it in context. I mean, you're accused of insider trading. How bad can going to see –

Hobbs Yeah, but it's the fact that contact was made at all. It just doesn't look good, it confuses the whole... I mean who knows what the public is going to make of it.

Flattery Well, if that's who it is you're trying to convince.

Hobbs Well, who else is there? You don't think Mac or Number 10 really give a damn about what I might or might not have done do you? I mean personally. They only care because the public might care.

Flattery And the public only care because the press care.

Hobbs Right.

Flattery Yes.

Hobbs So there it is.

Flattery Hmm. But still in the eyes of the law...

Hobbs Dennis, I really think we should come clean.

Flattery Well, you're the boss. I mean it could work, I just worry that...

Hobbs Could they sack me simply for speaking to the broker?

Flattery No, not in a million years.

Hobbs Are you sure?

Flattery Absolutely not. There's no breaches there, I mean even conduct... but as long as it was just a social conversation... it's conceivably misconduct but it's not gross misconduct so therefore they can't summarily dismiss you. And it's possibly a human rights thing as well. At the end of the day you can't sack someone for saying hello to someone.

Hobbs Well, it's a call, it's a call.

Flattery It's *not* a call. As far as I can work out these guys Kettley and, umm –

Hobbs Baxter.

Flattery These guys have weaselled their way to the top of the tree and are probably loving it up there, but no-one is above the law, and they can't unilaterally make those kinds of decisions.

Hobbs They're just powerful men, that's all I'm saying. They're just –

Flattery Fine, fine. But they cannot sack you, and if I sense the meeting is going nowhere then we'll just leave –

Hobbs Dennis, I'm not sure –

Flattery We will walk out and then they'll just have to do it in writing if they're… look, let's not waste our time being subjected to the party line brainwash. We'll say what we've got to say, we'll keep a proper record, and if they don't budge then we leave. *(pause)* Do you not think?

Hobbs OK. Well, I guess you're right.

Flattery So what's your instinct?

Hobbs I guess I cling to the idea that there's something to be said for telling the truth. Let's tell them about the call.

Flattery OK.

Hobbs If they ask us.

Flattery Sure.

Hobbs If they actually ask us.

Flattery Yes.

Hobbs Which they will, by the way.

Flattery Well...

Hobbs OK.

Flattery Well, I'll help the best I can.

Hobbs Thanks.

Scene 8

We now return to the meeting of scene 6.

Baxter And you had no contact with the broker of any kind?

Hobbs *(a very subtle start and confusion)* Umm? *(he looks questioningly at Flattery)* Yes; yes I did.

Baxter / Woh!

Kettley / Oh-oh-oh!

Hobbs Now just hear me out.

Kettley I don't fucking believe it. / What the... what the fuck were you thinking of? What the fuck were you thinking about?

Hobbs / Just hear me out.

Hobbs {/ Just hear me out.

Flattery {/ Will you let us / explain?

Kettley / Mac's been sticking up for you, he's stuck his neck out, against my advice, I might add –

Hobbs I'm sure.

Kettley Whatever, mate, what the hell happened?

Flattery If you'll just calm down we'll answer / all your questions.

Kettley / I think you're going to answer my questions whether / I'm calm or not.

Flattery / Just take it easy, OK? Just take it easy. OK? OK? Look. There was some contact with the broker, of a purely social nature.

Baxter When?

Hobbs Round about the time of the merger announcement.

Kettley So is the leak accurate?

Hobbs No, the leak is not accurate because I did not issue any instructions nor did I offer any advice.

Baxter But it's accurate in terms of a call being made from your office to the brokers at or around the time they suggest?

Hobbs That may be correct, yes.

Kettley *May* be correct?

Hobbs Yes. It may well be.

Both Kettley and Baxter sigh.

Kettley But you didn't talk about the merger.

Hobbs We did not talk about the merger.

Kettley So what the hell *did* you talk about if you don't mind me asking. How to fold a napkin?

Hobbs *(pause)* Err... we talked about Wimbledon.

Kettley Sorry?

Hobbs We talked about Wimbledon.

Kettley Wimbledon.

Hobbs Yes.

Baxter As in the tennis tournament.

A very subtle look from Kettley to Baxter.

Hobbs Yes.

Kettley What the hell were you thinking of?

Hobbs What happened was this. I know Jeff Bude reasonably well, which is to say we exchange Christmas cards and that's about it, but we were a doubles team at college together / –

Kettley / Brilliant. That's brilliant.

Hobbs / – and I received a couple of comps for a game in the second week and so I thought I'd ring him up and ask if he wanted to come along.

Baxter So, despite the... the embargo –

Kettley Despite common sense –

Baxter – you thought you'd –

Hobbs Yes.

Baxter Even though it might look like –

Hobbs I just didn't think anything of it. I just didn't consider –

Kettley OK, OK, OK. We've just got to think. We've got to think, now.

Hobbs OK.

Baxter Did Mr Bude actually go with you to Wimbledon.

Hobbs Err, no. Neither of us went in the end.

Kettley *Neither* of you went?

Hobbs Jeff couldn't make it, and I was just too busy in the end.

Kettley But if you had gone don't you think it would have handily shown that that's what you were actually talking about.

Hobbs Well, if you want to look at it that way.

Kettley It's not how *we* want to look at it.

Baxter And did you make the call before or after the merger was announced?

Flattery What difference does it make?

Baxter Well, if the call was made *after* the merger was announced then it doesn't matter what the call was about, Wimbledon or the price of fish or whatever because there would've been no privileged information to pass on, so we'd've already won more than half the battle.

Kettley Sure, I mean you shouldn't've made the call anyway but you'd've been in the clear re. the shares.

Hobbs Uh-huh.

Kettley So did you speak to Bude before or after the merger was announced?

Hobbs Yes, I've tried to think about that and I really don't remember.

Kettley You don't remember.

Hobbs Well, I know it was either the Tuesday or the Wednesday. But... you know, I just didn't connect the two events, so I can't be sure which came first or... I didn't think of them as related, so...

Baxter Now the merger was announced on the Wednesday.

Hobbs Yes.

Baxter The Wednesday morning.

Hobbs Yes.

Kettley But the committee sat on the Tuesday.

Hobbs That's right.

Baxter Now the key is there's a very specific window of opportunity for someone to potentially insider deal here. Before the committee sat there would have been no information, and after it was announced it's obviously not privileged any more. So the thing of it is is was the call made between the Tuesday meeting and the Wednesday announcement.

Hobbs Right.

Kettley Now Minister. Please. Just think very carefully. Did you ring your broker before or after the committee sat during which the merger was approved?

A two or three second pause.

Hobbs I don't remember.

Kettley Before or after?

Hobbs I don't know.

Kettley You don't know, or you don't remember?

Hobbs I don't remember.

Kettley Which is it?

Hobbs I don't know. I don't remember.

Flattery *(to Kettley)* What's the difference?

Kettley *(to Flattery, aggressively)* Err? *(to Hobbs)* OK, David, now just think.

Hobbs Yes, I have. I have thought.

Kettley Just think.

Hobbs Right.

Kettley Now I'll ask you again.

Hobbs / Yes, but I'll just –

Flattery / Excuse me –

Kettley *(to Hobbs)* Just… just / try.

Flattery *(to Kettley)* / Excuse me.

Kettley Minister.

Flattery *(to Kettley)* Excuse me.

Kettley *(to Flattery)* Err –

Flattery *(to Kettley)* Excuse –

Kettley *(to Flattery)* Excuse *me*.

Flattery *No*; I'm going to ask you to stop belittling my client and generally –

Kettley Sure. Ask away.

Flattery Look.

Kettley No; *you* look.

Baxter We're trying to work through this.

Kettley Yes, we're just trying to work through this, no-one's trying to catch anyone out or be aggressive or belittling or whatever. Because we have to know; we have to be sure.

Hobbs Yes, I understand, but if you're just trying to –

Kettley David, look, bottom line is you shouldn't've made the call at all.

Hobbs *(sarcastic)* Gee, do you think so?

Flattery I'm sorry, but it's just not a crime to say 'Hello, do you want to go to Wimbledon? No? OK, bye.'

Kettley Come on, mate, it's not about what's right and wrong, it's about what we can prove and what it looks like.

Baxter And it doesn't look good.

Kettley It really doesn't look good. And we can't prove it.

Baxter And we can't prove it.

Flattery But finally it's actually not that serious.

Kettley That's not for you to say.

Baxter Because finally we don't know what people are going to believe, do we? We don't know what the perception will be.

Hobbs Well, that's not my fault.

Kettley Maybe not, but it's certainly your problem. And at the moment it's our problem too.

Hobbs What do you mean 'at the moment'?

Flattery *(to Kettley)* Now listen. You're going to have to be very careful now, Kettley.

Kettley Beg your pardon?

Flattery You're straying dangerously close to giving us grounds for constructive dismissal here.

Kettley Right?

Flattery Do you know what that is?

Kettley Yes?

Flattery Are you sure?

Kettley Yes thanks, hot-shot. It's when you say 'Fuck off' to someone who works for you, and they take this to mean fuck off permanently and so they leave and then if you haven't got sufficient grounds to have fired them then you're buggered.

Flattery If Mr Hobbs' life is made difficult by his employer then he can resign, and his resignation will actually be, in the eyes of the law, a dismissal. And if you haven't followed the procedure and if the dismissal is unfair or without grounds then he can sue you for it.

Kettley That's fine, that's fine; sure, I have no objection to that –

Flattery Doesn't matter if you've got an objection or not; I'm telling you, that's the law.

Kettley Well I'm not worried about the law.

Flattery Well you will be if –

Kettley Look, this is not about the law.

Flattery Everything's about the law. Everything's about the law.

Kettley Look; don't you *get* it? Don't you *get* it? If it comes to all that you're going to be doomed anyway. Independent's words, not mine, by the way. You think you can still work up here after you've turned up to court every day and had it all out? There's not a single person who's gonna go near you again. You've got to be practical, David, OK? As soon as you go near a lawsuit or a courtroom you're never gonna make it through the door again. *(to Flattery)* I mean do you not see that?

Flattery Well I don't think *you'll* be going through the door again if you're found guilty of… well, first off it's not your place to –

Kettley Go ahead and sue me mate / if that's what you –

Flattery / You are being highly irrespons/ible and –

Baxter / OK.

Kettley Sue me; go on. Just grow a fucking backbone and / sue me. See how far you get.

Flattery / Right, for the record I'm going to / ask you to –

Baxter / OK, OK. Let's all just calm down.

Flattery I'm perfectly calm, I'm simply telling you that bottom line if Mr Hobbs has done nothing wrong then you can't get rid of him. That's the law.

Kettley And I'm simply saying that you're woefully out of date. Where have you been? This isn't a normal set-up. This isn't a place of work, we're not an employer. This is the *government*. We're not here to obey the rules, we're here to *make* the rules. The *law* has got no place whatsoever in this. Can you not see that? We have one imperative – we have to govern, we have to provide leadership, we have to manage, we have to *control*, OK? If we're in control we're all doing our job. And this situation is preventing us from being in control. Now I'm not interested in hearing anything from you other than practical and constructive suggestions about what you're prepared to do to salvage something from this mess, alright?

Scene 9

Flashback. Mac and Mason.

Mason Mr McConnolly, the public will forgive most things eventually but there's some things they'll never forgive. They don't mind you being crooked – after all, there's no-one more loveable than a loveable rogue…

You see, essentially the British readership is intelligent, but it's weak. And that's the paradox. I mean they have a highly developed conscience but they give in too easily to temptation. So we really want to read something sleazy, I mean this is not just the tabloids I'm talking about here, your middle class Home Counties gobble up those sex crimes on page three of the Telegraph like they're breaking meringues, but then they're intelligent enough to be disgusted in themselves for stooping so low and they suddenly feel guilty and they want to punish the source of their dirty little pleasure. Now are you going to hate the busty young blonde with her bright blue eyes and stay-wet lips who's too young and stupid to know any better or are you going to hate the unattractive late-middle-aged authority figure who's been mashing her up in his lunch hour. And of course the readers know they themselves would have done the same thing but they haven't been so lucky because although they too are unattractive and middle-aged they are not authority figures, so envy comes into it as well and all these elements combine to power up your witch hunt.

So everyone wants you to do it, the public love it because it means they can keep alive the dream that unattractive middle-aged men can fuck teenage girls, without which it's a little difficult getting up in the mornings beyond forty, and the press love it because the papers, well, the papers just sell themselves. But if you *do* do it – fucked for life.

So that's why I say you have to pick your scandal carefully, and let's face it; everyone has one – and this is good advice; make it financial and make it complicated enough for the public not to understand but simple enough for it to fizzle out in a few days and not leave too much of a stain on your reputation. Make it convoluted enough to make the public scratch its head, try to follow, get confused, and move onto other pages looking for the sex crimes. That's your best hope.

Scene 10

We return to the meeting of scene 8 etc. Enter Simpson.

Kettley Fuck me things must be serious.

People get to their feet if they're seated.

Hobbs Will, this is Dennis Flattery. Dennis, you know Will Simpson, um, Director of Communications over at Number 10.

Flattery Well, I watch tv.

Simpson Ha. Don't believe everything you see.

Flattery So I hear.

Baxter Hi, Will.

Simpson *(Nods to Baxter. Then, to Flattery:)* Sorry, are you David's lawyer?

Flattery Yuh.

Simpson OK. *(beat)* Alright, what's the progress? Angus?

Kettley Well, err, David is, err, David claims that he didn't instruct his broker, but he says he did make a call round about the, err, the time of the merger announcement, he rang him of a purely social nature but we don't know whether this took place before or after the merger was approved. But it was around about that time.

Simpson Is that a fair summary, David?

Hobbs Yes it is, yes.

Simpson You rang him or he / rang you?

Hobbs / I rang him. I rang him.

Simpson OK, OK. Give me one second. *(he thinks in silence for some time)* OK. The problem is this. The problem is that a story has attached itself to the government, OK? This is affecting our ability to govern. This is destroying our credibility. Look at the vote tonight. It's adding up. It's taking its toll. Let's stop the rot. Alright. What've we got? The story's out there. The press has bought it. It's everywhere. We're catching the flak. OK. Is there going to be an enquiry? Is there going to be a criminal investigation? Difficult to say and doesn't matter. If David's found guilty that's that. If not, well, same difference in a way because it will've been dragged through the press every day anyway and we're along for the ride, so just as much damage. OK? So we have to stop it now. *(Simpson looks up and Kettley gestures in agreement)* How do we stop it? Well, we either prove David's innocent, or we prove he's guilty, or we sack him anyway. Now we can't prove you're guilty, and thanks to this pissing around with the broker we're buggered on the innocent front too. So I have to tell you it's looking good for the sack, David.

Hobbs I'm sorry Will, but I'm not going to take this from anyone / other than –

Simpson / I'm specifically charged with ensuring you're on-side.

Hobbs Well...

Simpson OK?

Hobbs I'm sorry but I've made my position clear and... that's all I can do.

Simpson David, I'm telling you now this is not my way or the highway. It's my way or your way but I'm gonna tell you why it's gonna be my way.

Hobbs And why is that?

Simpson You gotta think about the future.

Hobbs Well, I am thinking about my / future. I am thinking about my future.

Simpson / Oh, come on now, David. Hear me out, OK? We all knew you were out the minute we read The Observer, right? Even you, David, surely. Even you *(to Flattery)*, no matter what you're gonna say now. That's just signed and sealed. We've seen it before; that's the way it goes. But here's a thing. We've got to shovel you out a.s.a.f.p., David, and you know it's not personal, it's not, it's just we can't give the scandal time to fester. That's the prerequisite. This is the PM talking now. Otherwise you're gonna turn the whole wash blue. That's why tonight's the night. But here's the plan; you're gonna take a hit now, you're gonna go to ground, sure, you'll languish in the background, five years, what do you know; they'll need a brain like yours in Opposition and before you know it you'll be back and bulletproof next but one. And that's a guarantee. I'm telling you now. But you can't funk this; you've got to do it our way cos if you don't and you try to hang on and let's be honest here you know we can't fire you yet but don't stick around, buddy, because I can tell you in ten years time the public will've forgiven everything but mess us about and we'll never forget. Not in a lifetime. You think you can't give up the drivers and the dinners? Well, think again, because if you don't give them up now you will not come back, David. You will not come back. *(his words sink in)* Now I understand you've got a statement. Forget it. You're not going to use it. You're gonna use our statement. Here it is.

He gives it to Kettley, who reads it out.

Kettley 'After much unwelcome and unjustified speculation in the media and in the House I have decided to step down as Minister for Trade forthwith. This in no way reflects on the veracity of these rumours, nor is it any sign of concord with those who have been calling for me to leave. The fact is that the media has descended to a new low of speculation and innuendo here, and I feel that these rumours are damaging not only the party that I love and have served faithfully for over a decade, but also they are systematically and quite deliberately eroding the quality of national debate. The issues that are most important to me, the issues which made me want to be Minister of State, are now seldom spoken of, it seems, and even more seldom reported. And this leaves us all impoverished, finally. Therefore, out of a sense of loyalty and responsibility, I have decided after much thought, and with the full support of the Secretary of State and the Prime Minister, to surrender my post here in the hope that my leaving will stop the vicious rumours and irresponsible journalism that have become so rife lately to the detriment of public life and the effectiveness with which we communicate and govern.'

Simpson Now you can't knock that. Hey? It's beautiful. Beautiful. Noble, calm, serene, dignified, and believe me, as soon as you go they'll love you. They want to kill you, but as soon as you're dead they'll want to canonise you. You'll be a hero tomorrow morning. That's the Great British way.

Hobbs Albeit a hero without a job.

Simpson Come on, David; go home and speak to your wife and kids. See what they think.

Hobbs Will, at least give me the weekend to think about it.

Simpson Cannot be done, David, cannot be done.

Flattery *(he goes as if to leave)* Well I have to tell you that we cannot agree to this. If there's going to be an official reshuffle then that's fine, and people come and go, sure, that's the Prime Minister's privilege, but we know that's not what we have here, and if there's any indication he's being forced out for something he didn't do… Now we've presented our case to you, you've shown less than no interest in what we've got to say, you've given us effectively a fait accompli here but we are not going to go for it, so go ahead and take your chances. It's a totally inappropriate statement and the whole thing amounts to coercion. Good evening, gentlemen.

Scene 11

Flashforward. Hobbs and Flattery.

Flattery But you have to hand it to Kettley, he's hit the nail on the head.

Hobbs How so?

Flattery It is a good question: how *do* you explain the rumours?

Hobbs Do you think I haven't thought about this?

Flattery And?

Hobbs Well, –

Flattery Does the story really from the brokers do you think?

Hobbs Well –

Flattery Really?

Hobbs I do have a theory.

Flattery Go on?

Hobbs *(to audience)* There's nothing unusual about an interview with MI5 once you become a Minister, I believe, but I was still surprised when they turned up one morning unannounced. A week or so after I was appointed, I think. Two guys from 5. We went into the inner office and I shut the door. They were very polite, very professional, but it was what you'd expect, which is to say it wasn't actually very enjoyable. In fact it was pretty grim. *(to invisible interlocuters, answering questions)* Umm... no. *(pause)* Yes, I'm sure. *(pause)*

Oh, sure; yes, but nothing more than the normal left-wing interests at college. *(pause)* Possibly at sixth form, too. *(pause)* No, although I know I gave out a few leaflets. Once or twice. *(pause)* Twice. Pretty harmless stuff. *(pause)* No, actually *I'll* be the judge of that and I'm telling you they were pretty harmless. *(he takes a list and looks through it)* Err... OK, I went to the Soviet Union once, and I've been to Israel and I've been to Saudi and... yes, that's it. *(Pause. Sigh.)* Look – OK, yes, I may have been around the odd one or two at college. *(pause)* I don't know; possibly once or twice, yes. *(pause)* No, nothing stronger. *(pause)* I knew a guy at college who sold various things but... well, he was a friend but... no, I never took anything... no, I never took any money from him either... Because I know I didn't... OK, well, yes of course he may have bought me the odd drink. *(pause)* Yes, I understand, I understand... No, I do. *(pause)* Of course. Well, a girl called Ruth Parks when I was about sixteen to eighteen, then single for a while... oh, maybe, from time to time... Look, this is... OK, Sarah someone, from Corpus Christi, I really don't remember her surname, Emma, err, Emma, Emma Jessop, from Trinity and a girl, I really don't know her name, she wasn't a student, she lived in the town. *(pause)* Yes. *(pause)* No, not since... not for many years. *(pause)* And then a girl called Susie Wright for about a year. *(pause)* She's an accountant. *(pause)* Occasionally, yes; parties or whatever. We're quite friendly. And then Rebecca, and that's it. *(pause)* Yes, I'm sure. Of course I'm sure. *(Pause. Sigh.)* Once when we were about sixteen a group of us were pushing over some traffic bollards or whatever and the police took all our names but nothing really happened. *(pause)* When I was elected President of the Union Society some people claimed that the election had been rigged. *(pause)* Because... I don't know, a lot of reasons; the whole thing was quite unpopular. *(pause)* No, not that I'd personally done it, just that I was the candidate of choice of the people who they thought might have done it. *(pause)* I forget. There may have been something in one of the student papers, I'm really not sure. *(pause)* That's it. *(pause)* That's it. *(Pause. Smiles.)* I'm sure you can. I'm sure you will.

Scene 12

A return to the meeting of scene 10.

Flattery It's a totally inappropriate statement and the whole thing amounts to coercion. Good evening, gentlemen.

Simpson What's your take, David?

Hobbs *(Pause. He looks to Flattery.)* Dennis, let's hold our horses here.

Flattery Sir, with respect –

Hobbs Yes, yes; look, I just want to... *(to Simpson)* I understand what you're saying and what you're trying to do, and I just feel that... *(Kettley flashes a supercilious look at Flattery here, perhaps)* Well, look, ultimately of course I'll follow Flattery's lead on this. Otherwise what's the point of him in a way.

Simpson Come on, David; you can do better than that.

Hobbs I just think you're trying to force our hand and play to our insecurities. I really do.

Flashforward.

(to audience) But it was only much later that it occurred to me I'd given 5 a full briefing without them having to spend a single penny on research; I just gave them the complete folder in five minutes. Volunteered the whole lot. I mean, was I *obliged* to answer those questions? Why didn't I think to ask anyone?

Back to the meeting.

Hobbs I just think you're trying to force our hand and play to our insecurities. I really do.

Simpson That's just not true, David.

Hobbs And why should I believe you? We all know that once I'm out I may not come back at all.

Simpson Well let's be sensible about this. I'm not guaranteeing this, I'm saying let's look at what normally happens, let's look for the patterns. What's believable. What's likely. What do we *think*.

Hobbs So...

Simpson I just think this is the best... I think it's your best shot, I think it's our best shot.

Hobbs *(he looks to Flattery and then back at Simpson)* Well, I'm sorry but we're just not gonna go for it.

Simpson Well, if that's the way you want it. But I have to tell you, if you use your statement we're going to use this.

Hobbs What's 'this'?

Flashforward.

(to audience) And *then* it occurred to me: how do I even know they were from MI5?

Back to the meeting.

Simpson hands him an A4 manila envelope. Hobbs opens it and studies the single sheet of paper in silence. The colour drains from his face.

Flashforward.

Hobbs *(to audience)* And at that moment I realised how little I knew about how it all fits together.

Back to the meeting.

Simpson So whadayasay?

Hobbs Where did you get this?

Simpson Don't force us to use this. Come on, David, we want to do the best for you, we really do, and this is breaking Mac's heart, you know it is, but if everyone's dragged down then the bad guys win and none of us can make the country great any more.

Flattery Oh please; oh please!

Simpson Well, either way you've got to see the bigger picture. Please don't force us to use this. Really.

Hobbs I just don't think people should be *treated* like that.

Flattery David, let's go.

Hobbs Dennis?

Flattery Let's go. *(to others)* I regret that we have been unable to reach a conclusion here tonight. We will revert to you in due course.

Simpson I'll hear from you in an hour.

Flattery In due course.

Simpson Yeah, like I say; in an hour.

Hobbs *(perhaps turning)* You're quite wrong, though, Simpson. In your statement. My leaving won't stop the speculation. They're just gonna move on to someone else. *(pause)* They might even get on to you one day.

Simpson Thanks, David. *(as in 'goodbye, David')*

Exit Hobbs and Flattery. There is a respectful pause. The others look to Simpson.

Scene 13

This follows directly on from the previous scene.

Simpson Well, it's a bad business. Don't think that it's not.

A pause.

Baxter Was that really... I mean does he really have to go?

Simpson What can I say? Sometimes you have to... I mean once you've made a big decision you have to ignore all the little decisions. Do you see? Otherwise you'll never get anywhere. And it's easy to feel sorry for Hobbs, and I *do* feel sorry for Hobbs, but do you want to lose Mac? Do you want to lose the PM? And then we'd lose Hobbs as well because we'd lose everything. It just comes down to time. Not enough time to find out what happened, not enough time to get our message across, not enough time to get it right, sometimes.

Baxter I just think it's a tragedy, really.

Simpson Well, that's life.

Baxter But do you really think he'll come back?

Kettley Do you really think he'll go, that's the question.

Simpson Yeah. Well, I hope he goes. And yeah, I hope he comes back, funnily enough.

Kettley Yeah.

Simpson What's your take on the leak, by the way?

Kettley Well.

Simpson Let's think. What do we know?

Kettley We know that Hobbs made a call to his broker. We just don't know when the call was made or what was the / subject of the discussion.

Simpson / No, no, forget all that. Let's go back. Further back. What's the root of the problem?

Baxter The root of the problem is that there's a potential case of insider dealing.

Simpson And how do we know that?

Baxter We know that because… well, we don't know it for sure.

Simpson Why not? Why don't we know it?

Kettley All we know is that two million's worth of

shares were bought by Hobbs' broker's firm around the time of the merger announcement.

Simpson And how do we know that?

Baxter Err... we know it because an investigative journalist published it.

Simpson And who was the hack and how do *they* know it?

Baxter The hack is Anthony Wilde from the Observer and they know it because they... they investigated. They got a tip-off. I'm not sure. But they're obviously pretty confident. And now everyone's run with it, of course.

Simpson And have we spoken to Wilde?

Kettley No. No-one's spoken to him. There's no point. He's not...

Simpson And the merger is between – / FirstCom and UBC International.

{**Kettley** / FirstCom and UBC International.

{**Baxter** / FirstCom and UBC International.

Simpson And why might anyone want to get at Hobbs?

Kettley Why are you assuming someone wants to / get at Hobbs?

Simpson / I'm not, I'm just saying we've rejected his coincidence theory, why are we, why are we placing so much stock in ours?

Baxter What's our coincidence theory?

Simpson Things are either coincidence or they're conspiracy. OK? We think Hobbs told the broker to buy the shares, that's the conspiracy. He's saying no, the broker just bought them off the cuff – it's just a coincidence and the *allegation* is the conspiracy.

Baxter OK?

Simpson There's three plausible options. Hobbs told his broker to buy the shares, someone there leaked it to the press and the story is bang on the money. That's the first option. And that's what we've assumed. However. Also possible is that Hobbs didn't instruct his broker, but someone, be it at the firm or the paper assumed – incorrectly – he did and disseminated accordingly. That's the cock-up theory. Thirdly is that Hobbs didn't buy the shares but someone wanted to make it look as though he had, so they plant the story. That's the conspiracy theory.

Kettley So which is it?

Simpson Well I don't know, but just imagine Hobbs is telling the truth. That's all I'm saying. Just for a moment. Because if he is, he's not out because he's unlucky. He's out because he's not wanted.

Kettley Well, look, let's all just keep our fingers crossed for the next hour and see what Hobbs does. The truth can wait thirty years as far as I'm concerned, but we need a result tonight.

Simpson Well. We'll speak when we hear.

Kettley Sure.

Baxter Sure.

Simpson I'll call you.

Kettley Yeah, or I'll call you.

Simpson Well, look, we'll speak.

Kettley Yeah.

Baxter OK, well, listen, Will, thanks for coming round.

Simpson Thanks for letting me help.

Baxter Thanks for helping.

Simpson What I'm here for.

Kettley Give my best to the boss won't you.

Simpson Oh no you don't.

Kettley Yeah, I'll see you mate.

Simpson *(he goes to leave yet turns back)* Here's the question we *should* be asking, by the way. Why was the *merger* approved? Why was the merger approved? *That's* the question we should be asking.

Exit Simpson.

Scene 14

Mason, Mac and Baxter.

Mac Mr Mason, I'm sorry and I understand the parties that you represent but surely they must see... This would create one of the largest media giants ever; certainly the largest in Europe. And your clients would become some of the most powerful men in the world. Now if you're formally engaged by –

Mason No, no, I'm not, I'm a private individual.

Mac Well I'm not sure I should even be speaking to you, but...

Mason That's not the way we want to go about it, Mac.

Mac I just have to tell you that it's *pretty* unlikely I can let a merger of that nature go through. I'm not saying it's impossible, I'm just saying... it goes against my instinct.

Mason OK, Mac, here's the deal. I wasn't going to put it in so many words but there we go. If that's the way you want to do it that's a matter for you. Can we speak? *(he gestures to Baxter)*

Mac Please, don't... this is as private as it gets.

Mason If you're happy trusting everyone.

Mac I don't trust everyone, but this is as private as it gets.

Mason Worried I'll double-cross you, eh?

Mac I'm just perfectly happy with Baxter being here. I hope you are too.

Mason Oh, it's perfectly alright with me, but... OK. Well, we know about the girl.

Mac: *(Pause. Perhaps even slightly laughing.)* What girl?

Mason Oh come on.

(They exchange a look of some intensity. Time passes.) Go along with the merger, Mac, or we're going to roll up our newspapers and cave in your skull. I swear to

God.

A pause.

Mac *(an almighty sigh)* Oh! So this is how you guys go about it, is it?

Mason I didn't ask you to have an affair, Secretary of State, I'm just trying to help my clients.

Mac And what if I were your client? How would you help me?

Mason *(slowly laughs)*

Mac You will have to excuse me now, Mr Mason. I'm running late.

Mason I'll be hearing from you soon, no doubt.

Baxter Thanks for your time, sir.

They have been making arrangements to leave.

Mason *(suddenly)* It's the hypocrisy I'm against, Mac. I don't mind the tastes, I've no objections to the tastes, to each his own, you know. If that's what you want… it's a free country, and we're only human after all. *(pause)* It's just the saying of one thing and the doing of another. That's what gets my goat. The hypocrisy of it all. Makes me feel I'm on the right side. Battling against people like you.

Mac *(sighs)* The tragedy is you probably do genuinely believe you're on the right side.

Mason I'll not take a moral lecture from the likes of you, mate.

Mac I've served this country faithfully and honourably

for thirty years and –

Mason Well, you should have thought of that earlier.

Mac Michael, I wonder if you realise just how misguided you are.

Mason Sorry? *(pause)* What did you call me?

Mac Nothing. Nothing. I just said I think you're misguided, that's all.

Mason I've been called a lot of things by a lot of people, Secretary of State, but I've never been called anything like that by anyone like you. Right. You've got two weeks to think about it.

Mac Yes. Yes I do.

Scene 15

This is a continuation of Scene 13.

Kettley *(sighs, looks at his watch etc.)*

Baxter What was that about? Are you after Simpson's job?

Kettley Everyone's after everyone's job, Baxter. That's what keeps the system together.

Baxter *(laughs)* Well, it doesn't feel together.

Kettley Yeah.

Baxter Listen, I think we should get Anthony Wilde in.

Kettley No need, mate.

Baxter Well I'm not sure I agree. I mean we don't know if Hobbs is going to go, and I just think if we –

Kettley There's no point. He's just...

Baxter He's the key link.

Kettley Right, but he's not going to say anything.

Baxter Is it not worth seeing him just to.. just to see him.

Kettley No need.

Baxter I'm going to get him in here and see what he says.

Kettley Baxter, I've already talked to him, it's a waste of time.

Baxter Oh, OK.

Kettley Yeah, all we can do is sit it out until we hear from *Flattery*.

Baxter OK.

Kettley Flattery will get him nowhere. Doesn't he see that?

Baxter Yes; thanks, Angus. *(as in 'grow up, Angus')*

Kettley It's been a long, long day, mate.

Baxter *(pause)* So you spoke to Anthony Wilde did you?

Kettley Err, yeah. Waste of time. If he's not going to say anything to me he'll not talk to anyone.

Baxter But it occurs to me you told Simpson you *hadn't* spoken to him.

Kettley Sorry?

Baxter Well you said to Simpson you hadn't spoken to

him.

Kettley Err.. I don't think I said that, no.

Baxter Umm, I think you did actually.

Kettley Right?

Baxter Well, I wonder why.

Kettley I don't know if I…well why wouldn't I? What are you talking about, Baxter?

Baxter Well, did you speak to him?

Kettley Yes I did. So what.

Baxter But you said you didn't speak to him.

Kettley What, Anthony Wilde?

Baxter Yeah, Anthony Wilde from the Observer. You used to work with him.

Kettley And I said this to Simpson.

Baxter To Simpson, right.

Kettley Well?

Baxter Well, it's just…

Kettley Who cares what I said to Simpson.

Baxter Well, don't you think it's a little odd?

Kettley Just give it a rest, mate.

Baxter Do you not think?

Kettley Just give it… look, sometimes you have to tell Will what he wants to hear, just to stop him going up these blind alleys.

Baxter OK.

Kettley OK?

Baxter Fair enough. Yup.

Kettley So.

Baxter *(pause)* But / surely –

Kettley / Oh! *(or another very audible sigh or expression of peevishness)*

Baxter / – a blind alley would be you saying you *hadn't* spoken to him when in fact you had.

Kettley What?

Baxter *Stopping* Will going up a blind alley would be to say yes, yes I have spoken to him –

Kettley OK.

Baxter – so there's no need for anyone else to –

Kettley OK.

Baxter – whilst all the while you hadn't.

Kettley But why would I want to do that?

Baxter Well you didn't do that; you did the opposite. You *created* a blind alley.

Kettley What?

Baxter You created a blind alley by saying you hadn't spoken to Anthony Wilde.

Kettley Baxter, –

Baxter Whereas in fact you had.

Kettley – I'm getting pretty fucking sick of this.

Baxter Hold on, hold on, hold on. Now in theory you

might say you *had* spoken to him just to stop anyone else speaking to them. Which might be what you're doing now.

Kettley No, it's not.

Baxter No, I'm just saying. But why then would you say to Simpson that you *hadn't*?

Kettley Well you tell me, mate.

Baxter *(pause)* Because you panicked.

Kettley Why would I panic.

Baxter Because on the one hand you might want to deny that you'd ever spoken to him. But on the other hand you might want to stop anyone else speaking to him.

Kettley Baxter, you're babbling.

Baxter Yes.

Kettley You're babbling.

Baxter I'm just thinking out loud.

Kettley Well, just keep those thoughts to yourself.

Baxter I'm just thinking out loud.

Kettley Yeah, well, keep them to yourself.

Baxter Just thinking out / loud.

Kettley / Give it a rest. Give it a rest.

Baxter *(longish pause)* Fair enough.

Both men brood for a moment.

Scene 16

Flashback.

Kettley Are you alright, sir?

Mac This UBC thing is blowing up in our faces.

Kettley Yes. Yes it is.

Mac What the hell are they... if I knew how much of a stink this was going to... *(sighs)* This is the last thing I need, I'm telling you. It's just the fucking *press*. And I'm not sure they're going to go away.

Kettley Well, they want their pound of flesh, sir, I have to tell you.

Mac Well they're not going to get it. We've got to draw a line under this, Angus.

Kettley Yes, sir.

Mac The merger... *(sighs)* I'm not going to put up with the media on the prowl like this. You know; searching and scraping about for a story. I've got better things to do than... and if they're not careful they'll upset the whole apple cart, and who knows what they might find. You know, anything can be made to look suspect when in fact...

Kettley I mean... we had to expect something from the press, sure, but nothing like this, surely. They've got it all –

Mac There's nothing wrong with that merger.

Kettley No.

Mac No. Right. There is nothing wrong with that

merger. I'm telling you. It was my call, and I made it, and if they don't like it then tough.

Kettley I agree.

Mac But they just take everything out of context. And it's all out of proportion.

Kettley It is.

Mac I made my decision, the merger went through, they're not happy about it, fine, that's their right, fine, but I resent the whole tone they take.

Kettley Yeah.

Mac I don't hear any complaints from the PM.

Kettley No.

Mac Look, let's not let this leave its mark. I can't be.. I can't allow myself to get bogged down in this. Every time my name gets mentioned now it's followed by the words 'controversial' and 'merger'. And sooner or later that's going to… I'm not going to take any more damage, Angus. Because frankly speaking it's starting to harm my prospects. *(he points to the Financial Times)* 'Beleaguered'! I can't allow the boss to read too much of that. At best I'm coming across like I don't know what day of the week it is and at worst it looks like I'm on the take and there's something dodgy about the merger decision.

Kettley Now, now, sir. No one's accusing you of that. Certainly not the latter anyway.

Mac I just want you to get rid of them OK? I'm sick of being on the damn front page.

Kettley Yeah of course. So what's the story?

Mac Just get them off this. Just…

Kettley Sure, well, *(sighs)* yeah, well it's going to take some doing. I mean, they're not letting go and it's not helped by a slow news week as well, so –

Mac Is there not something we've got that we can put out? I mean, anything.

Kettley Well, it's difficult, sir; I just don't think the red-tape campaign or the small business initiative or whatever is going to cut it with all respect. I mean –

Mac Look, just chuck a stone into the woods, alright? Make them look up from what they're eating.

Kettley Well I mean we can always plant something of course.

Mac What kind of something.

Kettley Well it would have to be pretty big.

Mac Angus, listen. If the press keep up this racket I'm going to be out on my ear. I've probably got another week and I'm not going out like that.

Kettley OK.

Mac I am specifically charging you with alleviating the pressure from the media. Does that seem clear?

Kettley Yes, sir.

Mac I am specifically charging you with / alleviating –

Kettley / Yes, I understand, sir.

Mac I don't care what you do, I don't want to know,

just do something, OK?

Kettley Yes. But I'm going to have to think.

Mac Well, think quickly, Angus, because I can't have another day like this.

Kettley No; sure. Sure.

Mac So I don't want to hear about it, OK? I just want to read about it.

Kettley Sir, I have to tell you I'm happy to do this but sometimes... I just want you to be aware that due to the magnitude of the story the decoy is going to have to be pretty big too.

Mac Angus, I want you to think about why you got involved in all this. Let's be honest, being a journalist was not enough, was it? Because we're moral beings, we... we want to make a difference. That's why we're here. And you don't need me to tell you how thankless it is. So we've got to be doing it for *something*. And you've seen, we *can* make a difference, and we can help people, and it *is* worth it. Think back five years and look at the difference. That's *us*. Do you see what I..? And I don't want to... I just think that you believe in me, OK, and I don't want to let you down and I think that – rightly or wrongly – I think that I've got something to contribute and I can't go out like this, and I need you, and I'll need you later on, and... look, let's not wreck everything, let's not waste everything, OK? You know the world we live in, you know what it's like. To do a great right do a little wrong. Angus, you and I are built for the top, and don't tell me you don't think that. So... and just think of what we could do *there*. Look at what we've done *here*.

Kettley *(thinks for a moment)*

Mac So what do you say?

Kettley Off the top of my head… look, we can at least have a look at… I don't know, was there any share activity at the time, just before, could it be… one could in theory look through the circulation list for the merger papers, see if anyone had a broker who worked at a firm that might have… well, sheer weight of numbers dictate you've got a chance of finding something there.

Mac Keep the merger out of the papers, Angus. OK? Just keep the merger / out of the papers.

Kettley / I mean we may have to… *(pause)* I'm just thinking here… we may have to lose someone, sir, and I just want to make sure that that's…

Mac I can't hear what you're saying.

Kettley Well, I just want to / know if

Mac / I can't hear what you're saying.

Kettley *(pause)* Right. Of course. I understand. I'll give you an update tomorrow.

Mac I don't want any updates.

Kettley OK. Just leave it with me.

Mac Just get on it, Angus. / Get on it.

Kettley / Right. *(pause)* Umm… no, don't worry. Don't worry.

Mac And Angus… listen, don't say anything to Baxter,

will you. Let's not get him involved.

Kettley Of course.

Mac I mean *(he gestures)*, you know.

Kettley Of course.

Mac *(pause)* Angus, I won't forget this.

Kettley Perhaps you should.

Scene 17

Baxter Well, you've got your merger, Mr Mason, well done.

Mason It's not *my* merger, mate; they came to me.

Baxter Well.

Mason But yes, it went through.

Baxter And we still have our agreement, of course.

Mason Sorry?

Baxter Our agreement.

Mason Oh grow up. Our agreement! You don't think it ends here, do you?

Baxter Err.. Mr Mason, I...

Mason This way everyone gets paid. Merger or no merger I'm gonna get my story out. Do you not see that? Forget UBC now. That's fine. Now why would I not use my story?

Baxter Mr Mason –

Mason I know you're attached to the old man and fair

enough – to each his own, as they say. I'm sure you've heard that expression.

Baxter Err… yes.

Mason A young man of your education.

Baxter Right.

Mason I mean you seem a nice enough young man and I'm sure you're very bright. Went to Oxford or something, I'll bet.

Baxter Well, Keele.

Mason A nice Oxford college and what have you, and now into the fast stream swimming with the big fishes. But I do have some advice for you, actually, and it's good advice. You guys sit up here running with your little stories or whatever and if you're doing some good so much the better and I'm sure that's why you got into this in the first place and so forth.

Baxter *(clears his throat)* Well…

Mason But you can't beat the press. You need us and we don't need you. So…err, so it really is that simple. And take a stand against us by the way and we'll smash your face into your neck.

Baxter Right.

Mason But none of that comes into play if everything is sweet and everyone treats each other nicely. That's what we want. You give us a little something or we, we, err… we take the whole lot. Now no-one wants that, so we always get our little something. *(pause)* Do you know how it works; your classic sex story?

Baxter *(he gestures)*

Mason You must have read some of your News of the World revelations or whatever and thought to yourself why on earth do the prostitutes or whoever they are go out of their way to say how good the guy was in bed? Did you ever wonder that? It just doesn't make any sense, does it? Well, what happens is this. We prepare two versions of the story. Oh, sure, we speak to the hooker but I wouldn't really call it an interview. I mean what's *she* going to say of any value? So we prepare two versions of the story. Then we have to time the call to the celebrity just right – the unsuspecting celebrity – because if we call him too early he may have a PR guy of his own who he can use and so forth. So we ring him early evening on Saturday night and say Look, we're just about to run a front pager on you tomorrow morning because the bad news is that hooker or teenage waitress etc. etc. from way back when has come crawling to us. So you let that sink in for a bit, and then you give them the good news, and the good news is that they've got a choice of stories. The first one is how you're the best lover this girl's ever had in her young life stroke varied career and you made her moan all night and you are a fucking love god. Fine, OK, but we're only gonna use this story if you sign the agreement we're about to fax over saying you'll give us an exclusive 'My Hell' story in a couple of weeks about how you broke your wife's heart but you're trying to patch things up and perhaps you need therapy. If you don't sign the deal then we go with story two, which says how you wear your socks in bed and you stink and you force her to shave and dress as a schoolgirl (or whatever the boys come up with). So you take a couple of minutes to think about it. And guess what they come back with. So we get our lead and then we get our follow-up. Sure, you've seen some of the bad-sex stories from time to time, but let's face it, what would *you* do?

Baxter *(laughs)* Yeah.

Mason So there you are.

Baxter Well, that's very interesting, Mr Mason.

Mason The celebrities... well, I do feel a bit sorry for them, believe it or not.

Baxter You do.

Mason Because, I mean... we're all weak, really. None of us are strong, are we. Not really. Not against that. But your tv presenters don't parade themselves as the moral guardians, you see. They don't preach, they don't dictate.

Baxter Mr Mason, the debate is on penny in the pound tax rise and health reform. Haven't you heard? No-one's talking about morality any more.

Mason Don't be daft, son. You've seen him parade his wife. You've seen him use his family. And he's part of the system. *The system*.

Baxter He's not part of any system.

Mason He's part of the system.

Baxter He's not; he's –

Mason He's the *system*, he's the estab/lishment.

Baxter / He's not... look, we're here to get *rid* of all that.

Mason He's the system, don't be / an idiot.

Baxter / I'm sorry, he is not part of that.

Mason I won't be contradicted.

Baxter Well if you don't want to be corrected / fair enough.

Mason / You fucking wankers really get my goat, do you know that? And yes I *do* take it personally and that's why I *am* going to fuck up that fucking piece of shit McConnolly good and proper, merger or no merger, because all you guys think you're the rulers of this place and I'm here to tell you that if you're going to be silly about it you can all just fuck off because I've been here for thirty years too you know and I don't appreciate being told what to do by the likes of you or the likes of Mac and your fucking loyalty to whatever it is you're loyal to. You make me laugh, you make me fucking laugh, do you know that? And let me tell you and proper about it I *am* going to get to that girl and she *is* going to talk and I am going to mash this fucking wanker until he wishes he'd gassed himself.

A pause.

Baxter Mr Mason, Alec McConnolly is going to be the best Prime Minister this country's had for sixty years. Do you not care about that, Mr Mason?

Mason What he does in his public life is his own business. It's his private life I take objection to.

Baxter Well, Mr Mason, thank you very much for your

views. I am now due at the House of Lords. I do hope you'll excuse me.

Mason So you take my message to your fucking boss and see if he still thinks I'm misguided.

Baxter Yes, I think I understand, thank you.

Mason You're talking to a man who gets the last word, mate.

Baxter Uh-huh.

Mason The last word, you hear?

Baxter Yes.

Mason Right.

Baxter Can I interest you perhaps in the opportunity to rethink?

Mason Fuck off.

Baxter Rethink your position?

Mason Fuck off.

Baxter Can we talk again tomorrow?

Mason Fuck off.

Baxter One last chance?

Mason Fuck off.

Baxter Very well, sir.

Mason Just fuck off.

Baxter *(laughs in genuine amusement and a little embarrassment)* Good evening, Mr Mason. Thank you very much for your time.

Scene 18

Mac He's got to be kidding. That man caught me on the back foot once but it's not going to happen again.

Baxter Let me be honest sir and say this could be pretty serious.

Mac I've bought into his culture now, do you know what I mean?

Baxter Yes.

Mac There's just never enough smokescreens. As soon as you put up your first smokescreen you're doomed to be putting them up for the rest of your life.

Baxter Yes.

Mac It's just bumps in the road all the way. The merger was meant to solve everything. And then that went down like a cup of cold sick and we had another crisis to resolve. And now we're back where we started; the merger may's well not have happened if Mason's going to double-cross us.

Baxter I have to admit we did not consider this as an eventuality.

Mac Did you not try and reason with him?

Baxter You don't reason with a dog that's foaming at the mouth, sir.

Mac OK. Well. Look. If he wants to try it on fine, but he's not going to beat the system.

Baxter So how do you want to play this.

Mac Hmm.

Baxter He's not going to listen to a word we say.

Mac This is not the time for words, Baxter.

Baxter Well, I hate to… this is none of my –

Mac Come on, mate.

Baxter Would the girl talk.

Mac Would the girl talk.

Baxter Would she.

Mac It's no longer a question of whether she'll talk.

Baxter Sir, surely that's the whole issue.

Mac That's not enough.

Baxter Sir, if we can just convince her that –

Mac Just get a handle on this. Do whatever you have to do but just get on it.

Baxter Yes, but –

Mac Just spook Mason. Spook him. Let's stare him out.

Baxter Sir, –

Mac Stare him out. We're not going to back down now.

Baxter I just think that if the girl's not going to talk then what can he do?

Mac Baxter, you're only getting half the picture here. I've painted myself into an impossible situation.

Baxter With respect I don't think she's going to talk and we'll be home and dry.

Mac *(slowly and clearly)* It is no longer going to be enough for her purely to remain silent.

Baxter Why on earth not?

Mac *(pause)* This is black, son. *(sighs)* Look, you know everything else, you may's well know this.

Scene 19

This is a continuation of Scene 15.

Kettley Actually, there was one slightly odd thing, one slightly odd moment. This was at my briefing with him the day after the Observer came out when it was all over the press.

Baxter What; something in the way it was reported?

Kettley No, it was nothing to do with that. Nothing to do with the Hobbs or the merger at all.

Baxter Well, is it relevant then, in a way?

Kettley No, probably not, but it's been rattling around in my head and I've only just noticed it.

Baxter Go on?

Kettley But I mean this was right at the beginning before we got on to the papers because this was the day when the news came through about the researcher, or it came through the night before so I told him that the researcher had died and I didn't think of it at the time but now I come to think about it... well... I said to him, like as soon as I got in, 'Secretary of State, I have some very sad news, a junior researcher who works here has been killed in a car crash.' And there was a pause *(pause)* and then he said –

Mac What kind of car crash?

Kettley *(pause)* Now does that not strike you as a particularly weird thing to say? What did he mean by that? And it hasn't struck me until now.

Baxter Well, I guess he meant was anyone else killed / I suppose.

Kettley / So why, so why didn't he just say was anyone else killed?

Baxter Well, I don't know… people don't always say what they mean, and especially if he was in shock or upset or whatever.

Kettley But he wa… I mean he didn't even know her; he'd never met her – why would he / why would he be upset?

Baxter / Oh come on, you don't need to know someone to be upset by something like that. It's just upsetting, you know. I mean he's obviously just in shock, you know – look, I mean he even went to her funeral for God's sake.

Kettley No, no, no, no, no. Surely *this* makes most sense: Secretary of State, I have some very sad news. A researcher who works here was killed last night in a car crash.

Mac Oh God no. Which researcher?

Kettley Why didn't he ask who it was? Why didn't he ask who it was? I mean he knows most of them. Why didn't he ask?

Baxter Well –

Kettley Why didn't he ask?

Baxter Look, every time you've described what he said to you you've said something completely different to him every time. How do you know for sure what you exactly said to him when you told him the news?

Kettley Why does it matter?

Baxter Well, because how do you know *this* didn't take place? *(to Mac)* Sir, I have some very sad news. Rachel Langford, a researcher here, has been killed in a car crash.

Mac Oh God. *(pause)* What kind of car crash?

Baxter Now that makes a *little* more sense, don't you think?

Kettley Yes, but that's not what I said.

Baxter Sorry?

Kettley That's not what I said.

Baxter That's not what you said or that's not what you *think* you said?

Kettley I… that's not what I said.

Baxter Which is it?

Kettley I –

Baxter Do you know what you said? Categorically do you know how you phrased it?

Kettley I *(sigh)* I really don't remember.

Baxter You don't remember.

Kettley I really don't remember.

Baxter Can you try?

Kettley I'm sorry; I just don't recall.

Baxter Is it possible you gave the name.

Kettley I really don't think I did.

Baxter Is it possible you gave the name.

Kettley I really couldn't say.

Baxter Is it or is it not / possible –

Kettley / Yes, yes, it's technically possible.

Baxter Technically possible?

Kettley I might have said it.

Baxter You might have said it.

Kettley Yes.

Baxter But you don't remember.

Kettley I just don't remember.

Baxter OK then.

Kettley Baxter, there's something bloody odd going on here.

Baxter *(shrugs)*

Kettley And it occurs to me also.

Baxter Yes?

Kettley There was something else with Rachel Langford. He was meant to turn up and shake her hand for the research prize and he wouldn't do it. I mean he just wouldn't do it. Now have you ever known Mac turn down a photo opportunity?

Baxter What's your point?

Kettley I don't know; but it's a little odd don't you think?

Baxter Do I think it's odd?

Kettley Yes.

Baxter No. / No I do not.

Kettley / Well hold on, hold on, how about if I told you this. How about if I told you this.

Baxter Yes?

Kettley Michael Mason was here.

Baxter *The* Michael Mason.

Kettley Yes.

Baxter When?

Kettley I don't know. A couple of weeks ago.

Baxter Why was he here?

Kettley I don't... something to do with the merger.

Baxter Why would he... so what's he got to do with the merger?

Kettley I don't know.

Baxter And what's he got to do with the crash?

Kettley Nothing. I don't know.

Baxter Well may I suggest that we leave it there, then.

Kettley Baxter, something's amiss here, I swear it.

Baxter May I suggest we leave it there.

The two men stare each other out for perhaps literally 30 seconds.

Scene 20

Mac *(to audience)* When I heard I just felt sick. I didn't feel anything, really; just… I felt sick for a couple of days. I wasn't sure, I couldn't tell, I couldn't prove it, but I could feel it. And I thought: this is the world you wanted to live in. In my heart when I spoke to Angus Kettley that first time about trying to distract the media I knew my instructions were probably going to destroy someone's career; sure, maybe I didn't know it was Hobbs, who I'd always liked and trusted, by the way, but I knew it would've had to've been someone. But I chose not to think about it. And then when I heard about the crash… And I don't know who did it; 5 or 6, the security and intelligence team in the Cabinet Office – does it really matter? Perhaps it actually was a genuine accident, just a coincidence, two days after me telling Baxter that Michael Mason should be cautioned in some way, calmed down, he wasn't to be trusted, needed a warning shot. And I told Baxter that Rachel was pregnant. Which she was. Or so she said. Perhaps she deliberately crashed, I don't know. We can't prove anything now. And at the funeral I felt nothing. And I still don't feel anything. I just store it away, I choose not think about it. I just observe, I watch the way I'm being buffeted towards high office, steered towards it by those around me as they clear my path and obscure my trail.

Scene 21

Kettley *(to audience)* I stayed on perhaps another six months but... *(pause)* We never spoke about that night, Baxter and I. I tried a couple of times but I suppose I was afraid of what I might hear. Or what I might say. No doubt he has his suspicions too, but, well, perhaps we've got each other over a barrel, and perhaps that's how it's going to work, or perhaps I'm utterly mistaken. After a while it got to the stage where we genuinely couldn't look each other in the eye any more. Then later we couldn't even talk to each other, not really. *(pause)* So, umm, I now work for a non-governmental organisation. We try to raise awareness of the importance of clean water in developing countries and various health issues; AIDS and malaria and so on. I travel quite a bit and write press briefings, and, err... you know, I think it's probably... well, it's obviously very different. McConnolly is now Chancellor, of course, and by all accounts doing fantastic things. Yeah; he's still on the way up, and just wait till we lose the next election – till *they* lose the next election; that'll really be the making of him. Simpson is still in his job, stockpiling his anecdotes I guess for when they leave office and he can write his memoirs. I still see him on tv quite a bit and I still like him. *(he stops and thinks and shakes his head)* And Baxter. What became of him? Well, I don't know. I believe he's still with Mac. I really couldn't say for sure. *(pause)* I've seen him once since I left; one morning – really early, I was running before work in St James's Park, it was like the first real autumn morning of the year and the air was all ... *(he sniffs happily)*, and I was at the Westminster end of the lake and I saw Baxter walking towards me, cutting through the park on his way to work. I had my cap on and all my running stuff, you know, so I really don't know if he was pretending not to recognise me or if he genuinely didn't recognise me, it really could have been either. And I made eye contact, I looked him in the eye, but just didn't get anything back. And I thought about turning round and going back after him but I didn't and I really can't explain why. I just kept on running and I looked across over the lake and I saw a couple of the pelicans perched on their roost – I always keep a look out for them over there. One of them seemed to yawn and he craned his neck and stretched out his great white wings and I thought he was going to take off over the water which is something you almost never see but after a brief flap he just settled back down again, and kind of nodded thoughtfully to himself. The air really smelled beautiful, actually; and I always feel really great round about that time on the run, taking great lungfuls of air, you know. *(pause)* I try and run most mornings.

Scene 22

This is a continuation of Scene 19. The two men's pagers ring again.

Baxter Ah, here it is! *(they both get out their pagers* *and check them)* Oh; he's gone.

Kettley Yeah.

Baxter Hobbs has made the statement.

Kettley Yes he has.

Baxter He's out.

Kettley He's out.

Baxter Thank God for that.

Kettley Yeah.

Baxter Yeah; that's that. Well, that was Hobbs. *(sighs in happy relief)* Just like you said.

A pause.

Kettley Yeah.

Baxter Bang on the money, Angus.

Kettley Right.

Baxter Bang on the money.

Kettley Yeah.

Baxter *(sighs)* Well, it's gonna be another long night.

Kettley *(sighs)*

Baxter Let's get onto the tv stations.

Kettley Yeah.

Baxter Well, we've already got Mac's response. Just give them that.

Kettley Yeah. Well, let's ring them.

Baxter Are you going to ring them?

Kettley Yeah, I'll ring them.

Baxter I'll get down to the House and see what we can mop up there.

Kettley OK. Sure.

Baxter Angus, do get some rest at some point, won't you.

Kettley Yeah. You too.

Baxter Yeah.

A long pause.

Baxter If you want me I'm in the lobby. *(he pats Kettley on the back or similar)*

Kettley Yeah, OK.

Exit Baxter. Kettley sits for a moment.

End.

MAHLER & RACHMANINOV

dedicated to the memory of Helen Mason

Characters
in order of appearance

Natalia Rachmaninov
Gustav Mahler
Alma Mahler
Sergei Rachmaninov

Mahler & Rachmaninov opened at the Landor Theatre, London on Tuesday 26 November 2002 with the following cast:

Natalia Rachmaninov	Angela Saul
Gustav Mahler	Adrian Fear
Alma Mahler	Danielle Urbas
Sergei Rachmaninov	John Atterbury

Directed by	Matt Lane
Designed by	Valerie Saint-Pierre
Lighting by	Stuart Griffith

Scene 1

We hear the slow movement of Rachmaninov's Second Piano Sonata and after a time the voice of an American radio announcer is added. Throughout this sequence the lights go up on Natalia, who is perhaps making a bed or similar.

Voice-over American troops launched a surprise attack on Fondouk in Central Tunisia today and are reported to be making good headway. This development coincides with signs of renewed activity in the north of the country. Germany infantry thrusts east of Mahnassy have been repelled by United States forces, while along the Mareth Line the British Eighth Army is edging forward against stiff resistance.

Meanwhile, on the other side of the world, Navy bombers raided the Japanese base on Nauru in the South Pacific. Nauru lies some 700 miles north-east of Guadalcanal.

The American people embarked today upon point rationing of meats, cheese, fats and canned fish. Federal Government spokesmen last night gave assurances that a number of independent packers have been authorised to rush supplies of beef to meat-famished areas where ration coupons would otherwise be of little value.

The British Foreign Secretary Anthony Eden left Washington this afternoon bound for Canada following his meetings with President Roosevelt this week. The President at his press conference this afternoon said discussions of post-war problems would continue with

Russia and other members of the United Nations. He offered an extremely optimistic picture of the degree of agreement between the British and American governments.

Police Commissioner Joseph F. Timility and six of his chief subordinates in the Boston Police Department were indicted today by the Suffolk County Grand Jury on charges of conspiracy to permit the operation of gambling houses and the registration of bets. The charges are misdemeanours.

In Los Angeles the composer and pianist Sergei Rachmaninov has died. He had cancelled a number of concerts this month due to illness. Rachmaninov was 69.

The flying ace Squadron Leader Keith 'Bluey' Truscott of the Royal Australian Air Force has been killed on escort duty in the Exmouth Gulf. Accompanying a Catalina flying boat from a long range mission Truscott was practising combat attacks when he misjudged the Catalina's closeness to the water and attempted to fly beneath it.

That was the news at seven o'clock.

Fade to black.

Scene 2

The scene begins in silence with Mahler and Alma awkwardly standing alone together, as if by chance, perhaps on a balcony after a formal dinner. A long pause.

Mahler The forest is very beautiful, don't you think?

Alma I'm sorry?

Mahler The forest.

Alma Yes?

Mahler It's very beautiful.

Alma Isn't it.

Mahler Yes.

Alma Extremely beautiful.

Mahler I beg your pardon?

Alma Umm… yes, it's very beautiful.

Mahler Yes, it is.

Alma It certainly is.

Mahler I quite agree.

Alma It really is a very beautiful forest.

Mahler Yes. Extremely beautiful.

A pause.

Alma And the trees?

Mahler The trees?

Alma No, I mean the lake. Sorry.

Mahler The lake.

Alma Yes. Umm... do you find the lake beautiful?

Mahler Of course.

Alma Of course you do, yes.

Mahler Who wouldn't?

Alma *(laughing a little falsely)* Well quite! Who wouldn't?

Mahler Who indeed?

Alma Yes. Probably no-one, I should imagine.

Mahler I'm sure.

A pause.

Alma Err... and is it... lakes in general you like?... Or just this particular lake?

Mahler No, no; I lake all likes.

Alma Oh lovely.

Mahler That is; I like all lakes.

Alma Of course.

Mahler Yes, I unwittingly transposed the words.

Alma You did?

Mahler Yes. Two words, both sounding very similar. I put them the wrong way round.

Alma Oh. I didn't notice.

Mahler You didn't?

Alma No.

Mahler You see, I unwittingly transposed the words.

Alma Yes. So you said.

Mahler That's right, yes.

Alma I suppose I must have transposed them back with equal… umm… unwittingness.

Mahler Ha! So I shouldn't have said anything.

Alma About the lakes, you mean.

Mahler Well, no, err… yes, about the lakes. My lake mistake.

Alma You know, I'm not sure there's such a word as 'unwittingness'.

Mahler No?

Alma No. Perhaps I should rather have said 'in equal innocence'. Or maybe 'with equal ignorance'. Not that you were…

A pause.

Mahler / The stars are very…

Alma / I understand you've just...

Alma Sorry, I –

Mahler No, no; –

Alma Oh, I was just about to say I understand you've just returned from Paris.

Mahler Yes, that's right. I've been back almost a week now.

Alma And you were conducting the Symphony Orchestra?

Mahler No, I was at the Opera House.

Alma The Opera House! Goodness.

Mahler Yes. Just for a few performances of *Tristan* and *Meistersinger*.

Alma Oh, I love Wagner.

Mahler You do?

Alma Oh, yes. Of all the composers in the world I consider him to be the most…

A pause.

It must be terribly exciting; travelling all the time, having your opinions listened to and so forth.

Mahler I'm not sure it's exciting. It's nicer than not travelling and having your opinions ignored, for example.

Alma Oh I'm sure it is. And…

Mahler Yes?

Alma I'm not sure if you remember, and in fact I'm certain you don't in fact, so…

Mahler / Yes?

Alma / Sorry, I...

Alma No, well I thought I might mention… I don't know if it's… but I thought… anyway, the thing is… and I don't know if you… in fact you probably don't, but… well, I'll say it anyway… (*pause, then very suddenly with great finality)* no it doesn't matter.

Mahler *(perhaps almost laughing)* Miss Schindler,

please. What is it?

Alma Very well.

Mahler Yes?

Alma All it was was I wrote to you.

Mahler You did?

Alma Yes. I was much younger. This was a long time ago. When you were first appointed.

Mahler Well, I must confess I –

Alma No, you wouldn't remember, of course not; it was the juvenile letter of a hot-headed young naïf.

Mahler Oh yes; I remember it now.

Alma Goodness! Really?

Mahler *(he reassures her with a shake of his head)*

Alma You must think me silly.

Mahler Don't be silly.

Alma Oh, well, as you know, then, I have always admired you.

Mahler Well, that's... awfully civil of you.

Alma I mean, it's just that you seem to have everything in a way.

Mahler Surely not. Whatever can you mean?

Alma Well; Principal Director of the Opera, prolific composer, respected and prominent if rather eccentric figure in Viennese life.

Mahler I am many things, Miss Schindler, but never

eccentric.

Alma Oh; come, come, sir! I saw you lick the spoon and return it absent-mindedly to the compote.

Mahler I never… did I?

Alma Oh yes.

Mahler Did I really?

Alma It was noted by many.

Mahler Goodness me.

Alma And by all accounts that is merely the tip of the iceberg.

Mahler But whatever must people think?

Alma Well, I would imagine they think of you as Principal Director of the Opera, prolific composer and prominent and respected if rather eccentric figure in Viennese life.

Mahler And what do you think?

Alma What do I think?

Mahler Yes.

Alma *(pause)* I think you have nice eyes.

Mahler Nicer than Gustav Klimt's?

Alma *(slightly flustered by the reference)* What a ridiculous question! As a painter I feel he is entitled to beautiful eyes. After all, it is through his eyes that his artistic vision is brought to life.

Mahler By that logic, therefore, I should have beautiful ears.

Alma Very well, Mr Mahler. I will allow that you have the nicest ears in Christendom.

Mahler Thank you very much. I hope to be remembered for them.

Alma I am quite certain you shall. For those if nothing else. *(pause)* That was a joke, Mr Mahler.

Mahler Oh, please. Call me Dr Mahler.

Alma It would be my absolute pleasure.

Mahler That's the spirit. But you see, you talk about my achievements and so forth. Really I've just been very lucky.

Alma Tush! There's more to it than that. Good luck doesn't just fly into your mouth like a roast chicken. I'm sure you've worked very hard.

Mahler Well, I suppose I...

Alma I too know what it is to work hard, Dr Mahler.

Mahler You do?

Alma Oh yes. I also write music.

Mahler Really?

Alma Not just music. I... I have written a number of short stories and I draw all the illustrations for them as well.

Mahler Tremendous. But you love music above all, though.

Alma Oh yes, sir. More than anything in the world.

Mahler Well, it seems we have that in common.

Alma In fact I've been thinking. I've had a really good idea, I think.

Mahler Go on.

Alma Well, wouldn't it be wonderful to compose a piece of music that reflects every event in a woman's life; her hopes, her dreams, her first love, her great achievements – you know; a sort of Adventures of a Noble Heroine.

Mahler Yes, well, that may indeed be entertaining. But you must remember. That type of programmatic device is all very well but nothing is more important than a good theme; a flexible but solid theme that will withstand a lot of development and so on. Look at Beethoven.

Alma Well, I see Beethoven as the most romantic composer in the world.

Mahler Yes, of course, but without those perfect little rhythmic cells to develop it doesn't matter how romantic he is.

Alma I rather see it the other way round. He could have three hours' worth of musical ideas but they won't count for anything unless the listener can engage with them.

Mahler Yes; that is the job of structure.

Alma No, no; emotion.

Mahler It's the same thing.

Alma No; all those musical ideas won't count for anything unless they have been inspired.

Mahler But what exactly do you mean? Inspired by what?

Alma Umm... I'm not sure. I just think... a great feeling. A great strength of feeling.

Mahler But a feeling of what?

Alma I don't know. Something inexpressible; something so rare and beautiful it can never be spoken of.

Mahler You must never make that mistake, Miss Schindler. Music is sound, just sound; horse-hair on cat-gut – that sort of thing. That's all. That's not to reduce the, the err...

Alma I know you don't believe that.

Mahler I must confess I don't know what I believe.

Alma Really?

Mahler *(he shrugs)*

Alma Well, may I say once again what a pleasure it has been, Dr. Mahler.

Mahler The pleasure has been all mine, Miss Schindler.

Alma Oh no; I won't allow that.

A very long pause.

The forest is still very beautiful.

Mahler Impossibly so.

Scene 3

An ageing and unwell Rachmaninov is seated. He perhaps slowly and carefully injects himself with medication and sits for a moment.

Rachmaninov The lights grow dim but still I work, pushing the truth away with my pen. *(he interrupts himself, perhaps putting on spectacles)* In his old age the monkey's eyes grow weak. *(quietly laughs)*

Lost in the wrong continent, trapped in the wrong century, an alien, a transient, stranger standing guard at the gatehouse of Time, boatman ferrying dead souls through the warm Pacific spray. Lately I have thought much of Tanayev. Dead for more than thirty years; died of pneumonia, caught by standing in the rain at Scriabin's funeral. I have though much of Scriabin, too. And indeed all the others; Scriabin, Tchaikowsky, Gogol, Tolstoy, Stanislavsky, Mahler, Toscanini, Charpentier, – that blessed concentration of brilliance. Actually Toscanini is still alive, isn't he. He sent me a Christmas card. Orthodox Christmas. Terribly thoughtful character.

Every time one hears of the death of a friend or a hero another piece of oneself is chipped away. The time comes when there is nothing left to chip away from.

Looking out over the water at night all I can hear is that A-minor circle of fifths from Bach's Englische Suite, endlessly resolving. A perfect little journey back to itself, describing its arcs like fireworks against the night sky.

The waves of the sea become ploughed earth, and I

remember the countryside of my youth. The brooding oak trees on the horizon at dusk and the silent acquiescence of the soil beneath my feet. And the bells of Moscow. I cannot escape from those bells, the chimes, the Gregorian calls to worship. The first time I heard a performance of my vespers I congratulated a young chorister who sang so beautifully. Patted him on the back and thanked him. Nice lad. Years later in Berlin Sergei Jaroff the conductor came up to me and told me he was that boy. And where is he now?

But still those bells ring; the call to commemorate, to remember, to keep things the same.

We hear Russian Orthodox bells pealing. This sound merges with and is gradually lost amid a cacophony of Western church bells ringing in the new year. Fireworks and happy crowds can also be heard.

Scene 4

Mahler Yes, and of course since my number is unlisted they wouldn't give it to me; perhaps suspecting me to be an interloper, so I had to ring the Opera House and thank goodness there was someone in the office, and so... anyway... the long and the short of it is that eventually I got through and picked up your message and got here in time although I must confess to not having had time to tie my shoelaces correctly, that is properly, and so of course with all the snow and ice and being in such a hurry... but that doesn't matter, of course. Of course not. Here I am, at last, and not too late, by which I mean you're still here and here we are.

So.

Alma Gosh!

Mahler Yes; as you know it is not just a beautiful night but a very special one.

Alma New Year's Eve.

Mahler Well, yes, and of course that can only add to the occasion.

Alma Gustav; have you seen all the skaters?

Mahler Yes! I know many of them by name and they cheerily waved to me and wished me luck. Which was rather appropriate, actually.

Alma How so?

Mahler Well, as you know… Look; I had all this planned but now I'm not so sure that… well, the thing is I was wondering… if you would marry me. *(pause)* That is… if you would agree to be my… if you would marry me. As I say. *(large pause)* Err… hello?

Alma I don't know what to say.

Mahler Please say yes. Just say yes. *(pause)* Err…

Alma Well, I don't know what to say. I'm –

Mahler Oh, Alma.

Alma I'm so flattered, Gustav, really I am.

Mahler But..?

Alma No, no but. Just.. I'm really flattered…

Mahler But?

Alma No; I'm really flattered *(she tries really hard not* *to say 'but')... and...* a bit confused.

Mahler Confused?

Alma No, well, maybe not confused. Well, maybe. Yes, perhaps a little startled. I mean...

Mahler No, I understand, of course.

Alma Yes. Well, I wonder if you do.

Mahler But my dear, of course. I can imagine it must...

Alma Well –

Mahler It must be... I mean it's rather sudden in some ways and is an extremely... serious... err –

Alma No, it's not that, it's –

Mahler What on earth is the matter?

Alma Do you really not know? Do you really –

Mahler No, I'm not sure I do. At least, I thought –

Alma Oh for goodness sake, Gustav; what about Anna?

Mahler What?!

Alma Well, what about her?

Mahler What on earth do you mean?

Alma What do you mean, what on earth... I can't believe you're genuinely surprised –

Mahler I *am* surprised.

Alma Incredulous, even.

Mahler Yes; I'm surprised and incredulous. I presume you mean Anna von Mildenburg.

Alma Well, of c – I can't believe you're being so intractable.

Mahler What?

Alma Gustav, you're in love with the girl.

Mahler I am not.

Alma You are.

Mahler I most certainly am not.

Alma You are. You are. You're obsessed by her.

Mahler I am *not* obsessed by her. I am *not*. How can I be? I haven't even seen her for *(the very briefest of pauses)* sixty-two days.

Alma But she's all you ever talk about.

Mahler Right! When I was with you, maybe. But I could hardly talk about *you* with you, could I? I used to save that for when I was with her.

Alma I just think you don't think… I don't think you know what you're doing.

Mahler What, do you think I haven't thought about this?

Alma Err.. well, no, I… well, yes, but… well, no. But...

Mahler Look, I really don't see what the problem is.

Alma Well, with the best will in the world –

Mahler Look –

Alma With the best will in the world I can't quite believe you.

Mahler But do you love me?

Alma I think... I love you but I'm not *in* love with you.

Mahler Oh, for fuck's sake.

Alma I'm trying to be honest.

Mahler So am I. I *am* honest. I love you. I love you, I'm *in* love with you.. Alma, I love you for God's sake.

Alma No you don't. No you don't.

Mahler I do.

Alma No you don't; you just think you do.

Mahler *(beat)* What's the difference?

Alma Please don't be awkward. I just think it's a little ridiculous that...

Mahler *(coldly)* Yes it is ridiculous. I'm totally ridiculous, that's right.

Alma Oh, Gustav; I'm not trying to hurt you, I just think that if this is serious, then we should –

Mahler Well of course it's serious. Of course it is.

Alma No, I know. I know, but I mean –

Mahler And if you don't mind me saying so I think it's a little rich coming from you.

Alma What's rich?

Mahler Well, surely if anyone's got anything to...

Alma What do you mean?

Mahler Well, for want of a better word; Klimt.

Alma What?!

Mahler Gustav Klimt.

Alma What about him?

Mahler Well, I'm not being funny and I don't mean to… but since you've been involved with him I just think in a way you should be… not *grateful*, exactly, but let's not deny it, I think… well, a lot of other men, that is, men in my position, by which I mean to say men who have achieved some kind of –

Alma What are you talking about? What the devil has Klimt got to do with it?

Mahler I would respectfully suggest that you know exactly what I'm talking about and furthermore you know full well what Klimt has got to do with it.

Alma I do not. I do not. Was I ever in love with Klimt? I don't know. I honestly don't know. Am I in love with him now? Certainly not. So it's got nothing to do with you. In a way it's got nothing to do with me, either. He's just someone I used to know. I can't help having met him before I met you. I'm sorry. Really I am. But me being fond of him then… that's no reflection on the way I feel about you now. It wasn't my fault. I wasn't to know. How was I to know you'd come along?

Mahler And how *do* you feel about me now?

Alma Oh, Gustav. I don't know. You make my head spin. I don't know what day of the week it is.

Mahler It's New Year's Day.

Alma Please don't make me cry.

Mahler Alma, please… And you're quite right to bring up Anna. I know… looking back.. I admit I made a mistake. I know I did. Just a small mistake. Just a small... series of mistakes.

Alma Oh!

Mahler *(pause)* I'm not good enough for you.

Alma *(pause)* Nor am I. *(pause)* Please don't say anything. Just... hold me and... please just hold me.

He does so.

Scene 5

Natalia St Lazybones. That's how he always signed his letters to me. Ever your loving St Lazybones. And sometimes when we were together. I would join him in his den and he would curl up against me and I would absent-mindedly scratch his tummy. 'You're just a bag of old bones' I would say. He would feign shock. 'Don't speak thus of St Lazybones'. And I would pretend to apologise; 'Sorry, I forgot just how venerable you are'. And he would smile and nod happily.

I remember once he was upset, terribly upset, not about anything in particular, just in low spirits I suppose, and he'd got it into his head that he was scared of dying and how difficult and futile life was and I was comforting him as best I could and we had this big bowl full of pistachios on the table and all the while he was edging nearer and nearer, the better to scoop up these pistachios. And I couldn't help it, I just started to laugh because there he was so doleful and gloomy yet obviously taking such a delight in these nuts and I laughed out loud and he suddenly realised what an incongruous sight he must be presenting and he laughed out loud too and even though I knew he was still sad he was also half-happy in a way. I loved him so much at that moment.

Often the littlest things would make him unhappy; inconsolable at times. And yet on other occasions he could be terribly brave and strong when you might have thought that he would have been sad and worried. I remember when he resigned from the IRMS, or at least he threatened to; well, yes – he actually handed in his resignation (he was the President, thinking about it, so I'm not sure who he could have handed it in to) – and we really needed the money, in fact, at the time. And what had happened was that one of the administrators, I don't think he even knew him, well, perhaps to ask him to prepare some letters et cetera from time to time, but no more than that and what had happened was that it turned out they had sacked this poor man simply because he was Jewish and I've never seen Sergei so angry; he seemed calm and quiet and serious nonetheless but you could barely bring yourself to look in his eyes he was so angry, something was blazing away in there and I was almost scared of him myself – not of him but of the intensity in him. He wrote his resignation letter there and then at the kitchen table and it almost scalded me to read over it before he sent it off. I think more than anything else he was revolted; he was appalled by this kind of thing and deeply ashamed - even though it was nothing to do with him he really was ashamed. And we never talked about what he thought of it, except when he came in that evening and told me what happened and from the way he said it and the way he looked at me I knew exactly how he felt and he knew I understood and we stood there for a moment together. And we also both knew we shouldn't talk about it, that talking about it would somehow cheapen it and it was too important for that and he wanted to hold onto it.

Whenever I knew he had to go away for his concert tours I would wish the time away before he went. I just longed for him to go. The thought of him leaving was so dreadful I couldn't wait for him to go as it meant he would be coming back sooner. And when he was gone I would ache for him, I really would physically ache for him, I would pull the curtains in his den every night just as if he was there and run my fingers along the lid of the piano where I would have ruffled his hair and I would say a prayer for him and imagine where he must be now. When he returned I would find myself almost in fear; not quite fear, no, certainly not fear, but some odd anxiety or trepidation at how happy I was going to be. When he came back I was so terribly happy it almost felt like I was unhappy in a way; I can't describe it. I would normally meet him at the station and we would ride back together and we wouldn't say a word, as if by some agreement never discussed we knew we had to keep quiet, that all words were a bit silly and would spoil everything and when we got into the house he would kiss me – my God! – full on the lips and I would smell all the foreign, unfamiliar smells on him and beneath them still the subtle smell of us somewhere, and I would hold on to him so tightly and feel him breathing and I would start to sob and he would hold me and hold me and hold me and never let me go. And I would close my eyes and feel my way around his face with my mouth, just trying to remember him all over again and make him mine again and trying to take it all in again and almost imagine he was still away so I could rejoice in him being back all the more. The infinite mystery of another human being.

And he always bought me one present for every city he had been to, but he would never give them to me until the next day because he knew they would be wasted on our first day together; he knew to wait until the novelty wore off a bit.

And I would always say to myself, Make the most of the time between the tragedies. Make the most of it. And I would hold him all the tighter.

Scene 6

The Mahlers are at a function or similar, quietly bickering in a corner.

Mahler Look, I know, I know.

Alma Well it's not going to come out.

Mahler We don't know that. We'll see.

Alma Well how am I going to enjoy the party now?

Mahler I don't... just… just don't think about it.

Alma Well how am I meant to stop thinking about it?

Mahler I don't know; use your imagination.

Alma *(to an unseen host, with much false politeness)*

Oh, yes, everything is wonderful, thank you very much.

Mahler *(similarly)* Yes, yes; all well.

Alma *(returning to him)* You're drunk.

Mahler I'll be the judge of that.

Alma You *are*.

Mahler It's a party. You're meant to be drunk.

Alma Just try to... just try to behave.

Mahler I wish I weren't here.

Alma I bet you do.

Mahler I do.

Alma I bet you do.

Mahler Yes, that's right; I do.

Alma I bet you wish you were with your precious... umm...

Mahler Precious what?

Alma Your little second violinist girl.

Mahler What?!

Alma Yes, that's right. What; you think I hadn't noticed? You wish you were with her now. I wish you were too.

Mahler I take it you mean –

Alma Oh, come on.

Mahler What;..?

Alma *(interrupting)* No; don't tell me her name. I don't wish to know her name.

Mahler Well, I barely know her name myself.

Alma But you know who I'm talking about.

Mahler Right; knowing all that I know about you I think I've got a pretty good idea of the focus of your current paranoia.

Alma What, there's nothing going on with her?

Mahler I'm not even going to answer that.

Alma I bet you're not.

Mahler For heavens sake, Alma, I've hardly even spoken to the girl.

Alma And the thought of her has barely crossed your mind, has it?

Mahler Look. Have you any idea how much work I've got to do? How far behind I am? How depressed I am? I can barely bring myself to cross the street every morning, let alone have an affair. Do you think I've got infinite energy?

Alma I'm sure you could find something. I know how… swoopy you can be.

Mahler The tragedy.. Sorry? How *what*?

Alma Swo… *(suddenly baffled and not sure)* you know; the way you… swoop on these girls. Anyway, that's not the –

Mahler The tragedy is, my dear, that my depression does upset you, even though you seem supremely indifferent to it. Not because you're worried about me or you wish I was in better health but because it means that your delicious little suspicions are probably wrong and instead of having something to righteously hate me for you are half-intelligent enough to realise that by rights you should be sympathetic and concerned for me instead; emotions, by the way, you are quite incapable of feeling.

Alma Yes, and all the while we can take shelter in the smooth lines of your brilliant argument. I wish *I* had an intellect.

Mahler So do I to be honest.

Alma I doubt it. You're probably glad this violinist girl doesn't have one which, by the way, I guarantee she doesn't.

Mahler What, because she's fallen in love with me she can't be intelligent, is that it?

Alma Ah, so she *has* fallen in love with you, has she?

Mahler Of course not, I'm just arguing.

Alma Well that's alright then. As long as we're just arguing everything must be alright.

Mahler You made the point; I'm just trying to... point out that you're wrong.

Alma It's always wheels within wheels, isn't it.

Mahler Yes, that's right, my dear.

A pause whilst they smile at their host.

Alma Yes; how convenient. And all the while we can focus on how difficult it is for you and how terrible it must be, but the reason you claim to be depressed – and you're not, by the way –

Mahler Thanks, doctor.

Alma – is because – shut up – is because you've allowed yourself to fall in love with this girl who let's face it sees you at best as some kind of avuncular curiosity and at worst some kind of hectoring roué.

Mahler I thought you said she was in love with me.

Alma It's not what I say that counts.

Mahler How right you are, my dear.

Alma And so you've managed to manufacture a little crisis for yourself either out of boredom or lust or I don't know what. Just a lack of contentment with me or with life. You see, if you want to know what the real tragedy is –

Mahler I wouldn't mind, yes.

Alma – it's not that you're depressed or that you're in love but the fact that you're so intelligent you're actually incapable of being depressed or being in love.

Mahler I don't accept the premise.

Alma 'I don't accept the premise'! How can you talk to me like that? I'm your wife, for God's sake.

Mahler In that case kindly act like it.

Alma I do.

Mahler Glad to hear it.

Alma But it is an act.

Mahler Oh, you really know how to needle, don't you.

Alma Please don't be difficult.

Mahler This is marriage; it's meant to be difficult.

Alma Yes; a fat lot you'd know.

Mahler I beg your pardon?

Alma I said what would you know about... *(immediately switching to the hostess)* Oh! Yes; lovely. Gustav and I were just admiring your marriage. That is... your watercolours. So beautiful. Really?... And was that each?... For the lot? Goodness!

Scene 7

Rachmaninov Another concert ends and I get another sleeper to another city and once again I am speeding through the darkness – whistles and smoke, whistles and smoke, back and forth, on and on. That endless 6/8 rhythm, falling within the great loop of another, larger rhythm; a rhythm that ends only when I return home again, to a home that only begins to feel like home when it is time to leave again.

So here I am. The hotel room. Tired. Tired. I got four bars into the second prelude tonight and just stopped. Just stopped and stared at my hands. What the hell the audience must have thought I do not know. Started again and it was all glossed over of course. After the concert I was so tired there was one autograph I forgot how to finish after the second loop. Not a great sign.

It occurred to me... If I just melted into the night no one would particularly notice and the world would keep on ticking away. Don't stop at the hotel, just keep going; out to the edges of the city and just keep going. I was tempted, tonight. Tomorrow's concert would be cancelled, and so would the rest of the tour eventually, there would be a degree of bewilderment, perhaps a parlour-game mystery feel to it all for a while, and then… business as usual. The venue would find a new booking, the agent would find a new client, and my wife...

And I realise that the thought of Natalia is too large to contain; the idea of her is so vast, like trying to picture America in its entirety, and a terrible guilt surrounds the thought of her, the guilt that because I want to die I must hate her in some way, hate her more than if I were betraying her in any of the other countless ways that men normally betray their wives. I know myself to be a dreadful man but I can't feel it, I can't feel anything, I can only remember it as one would remember the logic of it.

Every day sees me spending a fraction more energy than I replace, and now I find I have accumulated vast debts. Night after night I find myself sliding down, until there comes a time when I no longer have the strength to lift my eyes from the triangle at the far corner of the room where the two walls and the floor meet and the three shades of the same colour endlessly play themselves out against each other. I become absorbed by this meaningless conflict, the image appearing ever to shift from concave to convex, flipping in and out and after a while I can no longer believe it is just the corner of the room and it begins to take on the proportions of some odd, blank universe.

Things get blunted, and things get smudged, and after a while... It's all too close and mixed up and it seems that there are gaps I could get through, quite easily, great holes in the fabric of the world, these are the gaps, the cuts in my wrists I could make with my razor. So easy and beautiful. And I would do so, I long to do so, I just want to patiently score away at myself but I don't have the energy even to lift my eyes from that point on the far side of the room where the two walls meet the floor and the three shades of the same colour endlessly play themselves out. Too tired to die, it seems.

Sometimes I speak to her, some instinct forces me to telephone, and I prepare to protect myself from love as I hear her voice, scrambled and reassembled across the distance of a continent. And I cannot talk, I choke with sobs, so she has to do all the talking herself, she talks without response, just listening to me cry and she must be thinking God knows what all the while, and this makes me all the more guilty. But I can hear her and something from her is burrowing into me and I can be touched after all and that unbearable thought, the thought that she loves me – and I don't even know what it means, not really – but it finds its way into me and changes me imperceptibly; there is a glow as if it is still dark in the room but it has snowed during the night. And she reminds me, she says 'You're not unhappy, you're not; you're just tired'. And she's right. I'm just tired. But I'm *so* tired.

I got four bars into the second prelude tonight and just stopped. Just stopped and stared at my hands. What the hell the audience must have thought I do not know.

Started again and it was all glossed over of course. After the concert I was so tired there was one autograph I forgot how to finish after the second loop. Not a great sign.

Scene 8

The scene begins in silence – yet what a different silence from that at their first meeting. Mahler sits still in complete isolation. Alma is performing some task, perhaps. Eventually:

Mahler Do you know if / there's any –

Alma / Could you speak up?

Mahler Sorry?

Alma Could you speak up please?

A brief, unpleasant silence.

Alma Well, what were you going to say?

Mahler What what?

Alma What were you… I thought you were about to say something.

Mahler It was of no consequence.

Alma I'd really rather you said it.

Mahler Yes; it was of no consequence.

Alma So you said.

A pause.

Mahler It was just about milk.

Alma Sorry?

Mahler Milk.

Alma 'Milk'?

Mahler Yes: do we have any milk?

Alma I really don't know.

Mahler Right; thank you.

Alma I really don't know.

Mahler Well, that settles that.

Alma Yes. *(pause)* What do you want it for?

Mahler What do I what?

Alma What do you want milk for?

Mahler I thought I might drink it.

Alma You never drink milk.

Mahler I felt like milk.

Alma Sorry?

Mahler I felt like milk. I felt like it.

Alma Well you'll have to see if we have any. I really don't know if we do.

Mahler Yes; you said. *(pause)* Right.

He leaves. She remains motionless. We become aware of an old clock ticking in the silence. He returns with a glass of milk. There is a shift in the mood. He may sit back down.

Mahler Alma. I'm so sorry.

Alma For what?

Mahler *(pause)* Everything. I… I know you blame me.

Alma I don't..

Mahler No; that's alright. I understand. I think that if I'd been… perhaps if I'd been a better...

Alma Gustav, please don't…

Mahler No, I… Do you want to talk about it?

Alma Gustav, I…

Mahler I just should have been… better. I wish…

Alma Look, it's nobody's fault. Really it isn't.

Mahler I'm just so sorry.

Alma Look, it's not your fault. It's not anyone's. I saw there was *something* wrong a couple of weeks ago, and I didn't do anything about it; we both heard her coughing, I remember you said… and… but we just… how were we to know? I mean, are you supposed to run to the doctor every time you… There's just no way of knowing. And even if we had… We were just… we were just unlucky. That's all it was, finally.

Mahler I just wish…

Alma I know, I know. Look.

Mahler Oh, I'm so sorry. I'm so terribly sorry.

Alma Gustav, please, just…

Mahler I'm just… scared.

Alma Yes, I know. I'm scared too.

Mahler I know, I know. It's alright.

They embrace for some time, during which Alma says:

Alma I miss her. I miss her so much. I miss her so much. I miss her so much.

Mahler I know. I know. I know. It's alright.

The embrace ends.

Mahler Are you alright?

Alma Yes.

Mahler Are you alright?

Alma Yes.

Mahler You're sure?

Alma Yes.

Mahler You should get some rest.

Alma I will.

Mahler That's good. You should have some milk too.

Alma Thank you.

She gets up to leave.

Mahler Yes. There's something else. *(pause)* As you know, when Dr Blumenthal came to prescribe you your... well, we were worried about the state you might be in and so he, in a spirit of welcome enterprise, came up with an ingenious ruse whereby you would not be so alarmed by his presence. The formality of his presence, you know. *(pause)* Yes, and he proposed that he would examine me first; for fun, of course – to break the ice, you might say. A light-hearted little charade. But, err... the fact of the matter is... well, all was not what had been expected. And the upshot of his examination seems to be that I have a valve in my heart which doesn't work properly. In fact it doesn't work at all. And which explains... In short I am gravely ill, my dear.

Throughout this speech she has come to look upon him with a withering hatred.

And thus it seems entirely likely that I too, I'm very sorry to have to tell you, will also predecease you by a considerable margin.

He pauses. She still silently stares at him. This goads him into continuing.

Which may be a cause of some disappointment to you.

Another pause.

Or not. I really don't know.

A further pause.

Or perhaps even relief.

Alma *(eventually)* Oh yes. Oh, yes. One death wasn't enough for you, was it. Or at least –

Mahler Alma...

Alma – you can't even let me grieve for my own child without trying to take over that as well. Was this whole thing not enough about you? Was that it? Only half about you? She was only half yours; that wasn't enough, was it? You needed a tragedy that was all your own.

Mahler That's right, yes; I deliberately arranged my terminal –

Alma Oh, please!

Mahler – heart condition to give you –

Alma Oh, please!

Mahler – an extra and wholly undeserved challenge.

Alma You're poison, do you know that?

Mahler Yes...

Alma Pure poison.

Mahler I only organised the stupid examination to make you feel better –

Alma Yes, thanks.

Mahler – because you were so hysterical.

Alma And I'll bet some secret part of you is glad you're ill.

Mahler Yes, that's right; my work here is done, so now...

Alma I bet you're glad.

Mahler Well, I'll bet you were glad to actually have an excuse for being hysterical as opposed to your normal motiveless rants.

Alma You've got fishblood in those veins.

Mahler Go on.

Alma A small man writ large. That's you.

Mahler Yes, keep going.

Alma You disgust me. Did you know that?

Mahler I think I had a pretty good idea, yes.

Alma You're a fraud. Nothing but a fraud.

Mahler A fraud; yes.

Alma You make me sick. You make me physically sick. Sick. You –

Mahler Look. Let me tell you something.

Alma And how about your brother?

Mahler Let me –

Alma How about him?

Mahler Let me tell you something.

Alma What about your brother?

Mahler Well what about him?

Alma And after all these years you never mentioned him once. Not once.

Mahler Now listen.

Alma Yes; you can rot about it all day with Freud but you never think to breathe a word to me; me all the while sitting here –

Mahler If you were just sitting here –

Alma – yeah, just… and I've had enough, I can't –

Mahler If you were just –

Alma Enough!

Mahler If you were just –

Alma Enough! Do you not listen to a word I say?

Mahler Look. Do you think you could just say whatever it is you feel you've got to say, and then we can –

Alma I hate every single thing about you; you disgust

me, you revolt me, you –

Mahler Oh shut up.

Alma You make me sick.

Mahler Shut up.

Alma You make me sick.

Mahler Will you shut up?

Alma All your spleen, your bile, your selfish..

Mahler Listen you slut.

Alma What did you..?

Mahler You heard.

Alma You stinking Jew.

Mahler Oh-oh-oh!

Alma That's right.

Mahler Yes; I wondered how long it would take.

Alma Go and die.

Mahler Sixteen years of private tutors...

Alma I hope you die.

Mahler ...yeah, and that's what they taught you.

Alma Just leave me alone.

Mahler Piano lessons and French grammar and it turned out another anti-Semite just like your crippled father.

Alma Leave me alone before I kill you.

Mahler Ah, go away.

Alma I hope you die.

Mahler I will die.

Alma I hope you do.

Mahler I will do.

Alma I hope so.

Mahler Yeah, it doesn't matter; I will, so that's that.

Alma Just leave me alone.

Mahler What difference…

Alma Leave me alone.

Mahler What…

Alma Leave me alone.

Mahler What…

Alma Just leave me alone.

Mahler What difference does it make?

Alma Would you please –

Mahler Just tell me that.

Alma Just –

Mahler Just tell me that.

Alma Please, just –

Mahler Ah, *what difference does it make*? / Oh, what's the point? Just tell me that. What's the point? Like it's going to make a difference either way. A blind bit of difference and all the while it's a case of… ah, I mean the very fact that I've got to listen to this, that I've got to apologise for actually… that I'm the one who ends up having to... it's not even as though you had the first clue; not the first clue. Have you got any idea of what remorse is? Have you ever even... Do you have any idea? Have you ever stopped for one moment to think about what... oh, what's the point? What's the point? Ah!

Alma / Just leave me alone. I'm sick of you; physically sick of you, the way you parade yourself, your worn-out, woe-is-me façade, God, am I the only woman who doesn't fall for it, who sees right through it – you liar, you cheat, you thief, you disgusting little man; like everything's my fault, yes, always my fault while you're swanning around, God, your revolting little ambling innocent little... I've had enough of it, enough of it, enough; the way you poison everything and spoil everything and ruin everything, you've ruined me, and you've ruined us and you've ruined our little girl...

These speeches are delivered simultaneously. Hearing the reference to their daughter at the end of Alma's tirade Mahler screams and puts his hands over his ears. Immediately all is drowned out by music, perhaps the ten-note climax chord from the Tenth Symphony. Fade to black.

Scene 9

Natalia One morning I came into the study; he was working on an arrangement, I don't recall what it was (he used to hate orchestrating, I mean really loathe it; penal servitude he called it), and anyway I entered the room and he was used to this, because even though we would have separate rooms; that is he would work in there and I had my own study and we never really went in each other's rooms, but I did use to bring him tea mid-morning, and so on this particular morning I saw him in full concentration, working away, and he half-looked up, he looked up for the briefest of seconds over his papers and immediately returned to the page; an instinctive gesture and I was sure he hadn't fully noticed or wasn't thinking but he must have noticed something about my expression which puzzled him afterwards because he looked up again a few seconds later, more concerned this time. He saw something was wrong, and I told him what it was; I said that Gustav Mahler had died, it was in the newspaper, and he didn't say anything, he didn't say anything at all, he just looked out of the window at the trees in the garden; it was autumn and the leaves had made the lawn a sea of gold, and he just sighed; he gave a great, heavy sigh. I touched him, I put my hand on his hand but he didn't seem to notice, he just kept looking out at the garden in the rain.

We had lunch an hour or so later and I had made soup, and we ate our soup in silence, and when we had finished I went to clear away the things and he held my wrist, suddenly he held me, quite firmly, just squeezing my hand. He *had* noticed me touching him earlier, and now he was returning that touch, and trying to show that he needed me and loved me even if he didn't always communicate. And so he was sort of apologising as well. His sorrow at the news of Mahler's death was such that he could not be comforted, and yet he was sensitive enough to notice that I had been trying, and sensitive enough to know that he should now comfort me. So he held onto me and his eyes filled with tears.

I remember in New York when the two of them worked together on Sergei's Piano Concerto. Mahler was conducting the orchestra, the New York Philharmonic, and I think they made a sort of instant connection. Mahler said very little, but Sergei was amazed by the way he led the orchestra; he was the best conductor in the world at that time and the musicians were in awe of him and terrified to boot. He would rehearse and rehearse and rehearse with them and their fury gradually became transformed into a kind of brilliance. Mahler seemed to inhabit the music, he would live in the score before the performance and only rarely surface from the world that my husband had created for him. They just gave one performance together, and at the end of it the audience was literally stunned into silence for one, perhaps two complete minutes. Normally of course the 'bravo's start almost before the last note has ended but that night no one moved, people barely breathed, no one wanted the magic to end. Something holy had happened that night, something stirred, and people wanted to hold on to it for as long as they could before returning to their everyday lives. And when at last they applauded it was like no sound you ever heard. It was like the walls of Jericho. And of course eventually the applause died out, and the magic was over, and everyone quietly went on their way again, but something had happened that night, and everyone knew it, and in some strange way they could never explain it seemed that things could still turn out alright, that if this is what the world contained then perhaps it might all be worthwhile after all. And so everyone there took some small shard of perfection with them, and it kept them warm throughout the next working week, perhaps for many years after.

Scene 10

Alma It all started when I went dancing. It was Gustav's idea, funnily enough. Just something to occupy me while he was writing in the lodge. So I did; I went along and it was rustic and twee and the kind of thing that normally it would be very easy to be snide about except there was a man there, a young, very intense looking man and I secretly made it my mission to dance with him. At last he asked me. And I accepted. We danced together and he was funny and charming but all the while there was something deeper burning away in him and when I returned home I felt odd, listless and yearny in a way I can't explain. And the next day I realised I was looking forward to seeing him again, and the hour before the dance was almost unbearable; I suddenly realised how crushed I would be if he wasn't there, but there he was and when I saw him I realised that he had been longing to see me as well and we both crossed the room to each other and I smiled and he smiled too and we danced all night. He was called Walter, he was an architect; Walter Gropius. We walked back together and he was so clever and funny and *young* and I felt the most wonderful kind of vertigo. Then he began to write to me. Just jokey little letters, gossipy and arch, louche, clever, the very opposite of Gustav's dreadful earnestness. But we continued to dance, and continued to see each other, and one afternoon, almost as if we had never thought about it - although of course we had really thought of little else - he took me to his cabin out on the water's edge and I had never, ever, ever felt anything like that before in my life and I was so happy all I could do was laugh; I laughed and laughed like an idiot and held him to my chest and for the first time in ten years I felt alive and free and blessed. Nothing had happened to Walter yet, nothing had gone wrong in his life and he was all optimism and potential, and when I was with him I would get caught up and began to feel that perhaps *I* could have a second chance, not to do things differently, necessarily, just simply for the joy of doing them again.

Gustav, of course, burrowed further and further away from me into his music. I now saw that there was something odd and repellent about the way he walked, and once it had crossed my mind I never fully escaped from the suspicion that he was exaggerating his strange, ambling gait for attention or sympathy. And his ears were ridiculous; I tried to feel fond of him and I tried to find him handsome but I realised I actually hated the sight of him and his stupid, arrogant ears.

One day he intercepted one of Walter's letters. Whether by some strange compulsion or by sheer accident Walter had in fact addressed the letter to him. Gustav's reaction was predictably cloying, telling me he loved me and other such slop. He had really become pitiful in the past few months; fawning, clingy and spineless. I was ashamed of him, I was ashamed to be with him, finally he made me ashamed of myself. The discovery came just as we were preparing to leave for New York, and the passage became two botched getaways. We never talked about Walter; we never talked at all. We had to stay in the same hotel, of course, but we had a large suite so I barely saw him and we slept in separate rooms. While he was at his rehearsals and concerts I would stay in the hotel. I would sit out on the balcony and gaze down at the traffic, and feel myself slowly dissolving into the chaos below; the confusion, the innocent discord of a world full of people. Real people. Other people. Normal people.

Scene 11

Connecting the previous scene to this is the sound of an orchestra tuning up whilst an audience chatters and coughs. The lights go up and we see both Mahler and Rachmaninov together in the green room of Carnegie Hall. They are both utterly absorbed in their preparations: Rachmaninov may be seated in deep concentration whilst Mahler paces or labours over tempi. By now Mahler is handkerchief-consumptive (he is at this point older than Rachmaninov and only a few months away from death).

Mahler Four before 4.

Rachmaninov Yes?

Mahler You want it to hold back slightly.

Rachmaninov Err… that's right. Just a small…

Mahler Just holding back for that one bar...

Rachmaninov Yes.

Mahler And then *a tempo* one before 4.

Rachmaninov What did you think in the rehearsal?

Mahler Just… yes. That was fine.

Rachmaninov I don't want to make too much of it.

Mahler No, I don't think you do. That's fine: how it was in the rehearsal is fine.

Rachmaninov Good.

A pause.

Mahler You know, that Adagio theme really is the most beautiful melody.

Rachmaninov Thank you. Thank you very much.

Mahler It was all I could hear last night.

Rachmaninov Really?

Mahler Yes.

Rachmaninov Well.

A pause.

Mahler Don't worry about those horns at 26. We did some work after you left.

Rachmaninov No, that's alright.

Mahler They'll be *just* audible. Just.

Rachmaninov Yes; we want them to be…

Mahler You've got to… *feel* them rather than hear them.

Rachmaninov That's it exactly. Just a cushion of sound.

Mahler Yes. They'll be like velvet. Please don't worry.

Rachmaninov No; I shan't.

Mahler Very well. *(now more to himself)* So, then… *(he traces a tempo)*, yes… and… *(He continues in this vein following the successive speeds of the movement. He turns away, and Rachmaninov also begins to mark out little passages either mentally or on a surface. A door opens and we hear the orchestra tuning up. The door is closed again, and they surface from their reveries.)* What's the absolute fastest you're going to take the accelerando at 54?

Rachmaninov How fast does it become? *(with the sense of 'Do you mean "how fast does it become?"')*

Mahler Yes.

Rachmaninov Well, they start *(he gestures a beat)* and then… *(he beats four bars of 4/4 in increasing time)*

Mahler Exactly like that?

Rachmaninov Exactly like that.

Mahler And then the rit.

Rachmaninov Yes; four bars to the Lento. And you know what I'm doing with that.

Mahler Yes, yes; that's fine. It has a momentum there.

Rachmaninov Yes.

Mahler Good.

A door opens again and stays open. We hear the crowd and the two men are galvanised into their very final preparations. After checking themselves there is a moment of stillness, each waiting for some cue.

Mahler Well, may I wish you the very best of luck.

Rachmaninov Thank you. Thank you very much. And the very best of luck to you too.

Mahler Thank you.

A pause.

Well.

He goes to shake Rachmaninov's hand, but Rachmaninov, by tradition concerned for his fingers, gestures to this effect and without any sense of awkwardness or reprimand Mahler converts his offered handshake to an affectionate yet respectful pat on the arm or back etc. Mahler exits, and we hear the applause for him. Rachmaninov is left alone in the room. After a moment he also exits and we hear more applause, then silence. Blackout.